Cheryl Pelteret

Alicia Artusi   Gregory J. Manin   Claire Thacker

engage

2ⁿᵈ edition ◄◄◄◄◄◄

Teacher's Book

1

OXFORD
UNIVERSITY PRESS

Great Clarendon Street, Oxford, OX2 6DP, United Kingdom

Oxford University Press is a department of the University of Oxford.
It furthers the University's objective of excellence in research, scholarship,
and education by publishing worldwide. Oxford is a registered trade
mark of Oxford University Press in the UK and in certain other countries

ISBN: 978 0 19 453777 3

Printed in China

This book is printed on paper from certified and well-managed sources

ACKNOWLEDGEMENTS

Special acknowledgement is due to Helen Halliwell for the Unit tests and
Pairwork activities.

Illustrations by: Tony Forbes

Contents

Overview of *Engage* 2nd edition

With fresh content and a full range of digital products *Engage* **2nd edition** appeals to a new generation of adolescent learners, providing them with new and exciting ways to interact.

Engage **2nd edition** builds on the success of the original, with completely revised content, ensuring that topics are meaningful for today's students.

Engage **2nd edition** uses a wide range of topics to contextualize new language, combining a strong visual impact with an exceptionally clear, well-paced syllabus.

Engage **2nd edition** is easy for both teachers and students to use. It is stimulating but not confusing; structured but not rigid; straightforward without being simplistic. Its up-to-date design and strong visual impact motivates students to want to learn English. The material actively encourages students to truly **engage** with the process of learning English at every level, connecting with each other, and with the wider world.

Topics

By focusing on a different topic in each teaching unit, students use English to **engage** with the world around them. Sometimes this is through factual presentations, sometimes through fictional characters and situations – but always with the aim of teaching students about a particular aspect of the real world. A wide range of topics and formats is used, mixing cultural and cross-curricular features with more light-hearted presentations.

Vocabulary

In *Engage* 2nd edition, vocabulary provides the gateway to the unit topic. Each teaching unit presents two sets of vocabulary, using a mixture of textual and visual input. Together, the topic and vocabulary set give students the tools they will need for subsequent reading comprehension and grammar practice, and for skills work at the end of the unit. All the items are modeled on the **Class Audio CDs** for students to listen and repeat as a class.

Additional vocabulary input is provided by the **Workbook**, where **Extend your vocabulary** exercises introduce a further set of words related to the topic of the relevant Student Book lesson.

Grammar

Engage 2nd edition features two single-page grammar lessons per unit. Most lessons present and practice a single small point, rather than covering several points at a time. Some lessons focus on two related points. Verb forms and other complex areas of grammar are divided over a number of lessons and units. This focused, step-by-step approach makes new language more accessible and easier to digest.

Comprehensive grammar charts are given on the page, so that students have a correct model to work from at all times. Grammar practice activities are carefully graded, from recognition exercises at the start of the lesson, to sentence production at the end, with the result that students can see real progress as they work their way through the lesson.

Each unit now also has a **Grammar reference** page as the first page of the relevant unit in the Workbook. This provides students with examples and rules to help them further understand the grammar area and to encourage self-study.

Communication

Each grammar lesson ends with a short **Over to you!** activity, which provides the opportunity for meaningful, personalized practice in the form of a simple speaking activity. A guided preparatory stage, usually written, builds students' confidence before they speak. All **Over to you!** activities can be done either as a whole class, or if conditions allow, in pairs.

Skills

Special attention is given to the gradual, controlled development of the four skills (reading, listening, speaking, and writing), through the **Living English** and **Round-up** sections at the end of every unit. All four skills areas feature in every unit: reading, listening, and speaking on the Living English pages and writing on the Round-up page. There is extra reading practice in every Workbook unit.

From the very first unit, *Engage* 2nd edition aims to build students' competence in both receptive and productive skills. Simple strategies help students learn how to read and write more effectively, while speaking lessons include more guided exercises on pronunciation within the context of short dialogues. For both speaking and writing, a short, carefully structured model is provided on the page, so that students have a clear framework on which to build their own ideas. Listening scripts and activities are deliberately short and simple to begin with, in order to help students gradually recognize the sounds of spoken English. Levels 2 and 3 build on this by introducing a series of basic listening strategies.

Learning

It is important that students learn to take control of their learning and study techniques from the earliest opportunity. *Engage* 2nd edition addresses this need by including study skills as part of the **Review** lessons. These cover a range of areas – from the basics of understanding instructions in the coursebook, to ways of using English outside the classroom – and always include a follow-up practice activity.

Mixed ability

The flexibility of *Engage* 2nd edition makes it ideal for mixed-ability classes. An example of this is the series of vocabulary and grammar-related puzzles in the **Magazine** section of the **Student Book**, to which fast finishers are directed at the end of each grammar lesson.

The core material itself is also easy to adapt to the needs of different groups or individuals, allowing the teacher to place more or less emphasis on listening, speaking, reading, or writing as appropriate.

The photocopiable **Reading worksheets** (one per unit) and **Grammar worksheets** (two per unit) on the **Teacher's Resource MultiROM** are designed to cater for students at different stages of learning, with both support for weaker students, and freer extension activities for the more able students. These activities are graded and get progressively harder throughout the worksheet: basic (★☆☆); harder (★★☆); and more challenging or freer practice (★★★).

Further suggestions for graded follow-up activities are given in the **Teacher's Book**.

Cross-curricular content

A strong emphasis on real-world topics provides an excellent springboard for dealing with other areas of the curriculum. Throughout *Engage* 2nd edition, students are encouraged not just to learn a series of words and structures, but rather to use English as a tool for expanding their knowledge of the world around them. Features on music, movies, and popular culture sit comfortably alongside texts about geography, history, and technology. Whatever the topic, the aim is to make it informative, accessible, and relevant.

In addition, the material gives numerous opportunities for reinforcing basic values and areas of general education. For instance, the importance of tolerance and respect for others is a theme which runs throughout each book, as demonstrated by the inclusion of a diverse range of nationalities, cultures, and social backgrounds in the presentations and reading texts. Other areas seen in *Engage* 2nd edition include gender equality, consumer education, and health.

The unit summaries in this **Teacher's Book** list the values and cross-curricular subjects covered in each unit.

Photocopiable **Cross-curricular worksheets** (four per level) on the **Teacher's Resource MultiROM** link to the themes and grammar of the corresponding **Student Book** units as well as to the school subjects that students typically study in their own language, such as history, math, art, science.

Recycling

New language is constantly recycled at each stage of the course. Each new vocabulary set is immediately practiced, and then actively used in subsequent reading, grammar, and skills lessons. All vocabulary sets and grammar points are systematically reviewed in **Review** units. **Round-up** lessons also bring together all the main language covered in the unit for a final writing task and self-assessment activities.

An additional resource for reviewing recently acquired language is through the **Project** pages of the **Magazine** section. The projects have been carefully designed so that students review and actively use the most important language from the previous two units. The **Teacher's Book** also offers ideas for multimedia extension activities to recycle material in a fun and interactive manner.

Further practice is provided in the **Bonus lessons** on the **Teacher's Resource MultiROM**. Two of the four **Bonus lessons** in each level provide extra review and consolidation of language areas covered in a previous level of the series.

Extension

Engage 2nd edition features a range of extra resources, which can be used with the whole class, as extra self-study material, or as extension with individual students:

- the **Magazine** section provides puzzles and guided projects in the **Student Book**;
- two **Extend your vocabulary** exercises are provided per unit in the **Workbook**;
- the **Teacher's Book** includes suggestions for warm-up activities and extra follow-up activities where appropriate;
- one photocopiable **Pairwork activity** per unit, plus teacher's notes and extension activities are provided in the **Teacher's Book**;
- two **Bonus lessons** (see **Teacher's Resource MultiROM**) per level introduce students to additional vocabulary and grammar areas which are not taught in the main **Student Book**;
- the **Teacher's Resource MultiROM** offers a wealth of supplementary and extension material.

Assessment

Assessment is an important feature of *Engage* 2nd edition. Printable and photocopiable tests provide a convenient method of assessment for both teacher and student. *Engage* 2nd edition offers assessment options at various stages of the course. Graded **Unit tests** allow for assessment of weaker and stronger students, while specific **Listening tests** and **Speaking tests** also assess key skill areas. See the **Teacher's Resource MultiROM** for a full list of tests. All tests are available as both editable Microsoft Word documents and non-editable Adobe pdf documents.

Self-assessment and Common European Framework of Reference

Engage 2nd edition is linked to the Common European Framework of Reference (CEFR – see page xii and the **Teacher's Resource MultiROM** for more details) and actively promotes the development of a Language Portfolio for each student. The **Student Book** also encourages students to reflect and review their understanding of unit grammar points in the **I can ...** section of the **Round-up pages**.

Using the Student Book

Teaching units are divided into five sections. All the material is organized so that one page represents one lesson and teaches one point.

Introducing the topic introduces vocabulary related to the topic of the unit, and is followed by three sections of two pages each: **Exploring the topic, Building the topic, and Living English.**

Exploring the topic features a reading text which contextualises the vocabulary introduced on the previous page. This section also introduces the first of two grammar areas.

Building the topic extends the theme with a second set of vocabulary shown within the context of text and visuals, followed by grammar presentation and practice.

Living English aims to practice all the vocabulary and grammar presented in the unit, with reading, listening, and speaking practice, and integrated learning skills.

The last page, **Round-up**, encourages students to consolidate everything learned in a writing activity and self-assessment (**I can ...**).

Introducing the topic

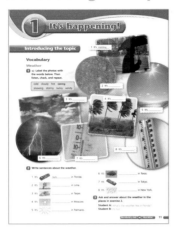

Vocabulary

Introducing the topic opens each unit. This page is an illustrated presentation of vocabulary related to the unit topic. In most cases, activities involve some form of labeling or matching of words to visuals, sometimes requiring students to choose the correct word to complete a caption or definition.

The answers are always recorded on the **Class Audio CDs**, allowing students to hear the new words, either alone or in short phrases, and to practice saying them as they repeat.

> You may wish to play the recording twice at this point – once for students to check their answers, then a second time for them to listen and repeat. Alternatively, you could model the words yourself.

Exploring the topic

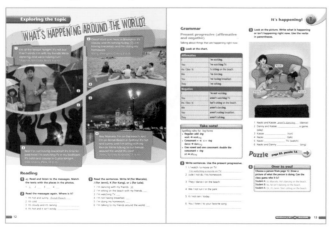

Reading

This double page section starts with a reading text of different genres (e.g. magazine and newspaper articles, blogs, e-mails, online chats, profiles, advertisements). Although the text includes a new grammar structure, students are not actively using the new grammar on this page.

At some point during each reading lesson, students have the opportunity to listen to the complete text as recorded on the **Class Audio CDs**, at the same time as they read the text on the page. This has the advantage of exposing students to the sounds of a new grammar structure before they come to study it in the next lesson. Reading and listening at the same time also familiarizes students with the relationship between the written and spoken word in English, and gives them extra listening practice.

Grammar

The right-hand page of **Exploring the topic** formally presents the new grammar structure first seen in the reading text on the opposite page. The headings on the page describe the new language in both structural and functional terms. A more detailed explanation of usage is given in the *Grammar reference* on the opening page of the **Workbook** unit, and you may wish to draw students' attention to this during the lesson.

Form is modeled using a comprehensive grammar chart, which features sentences taken or adapted from the previous page where possible. The advantage of having a completed chart on the page is that students always have a correct reference to help them.

Sometimes a *Take note!* box appears after the grammar chart. This draws attention to a particular grammatical detail – such as a spelling rule – which students will need in order to correctly produce the target language.

> Once students have looked at the grammar chart in the book, it can sometimes be a good idea to get them involved in filling in an "alternative" chart on the board, using different example sentences. This provides you with an opportunity to clear up any difficulties with either form or meaning, using the students' mother tongue if appropriate. It also serves to highlight common mistakes.

Grammar practice is generally provided in the form of three graded exercises, followed by an *Over to you!* activity. The exercises begin with simple recognition, for example matching or choosing the correct answer. The aim is to get students accustomed to seeing and identifying the new structure, before moving on to production at the level of individual words and verb forms, and phrase and sentence-level production in the final grammar exercise.

At this point in the lesson, a *Puzzle* symbol directs fast finishers to the *Magazine* section at the back of the book. Here they will find a word puzzle, brainteaser, or other fun activity which uses the vocabulary and grammar from **Exploring the topic**. You can, of course, use the puzzle as a fun activity for the whole class, or for fast finishers who have finished the grammar activities ahead of the other students. Answers to all the *Magazine* activities are given within the teaching notes for the corresponding lesson.

At the end of this lesson, *Over to you!* gives students the opportunity to personalize the new language and exchange information in a meaningful way. A written preparatory stage often builds students' confidence by ensuring that they have had time to plan what they are going to say.

All *Over to you!* activities have been designed so that they can be successfully completed either as teacher-led exchanges in open class, or alternatively in pairs and groups.

Building the topic

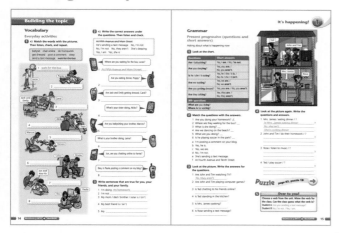

Vocabulary

In **Building the topic**, the *Vocabulary* page introduces a different perspective on the unit topic, and presents a new set of words, which are taught, modeled, and practiced. Although not a formal reading lesson, the *Vocabulary* page in **Building the topic** usually includes some reading matter. The purpose of this is to contextualize the new words, and to expose students to the new structure that they will study on the following page.

Grammar

The new language presented in the *Grammar* lesson usually builds on the previous grammar point, e.g. presenting the negative or question forms of a new tense.

Living English

The last two pages of each unit deal specifically with skills work. The left-hand page always features a reading text and related activities, while the right-hand page always covers listening and speaking. Writing is covered on the **Round-up** page. We recognize that different school systems and classroom conditions require teachers to place more or less emphasis on certain skills. By dealing with each skill as a separate lesson, this section of the unit gives you the flexibility to choose the material which best suits your own requirements.

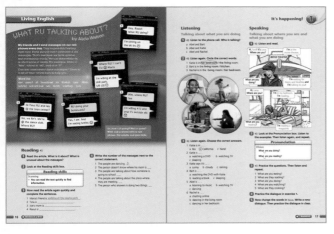

Reading

Skills reading texts in **Living English** are longer than those in **Exploring the topic**. They deal with an aspect of the unit topic, often with a factual focus, and actively use the vocabulary and grammar of the unit. Any new vocabulary – whilst kept to a minimum – is included in the *Word list* at the end of the **Teacher's Book**, and the language structures are strictly limited to what students have seen so far. The accompanying exercises are designed to gradually build up students' reading comprehension skills. The first exercise focuses on global comprehension, while the second requires a more detailed understanding of the text.

Some of the **Living English** reading texts in Levels 2 and 3 test reading comprehension through four-option multiple choice question activities. This reflects the type of activities that students encounter in their school exams and helps to bridge the gap between lower and upper secondary.

Approximately half of the *Reading* lessons include *Reading skills* boxes, around which the comprehension activities are based. These boxes help students to acquire and practice simple but important strategies from the very first unit onwards.

In order to help students remember reading strategies, it is a good idea to review them from time to time, e.g. if they have recently looked at how to use photos to predict the content of a text, it is worth encouraging students to do this whenever possible with subsequent reading texts.

All reading texts are recorded on the **Class Audio CDs**, for additional listening practice.

Listening

Listening scripts usually follow on from the topic of the reading text, and once again the emphasis is on building students' confidence through gradual exposure. There is an initial context check question, followed by more detailed comprehension questions. In the lower levels of the course, scripts are short, and tasks are generally limited to recognition, so that students do not have to decode several levels of information and write answers at the same time. As the series progresses, scripts become longer, and tasks increase in complexity.

When doing detailed listening activities with the class, it is good practice for students to listen to the recording at least three times. Before playing the recording, give your students time to read the comprehension questions through so that they can predict the information, vocabulary, and structures they are going to hear. On the first listening, encourage them not to write anything down, but simply to listen and try to get a general idea. After they have listened, give them a few minutes to try and answer as many questions as they can from memory.

On the second listening, students can check and complete their answers. If necessary, repeat this stage. The third time around, students correct their answers. You may wish to pause the CD at relevant points during the recording so that students can see exactly where the answers are given.

All scripts are recorded on the **Class Audio CDs**, and reproduced either on the **Student Book** page or in the teaching notes.

Speaking

Speaking lessons provide a fun context in which to review some of the language seen in the unit. A simple model dialogue is presented by means of a short comic strip or conversation, with different characters appearing throughout each level of *Engage* 2nd edition. Unlike the other levels, Level 3 uses a new set of characters for each conversation.

After reading and listening to the dialogue for the first time, students' attention is drawn to a particular area of pronunciation, which is highlighted in a *Pronunciation* box. Specific examples from the dialogue are given for students to listen and repeat. As a follow-up activity, there is an exercise featuring other examples. To consolidate pronunciation work, students are then encouraged to practice the model dialogue on the page.

In pronunciation exercises, the emphasis is mostly on recognition, particularly in the early levels of *Engage* 2nd edition. However, it may be appropriate with some groups to ask the class to repeat the example sentences for extra practice before returning to the dialogue. Teenage students often feel intimidated by pronunciation activities, so it can be a good idea to repeat as a whole class, rather than asking individual students to repeat individually.

When practicing the model dialogue, students will benefit from listening to the recording again. One way to organize this is to stop the CD after each sentence initially and have the whole class repeat in chorus. Do this as many times as necessary for your students to feel comfortable with the dialogue.

Finally, students adapt the model dialogue to make their own personalized versions, by substituting their own ideas for the words in blue. An initial written stage gives them the chance to prepare before performing the dialogue in class – either in front of the whole group or, if appropriate, in pairs or small groups.

Round-up

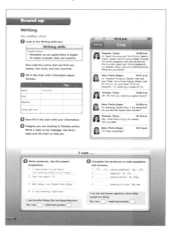

Writing

Writing lessons are based around a model text, which is carefully structured in such a way that students can follow it exactly when they produce their own compositions. A chart helps students to analyze the model and note down the important information. As a result, they are able to see which parts of the model text can be changed, before thinking of their own ideas and writing them in their own chart. At this point, most students will be ready to write.

For weaker groups, it might be helpful to go through the model text together and ask students to identify exactly which words and phrases they can change to produce their own piece of writing. If necessary, write the model on the board with the relevant words gapped out, so that students can write it down in their notebooks and then complete it.

In the majority the teaching units, the *Writing* lesson includes a simple strategy in the form of a *Writing skills* box, followed by a short practice activity. Strategies begin with areas such as using subject pronouns with verbs, simple word order, and the use of capital letters for names.

I can ...

Self-assessment is an important tool for helping students to review and reflect on their learning of English. The two activities in this section review the grammar areas taught in the main unit, and allow students to reflect on how well they understand them. Students should assess whether they think they can use the grammar point with little difficulty, or whether they need extra practice. The **Teacher's Resource MultiROM** has a wealth of material for further practice.

Welcome

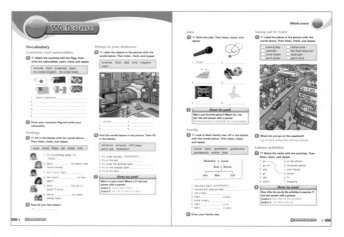

Each level of *Engage* 2nd edition features a seven-page *Welcome* unit . In Levels 1, 2, and 3, the aim is to review language from the previous level. In the case of Starter level, the *Welcome* unit practices assumed language areas to allow students to start the course with a very basic level of English.

Review

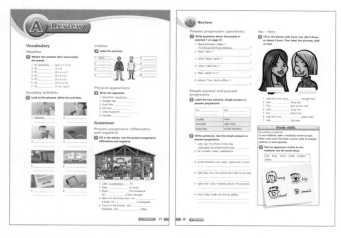

Engage 2ⁿᵈ edition features two *Review* pages after every two **Student Book** units. Each vocabulary set and each grammar point is individually reviewed. A *Study skills* section introduces students to basic strategies for organizing and taking control of their own learning.

Engage Magazine

At the back of the **Student Book** is a *Magazine* section, which features puzzles and guided projects.

The puzzles are designed as a fun extra activity to be completed when students reach the end of a *Grammar* page. In mixed-ability classes, they can be used as a reward for fast finishers. Alternatively, they can be used with the whole class as a warm-up or end-of-lesson activity. Each puzzle is linked to the vocabulary and grammar of the relevant *Grammar* page.

There are four *Project* pages in the *Magazine* section, each designed to review – and encourage active use of – the language taught in the previous two units. They are easily adapted to suit the needs of your students. They can be completed individually or in small groups, in class or as homework.

A clear model is shown on the page, broken down into short pieces of text. Students first read the model and match each piece of text with a category or question. This helps them identify the subject of each paragraph, and the language used. Step by step instructions are given on the page to guide students to produce their own projects.

Project work gives stronger students the opportunity for freer writing. This is always to be encouraged, even if it results in many more mistakes being made.

The weakest students, on the other hand, will sometimes need extra guidance to follow the model and adapt it. As with *Writing* lessons (see opposite), a useful first step is to look through the model with the students and help them identify the words and information that can be changed.

Workbook

For every **Student Book** unit , there are five pages of extra vocabulary and grammar practice in the **Workbook.** Each workbook unit contains:

- one page of **Grammar reference**, including the word lists for the vocabulary sets;
- four pages of extra **Vocabulary** and **Grammar** practice;
- two **Extend your vocabulary** activities;
- an extra **Reading** text with comprehension providing further practice of the reading skill that they have seen in the main unit.

Other components

Student MultiROM

The Student Book and Workbook includes a **Student MultiROM**, which, when used in a computer, contains:

- three graded **Grammar** exercises for each grammar point in the **Student Book** (total of six exercises per unit);
- two **Vocabulary** exercises for each vocabulary set in the **Student Book**;
- two word lists with interactive audio and artwork per **Student Book** unit;
- one **Speaking** activity per unit;
- two games corresponding to each **Review** unit.

When used in a CD player, the **Student MultiROM** contains the recordings of:

- the **Listening** sections in the **Living English** pages of the **Student Book**;

- the **Speaking** dialogues in the **Living English** pages of the **Student Book**;
- the **Pronunciation** activities in the **Living English** pages of the **Student Book**.

Teacher's Book

One of our principal aims in producing the material in *Engage* 2nd edition is clarity. For ease of reference, the **Teacher's Book** is designed so that each double page of teaching notes represents an open page of the **Student Book**.

The teaching notes are presented as step-by-step lesson plans. The notes for each activity simply state the aim, list the steps needed to complete the activity, and, where appropriate, the audio script and answers. There are no paragraphs or long explanations on the page.

The overall contents and aims of the unit are given in the **Unit summary** at the start of the notes for each unit; individual lesson aims are listed at the top of each page.

Within the notes there are occasional suggestions and background notes providing extra support for the teacher. These include ideas for warm-up activities at the start of a class; suggestions for simple follow-up or extension activities, graded according to level; background notes on matters of cultural or historical interest arising from reading or listening texts; and notes highlighting particular pitfalls to be aware of when teaching a given area of grammar.

In addition, a comprehensive Workbook answer key is provided at the back of the **Teacher's Book**.

The **Teacher's Book** contains:

- an introduction to the course;
- background information on the Common European Framework of Reference;
- a **Welcome self-assessment** checklist;
- Student Book contents pages;
- teaching notes for all units including audio scripts, and answers for all Student Book exercises;
- teaching notes for **Review** units, **Engage magazines,** and **Projects**;
- the full **Workbook** answer key;
- overprinted answers on embedded **Student Book** pages, so teachers can see exactly what the students see;
- eight photocopiable **Unit tests**;
- eight photocopiable **Pairwork activity** worksheets, with teaching notes;
- photocopiable **Word list** arranged by unit.

Class Audio CDs

The **Class Audio CDs** contain the following **Student Book** listening tracks:

- all vocabulary activities;
- all presentation texts;
- all skills reading texts;
- listening activities;
- speaking dialogues;
- and pronunciation exercises.

iTools

Engage 2nd edition **iTools** provides a powerful classroom resource for the teacher. In addition to a fully interactive **Student Book**, each iTools disk contains extra support material.

iTools contains the complete content of the **Student Book** and **Workbook**, designed to be projected in class. To take full advantage of its rich interactive content, it should be used on an interactive whiteboard, but may also be used with a computer connected to a data projector.

Features of iTools include:

- fully interactive **Student Book** content including full class audio;
- answer keys and audio scripts which can be turned on or off;
- complete **Workbook** contents with answer keys;
- the ability to alternate between corresponding **Student Book** and **Workbook** pages at the touch of a button;
- Video material featuring four short documentary style reports and a selection of short interviews with American teenagers, with accompanying worksheets. When used with an interactive whiteboard, the video clips can be launched directly from the icon on the worksheet.

Teacher's Resource MultiROM

The **Teacher's Resource MultiROM** contains the following additional material:

Student Worksheets

- eight two-page photocopiable **Grammar worksheets** with graded activities for each grammar point;
- eight photocopiable **Reading worksheets**;
- eight photocopiable **Speaking worksheets** with extension dialogue activities and pronunciation; audio tracks can be found on the audio section of the disk;
- eight photocopiable **Writing worksheets**;
- eight **Pairwork activities** for further communication and fluency practice;
- four photocopiable **Progress checks** with one activity per per two units;
- four **Extended Reading Worksheets** extracts from Oxford Bookworms Library readers, written especially for *Engage* 2nd edition. Extracts have been chosen carefully so that they allow for a gradual transition between levels.

  The vocabulary and grammar syllabus of *Engage* 2nd edition is broadly in line with the Oxford Bookworms Library syllabus. As a result, students nearing the end of Starter Level will be able to enjoy readers from the Bookworms Starters range. As they work their way through Level 1, they will be able to make the transition to Bookworms Stage 1 readers, moving on to Bookworms Stage 2 for *Engage* Level 2, and Bookworms Stage 3 for *Engage* Level 3;
- full answer keys and audio scripts.

Review and extension

- four **Cross-curricular worksheets** with extended reading and web-based project work;
- two **Bonus lessons** which provide extra review and consolidation of language areas covered in a previous level of the series;
- two **Bonus lessons** which present and practice additional vocabulary and grammar areas which are not taught in the main Student Book.

Assessment

- a series **Diagnostic test** to help place students at the correct level;
- three two-page **Unit tests** covering vocabulary, grammar, and reading per unit (one basic (★☆☆), one standard (★★☆), and one challenging (★★★));
- eight **Review tests** (two per Review unit) covering vocabulary, grammar, and reading;

- eight **Listening tests** (two per Review unit);
- eight **Speaking tests** (two per Review unit);
- two **End-of-year tests** covering vocabulary, grammar, and reading;
- two **End-of year listening tests**;
- full answer keys for all written tests and criteria for marking **Speaking tests**;
- a **Student Language Portfolio** containing:
  - an introduction to the Common European Framework of Reference and Student Language Portfolio;
  - a *Welcome self-assessment*;
  - eight *Unit self-assessment* checklists;
  - an *End-of-Year self-assessment* with descriptors from levels A1, A2, B1, and B2 of the Common European Framework of Reference.

Planning

- a **Teaching calendar** to help keep track of teaching objectives and observations;
- a **Class planner** to record aims, stages, and timings for each lesson;
- a **Student record** to note students' individual progress in key skills and in test results.

DVD

Two **DVDs** accompany the series, with four documentaries and a selection of short interviews with American and British teenagers for each level. The material deals with different cultural aspects of the English-speaking world, and is linked to the language syllabus and topical themes of the **Student Book**. The video clips are designed to be used after completion of each **Review** unit, or after every second main unit.

The **DVD** also contains printable worksheets, teaching notes, answer keys, and scripts. These can be accessed when the disk is used with a computer.

In addition to the comprehension questions on the worksheets, there are multiple-choice questions displayed on screen after each documentary. The correct answer can be selected with the remote control if viewed on a DVD player, or using a mouse if viewed on a computer.

There is also an on-screen language check feature which focuses students' attention on examples of the target grammar areas in the documentary reports.

Common European Framework of Reference (CEFR)

The Common European Framework of Reference (CEFR) was designed to promote a consistent interpretation of foreign-language competence among the member states of the European Union. Today, the use of the CEFR has expanded beyond the boundaries of Europe, and it is used in other regions of the world, including Latin America, Asia, and the Middle East.

The CEFR is a description of linguistic competence at six levels: A1, A2, B1, B2, C1, and C2. The descriptors were written to help both learners and education professionals to standardize assessment.

The CEFR definitions of linguistic competence are as follows:

A	Basic User	A1	Breakthrough
		A2	Waystage
B	Independent User	B1	Threshold
		B2	Vantage
C	Proficient User	C1	Effectiveness
		C2	Mastery

The CEFR provides teachers with a structure for assessing their students' progress as well as monitoring specific language objectives and achievements. Students respond to the CEFR statements in the **I can…** section at the end of each unit.

Engage 2nd edition aims to enable students to move from no English or level A1 and into level B2 at the end of the four years of the course.

Descriptions of the CEFR levels covered in *Engage* 2nd edition

Basic User

A1 Can understand and use familiar everyday expressions and very basic phrases aimed at the satisfaction of needs of a concrete type. Can introduce him / herself and others and can ask and answer questions about personal details such as where he / she lives, people he / she knows and things he / she has. Can interact in a simple way provided the other person talks slowly and clearly and is prepared to help.

A2 Can understand sentences and frequently used expressions related to areas of most immediate relevance (e.g. very basic personal and family information, shopping, geography, employment). Can communicate in simple and routine tasks requiring a simple and direct exchange of information on familiar and routine matters. Can describe in simple terms aspects of his / her background, immediate environment and matters in areas of immediate need.

Independent User

B1 Can understand the main points of clear standard input on familiar matters regularly encountered in work, school, leisure, etc. Can deal with most situations likely to arise whilst traveling in an area where the language is spoken. Can produce simple connected text on topics which are familiar or of personal interest. Can describe experiences and events, dreams, hopes, and ambitions, and briefly give reasons and explanations for opinions and plans.

B2 Can understand the main ideas of complex text on both concrete and abstract topics, including technical discussions in his / her field of specialization. Can interact with a degree of fluency and spontaneity that makes regular interaction with native speakers quite possible without strain for either party. Can produce clear, detailed text on a wide range of subjects and explain a viewpoint on a topical issue giving the advantages and disadvantages of various options.

Language Portfolio

The Portfolio, as proposed by the Council of Europe, is a folder kept by students, which details their experiences of languages and language learning. This includes the student's native tongue as well as any other languages with which the student has had contact. A Portfolio comprises a Language Biography, a Language Passport, and a Dossier. *Engage* 2nd edition offers practical solutions to help students build up the three sections of their Language Portfolio:

Language Biography

- A **Welcome self-assessment** (see page xiii) to help students evaluate what they remember and set learning objectives at the start of the year.

- Checklists for students to assess their own language skills in terms of "What I can do". In the **Student Book** these are found in the **Round-up** section at the end of each unit. Additionally, there are **Unit self-assessment checklists** in the CEFR portfolio section of the **Teacher's Resource MultiROM** with checklists for the skills and language covered in each unit, and a checklist of learning activities outside the classroom.

Language Passport

- An overview of the level attained by the student in English at the end of the year in the form of a checklist in the **End-of-Year self-assessment**. This provides the student with an overall self-evaluation of their language skills, using descriptors from the CEFR.

- Descriptors from levels A1, A2, B1, and B2 of the CEFR are provided within this document.

Dossier

- Samples of the student's work, including tests, written work, projects, or other student-generated materials.

In brief, the **Biography** details day-to-day experience of language. The **Passport** summarizes the experiences, and the **Dossier** is evidence of the experience.

Ask students to keep their self-assessment and checklists in their portfolio folder. Finally, encourage students to choose several pieces of their work from different points in the year to compile the dossier of their portfolio.

Welcome self-assessment

What I remember

Useful grammar:

....

....

....

Useful vocabulary:

....

....

....

Objectives

One thing I need to improve:

....

....

....

How can I improve this?

....

....

My English

What do you do in English outside class?

- ☐ Do homework
- ☐ Learn new words
- ☐ Study for a test
- ☐ Listen to music
- ☐ Read something in English
- ☐ Watch a TV show or a movie
- ☐ Use the Internet
- ☐ Write an e-mail or chat
- ☐ Speak to someone in English

Other activities

....

Student record sheet

Name: ....

Class / Grade: ....

| | Date | Classwork: Continuous assessment | | | | | | ★★☆ |
| | | Grammar | Vocabulary | Skills | | | | Unit test results |
				Reading	Listening	Speaking	Writing	
Unit 1								/ 60
Unit 2								/ 60
Unit 3								/ 60
Unit 4								/ 60
Unit 5								/ 60
Unit 6								/ 60
Unit 7								/ 60
Unit 8								/ 60

Class Audio CDs track list

CD 1

CD 2

Contents

Reading	Listening	Speaking	Writing
What's happening around the world? What RU talking about? Reading skills: Scanning	Talking about what you are doing	Talking about where you are and what you are doing Pronunciation: Elision	An online chat Writing skills: Capital letters
Follow the money – Part 1 Follow the money – Part 2 Reading skills: Using pictures	Clothes and physical descriptions	Describing what you look like and what you are wearing Pronunciation: h sound at the start of words	A personal blog Writing skills: Word order: position of adjectives
Fun food facts! Healthy eating – your way! Reading skills: Reading questions first	Favorite food	Making requests Pronunciation: Weak form of some	A report about a favorite meal
Advertisements Teen trivia quiz	Radio advertisements	Asking for things in a store Pronunciation: Intonation in questions	A consumer profile Writing skills: Using paragraphs
The sleepover Teen trouble Reading skills: Looking for key words and phrases	Talking about what to do on the weekend	Making suggestions Pronunciation: Responding to suggestions	An e-mail to a friend
Great names Famous firsts Reading skills: Using headings	Famous politicians	Giving personal information Pronunciation: th sound in ordinal numbers	A biography of a famous person Writing skills: Dates and time expressions
Music past and present Music in a virtual world Reading skills: Getting the general idea	Talking about a concert	Talking about activities in the past Pronunciation: Past tense -ed endings	A profile of your favorite band
Mysteries around the world Did he know his name?	Easter Island mystery	Talking about yesterday Pronunciation: Intonation in yes / no questions	An e-mail about a day out Writing skills: Ordering events

Unit summary

Vocabulary

Countries and nationalities: *Australia, Brazil, Guatemala, Japan, the United Kingdom, the United States; American, Australian, Brazilian, British, Guatemalan, Japanese*

Feelings: *angry, bored, happy, sad, scared, tired*

Things in your bedroom: Objects: *cell phone, computer, MP3 player, pencil case, skateboard;* Furniture: *bookcase, closet, desk, lamp, magazine, watch*

Jobs: *actor, athlete, dancer, doctor, singer, soccer player*

Family: *brother, father, grandfather, grandmother, grandparents, mother, sister*

Going out in town: *bowling alley, clothes store, cybercafé, fast food restaurant, movie theater, skate park, sports center, sports store*

Leisure activities: *go online, go out with friends, go shopping, play computer games, talk on the phone, watch TV*

Grammar

be (affirmative, negative, questions, and short answers)

Possessive adjectives

Possessive *'s*

this / that / these / those

there is / there are

can (affirmative, negative, questions, and short answers)

Imperatives

Simple present (affirmative, negative, questions, and short answers)

Question words

Cross-curricular

Multiculturalism; geography

Welcome

Vocabulary

Countries and nationalities

1 🔊 Match the countries with the flags. Then write the nationalities. Listen, check, and repeat.

> Australia   Brazil   Guatemala   ~~Japan~~
> the United Kingdom   the United States

1 Japan, Japanese
2 Australia, Australian
3 Brazil, Brazilian
4 the United States, American
5 Guatemala, Guatemalan
6 the United Kingdom, British

2 Draw your country's flag and write your nationality.

Feelings

3 🔊 Fill in the blanks with the words below. Then listen, check, and repeat.

> angry   bored   ~~happy~~   sad   scared   tired

1 It's my birthday today. I'm happy.

2 Ben's scared. He doesn't like horror movies.

3 It's 11 p.m. She's tired.

4 My mom's angry. I'm late again!

5 She's bored. This isn't a good TV show.

6 We're sad. Our team always loses!

4 How do you feel today?
I'm _____

4   → Workbook p.W2

Things in your bedroom

5 🔊 Label the objects in the picture with the words below. Then listen, check, and repeat.

> bookcase   ~~closet~~   desk   lamp   magazine   watch

1 closet   2 lamp
3 watch   4 bookcase
5 desk   6 magazine

6 Find the words below in the picture. Then fill in the blanks.

> cell phone   computer   MP3 player
> pencil case   ~~skateboard~~

1 It's under the bed. skateboard
2 It's on the bed. pencil case
3 It's under the bedside table. cell phone
4 It's on the bedside table. MP3 player
5 It's on the desk. computer

7 **Over to you!**
What's in your room? Where is it? Ask and answer with a partner.
Student A: Do you have a desk?
Student B: Yes, I do. It's next to my bed.

Vocabulary

Countries and nationalities

1 Review of vocabulary set: countries and nationalities 💿 1.2

- Match the countries with the flags and write the nationalities.
- Play the CD. Listen, check, and repeat.

2 Personalization of nationalities

- Draw your country's flag. Write your nationality. Check answers.

ANSWERS
Students' own answers.

Feelings

3 Review of vocabulary set: feelings 💿 1.3

- Look at the pictures. Fill in the blanks.
- Play the CD. Listen, check, and repeat.

4 Personalization of feeling adjectives

- Write down how you feel today.
- Check answers.

ANSWERS
Students' own answers.

Things in your bedroom

5 Review of vocabulary set: things in your bedroom 💿 1.4

- Label the objects.
- Play the CD. Listen, check, and repeat.

6 Vocabulary practice for things in your bedroom

- Find the things in the picture.
- Fill in the blanks.
- Check answers.

Over to you!

7 Personalization of things in your bedroom

- Work in pairs.
- Ask and answer questions about your partner's room. *What's in it? Where is it?*

Further practice
Workbook   page W2

Jobs

1 ◀)) **Write the jobs. Then listen, check, and repeat.**

1 _singer_   2 _doctor_

3 _athlete_   4 _soccer player_

5 _actor_   6 _dancer_

2 | **Over to you!**

Who's your favorite person? What's his / her job? Ask and answer with a partner.
My favorite person is Ji-Sung Park. He is a soccer player.

Family

3 ◀)) **Look at Mei's family tree. Fill in the blanks with the words below. Then listen, check, and repeat.**

brother father ~~grandfather~~ grandmother
grandparents mother sister

Keisuke = Lena

Ana = Norie

Joe   Mei   Lili

1 Keisuke is Mei's _grandfather_ .
2 Keisuke and Lena are Mei's _grandparents_ .
3 Joe is Mei's _brother_ .
4 Mei's _mother_ is Ana.
5 Norie is Mei's _father_ .
6 Mei's _sister_ is Lili.
7 Mei's _grandmother_ is Lena.

4 **Draw your family tree.**

Going out in town

5 ◀)) **Label the places in the picture with the words below. Then listen, check, and repeat.**

1	bowling alley	8	clothes store
5	cybercafé	7	fast food restaurant
3	movie theater	4	skate park
2	sports center	6	sports store

6 **Where do you go on the weekend?**
I go to the bowling alley with my friends.

Leisure activities

7 ◀)) **Match the verbs with the activities. Then listen, check, and repeat.**

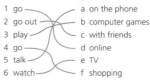

1 go   a on the phone
2 go out   b computer games
3 play   c with friends
4 go   d online
5 talk   e TV
6 watch   f shopping

8 | **Over to you!**

How often do you do the activities in exercise 7? Ask and answer with a partner.
Student A: How often do you go online?
Student B: I go online every day.

➜ Workbook pp.W2–W3   **5**

Jobs

1 Presentation and practice of vocabulary set: jobs ⊚ 1.5
- Write the jobs.
- Play the CD.
- Listen, check, and repeat.
- Check answers.

Over to you!

2 Personalization of words for jobs
- Think about your favorite person and their job.
- Ask and answer questions with your partner.

Family

3 Presentation and review of vocabulary set: family ⊚ 1.6
- Look at the family tree.
- Fill in the blanks.
- Play the CD.
- Listen, check, and repeat.
- Check answers

4 Personalization of family words
- Draw your family tree.
- Compare with a partner.
- Check answers with your partner.
- Check answers as a whole class.

ANSWERS
Students' own answers.

Going out in town

5 Presentation and review of vocabulary set: going out in town ⊚ 1.7
- Label the places.
- Play the CD.
- Listen, check, and repeat.

6 Personalization of going out in town
- Work in pairs.
- Ask and answer to find out where your partner goes on the weekends.
- Check answers with your partner.
- Check answers as a whole class.

ANSWERS
Students' own answers.

Leisure activities

7 Presentation and review of vocabulary set: leisure activities ⊚ 1.8
- Match the verbs with the activities.
- Play the CD.
- Listen, check, and repeat.

Over to you!

8 Personalization of leisure activities
- Work in pairs.
- Ask and answer questions to find out how often your partner does the activities in exercise 7.

Extra activity (all classes)
Review countries and nationalities
- Divide the class into two teams.
- One team says a country, e.g. *Brazil*.
- The other team responds with the corresponding nationality, e.g. *Brazilian*.
- The teams change roles.
- The game can be played with any set of related words, e.g. family "opposites" (*mother / father, sister / brother*, etc.), leisure activities – verb and phrase, e.g. *play computer games; watch TV*, etc.

Further practice
Workbook   pages W2–W3

Grammar

be (affirmative and negative)

1 Grammar chart: *be* (affirmative and negative)

- Look at the chart.
- Fill in the blanks with the short affirmative and negative forms of *be*.
- Check answers.

> **Note:**
> - In English we use a subject pronoun before the verb *be*, e.g. *I am Akiro.* (NOT ~~Am Akiro.~~)
> - We use *be* with age, e.g. *I am twelve.* (NOT ~~I have twelve years.~~)

2 Review and controlled practice of *be* (affirmative and negative)

- Read Nikos's message.
- Fill in the blanks with the affirmative form of *be*.
- Check answers.

3 Further practice of *be* (affirmative and negative)

- Read Rudi's message.
- Fill in the blanks with the affirmative or negative form of *be*.
- Check answers.

| **Further practice**
Workbook page W4

 Welcome

Grammar

be (affirmative and negative)

1 Look at the chart. Fill in the blanks with the short affirmative and negative forms of *be*.

Affirmative			Negative	
I (1) 'm	fourteen years old.		I (2) 'm not	from Japan.
You (3) 're	my brother.		You (4) aren't	Greek.
He (5) 's / She 's / It 's	from Greece.		He (6) isn't / She isn't / It isn't	tired.
We (7) 're	a happy family.		We (8) aren't	in the same class.
You (9) 're	best friends.		You (10) aren't	at school today.
They (11) 're	teachers.		They (12) aren't	happy.

2 Look at the webpage. Read Nikos's message. Fill in the blanks with the affirmative form of *be*.

3 Now read Rudi's message. Fill in the blanks with the correct form of *be*, affirmative (✓) or negative (✗).

engage world — Meet new friends from around the world!

Nikos

Hi, everyone. I (1) 'm _____ Nikos. I (2) 'm _____ fourteen and I (3) 'm _____ from Greece. My mother and father (4) are _____ Dimitra and Yannis. They (5) 're _____ teachers. My brother, Costas, (6) is _____ sixteen and my sister, Popi, (7) is _____ nineteen. They (8) 're _____ students. I (9) 'm _____ in my bedroom. My brother and sister (10) are _____ in the living room. Our apartment (11) 's _____ big and very nice. We (12) 're _____ a happy family! ☺

Rudi

Hi, Nikos! My name (1) is _____ (✓) Rudi. I (2) 'm _____ (✓) thirteen years old. My home (3) is _____ (✓) in Zurich, Switzerland. School (4) is _____ (✓) cool. I (5) 'm _____ (✓) very busy with exams this week, and I (6) 'm _____ (✓) tired. My best friends (7) are _____ (✓) Hans and Roger, but they (8) aren't _____ (✗) in my class. They (9) 're _____ (✓) fourteen years old. Hakan (10) 's _____ (✓) a good student, but Alex (11) isn't _____ (✗) happy at school. He (12) 's _____ (✓) late every day and his homework (13) isn't _____ (✗) good. ☹

→ Workbook p.W4

be (questions and short answers)

1 Fill in the chart with the correct form of *be*.

Questions	Short answers
(1) __Am__ I from Greece?	Yes, I (2) _am_ . / No, I (3) _'m not_ .
(4) _Are_ you fourteen?	Yes, you are. / No, you (5) _aren't_ .
(6) _Is_ he / she / it tired?	Yes, he / she / it (7) _is_ . / No, he / she / it isn't.
(8) _Are_ we good students?	Yes, we (9) _are_ . / No, we aren't.
(10) _Are_ you happy?	Yes, you are. / No, you aren't.
(11) _Are_ they teachers?	Yes, they are. / No, they (12) _aren't_ .
Personal questions	
Where (13) _are_ you from?	
What (14) _is_ your name?	
How old (15) _are_ you?	

2 Write questions with *be*. Then write the answers.

1 where / Nikos / from / ?
Where's Nikos from ?
He's from Greece .

2 his mother and father / teachers / ?
Are his mother and father teachers ?
Yes, they are .

3 Where / Nikos's / brother and sister / ?
Where are Nikos's brother and sister ?
They're in the living room .

4 Where / Rudi / from / ?
Where's Rudi from ?
He's from Zurich, Switzerland .

5 How old / his friends / ?
How old are his friends ?
They're fourteen .

6 Hakan / a good student / ?
Is Hakan a good student ?
Yes, he is .

7 Alex / happy / at school / ?
Is Alex happy at school ?
No, he isn't .

8 Alex / late / every / day / ?
Is Alex late every day ?
Yes, he is .

Possessive adjectives

3 Match the subject pronouns with the correct possessive adjectives.

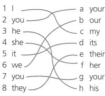

1 I — a your
2 you — b our
3 he — c my
4 she — d its
5 it — e their
6 we — f her
7 you — g your
8 they — h his

4 Fill in the blanks with possessive adjectives.

1 I'm from the U.S., but _my_ mother is Japanese.
2 I'm twelve. _My_ brother is fourteen.
3 We're at school today. _Our_ school is Weston High School.
4 Is that the new girl? Yes, _her_ name is Alice.
5 This isn't Sam's cell phone. _His_ cell phone is white.
6 My best friends are in my class. _Their_ names are Sue and Lidia.

Possessive *'s*

5 Write sentences. Use the possessive *'s*.

1 Susie / pen / be / new
Susie's pen is new .

2 Luca / notebook / be / small
Luca's notebook is small .

3 Max / skateboard / be / old
Max's skateboard is old .

4 Kevin / eraser / be / big
Kevin's eraser is big .

5 Eva and Marie / bags / be / new
Eva and Marie's bags are new .

6 Dan / ruler / be / short
Dan's ruler is short .

7 Andy / computer / be / expensive
Andy's computer is expensive .

8 Geoff / cat / be / angry
Geoff's cat is angry .

be (questions and short answers)

1 Grammar chart: *be* (questions and short answers)

- Fill in the chart with the correct form of *be*.
- Check answers.

> **Note:**
> - Use *Where* to ask questions about a place or position.
> - Use *What* when you are asking for information about something.
> - Use *How old* to ask about the age of someone or something.

2 Review and controlled practice of *be* (questions and short answers)

- Look at the sentence skeletons.
- Write questions with the correct form of *be*.
- Write the answers using the information on page 6.
- Check answers.

Posessive adjectives

3 Controlled practice of possessive adjectives

- Match the subject pronouns with the correct possessive adjectives.
- Check answers.

4 Review and controlled practice of possessive adjectives

- Fill in the blanks with possessive adjectives.
- Check answers.

Possessive *'s*

5 Review and controlled practice of possessive *'s*

- Look at the sentence skeletons.
- Write sentences, using the possessive *'s*.
- Check answers.

Extra activity (all classes)

Practice *be* (affirmative, negative, questions, and short answers), possessive adjectives and possessive *'s*

- Hold up a student's item, e.g. Eliza's pencil case, and ask, *Is this Robert's pencil case?* Elicit these responses from students: *No, it isn't. It isn't his / Robert's pencil case. It's Eliza's. It's her pencil case.*
- Do the activity several times with different items.

Further practice
Workbook pages W4–W5

Demonstratives: *this / that / these / those*

1 Review and controlled practice of demonstratives: *this / that / these / those*

- Fill in the blanks with *this*, *that*, *these*, or *those*.
- Check answers.

> **Note:**
> - *This / That + be + a / an* + singular nouns
> - *These / Those + be* + plural nouns
> - *What's + this / that?* (Answer: *It's / This is / That's …*)
> - *What are + these / those?* (Answer: *They are …*)

there is / there are

2 Review and controlled practice of *there is / there are*

- Look at the picture.
- Fill in the blanks.
- Check answers.

> **Note:**
> - In English we use *there is / there are* to say that something exists. We do not use *have*.
> - We use *there is + a / an* + singular noun, and *there are* + plural noun.
> - The short form of *there is* is *there's*. There is no short form of *there are*.

3 Further practice of *there is / there are*

- Look at the picture.
- Write questions with *Is there / Are there*.
- Write short answers.
- Check answers.

can (affirmative and negative)

4 Review and controlled practice of *can* (affirmative and negative)

> **Take note!**
> - *can* is a modal verb. Modal verbs have the same form for all persons, singular or plural.
> - The negative of *can* is *cannot* (short form *can't*).

- Write sentences.
- Use *can* (✔) and *can't* (✗).
- Check answers.

Welcome

Demonstratives: *this / that / these / those*

1 Fill in the blanks with *this, that, these,* or *those*.

1 **That** is my dad.
2 **This** is my cell phone.

3 **Those** are my sneakers.
4 **These** are your books.

there is / there are

2 Look at the picture. Fill in the blanks with *there is, there are, there isn't,* or *there aren't*.

1 **There are** two mountains next to the beach.
2 **There aren't** any foxes.
3 **There are** two butterflies next to the waterfall.
4 **There are** ten birds in the trees.
5 **There isn't** a bear.
6 **There is** a lake in front of the waterfall.

3 Write questions about the picture. Then answer the questions.

1 **Is there a penguin** ? (penguin)
  No, there isn't .
2 **Are there any foxes** ? (foxes)
  No, there aren't .
3 **Are there any trees** ? (trees)
  Yes, there are .
4 **Is there a beach** ? (beach)
  Yes, there is .
5 **Is there a chair** ? (chair)
  No, there isn't .
6 **Are there any monkeys** ? (monkeys)
  Yes, there are .

8   ➔ Workbook p.W5

can (affirmative and negative)

> **Take note!**
> - We use *can* to talk about abilities.
>   I can swim.
>   Susie can't ski.
>   Can you ice-skate? Yes, I can. / No, I can't.

4 Write sentences. Use *can* (✔) and *can't* (✗).

1 My brother / ski (✔) / ice-skate (✗)
  My brother can ski .
  My brother can't ice-skate .
2 You / swim (✔) / dive (✗)
  You can swim .
  You can't dive .
3 I / dance (✔) / jump high (✗)
  I can dance .
  I can't jump high .
4 Your parents / dance (✔) / run fast (✗)
  Your parents can dance .
  Your parents can't run fast .
5 We / play soccer (✔) / play tennis (✗)
  We can play soccer .
  We can't play tennis .
6 She / ride a horse (✔) / jump high (✗)
  She can ride a horse .
  She can't jump high .
7 They / swim (✔) / play soccer (✗)
  They can swim .
  They can't play soccer .

can (questions and short answers)

5 Answer the questions. Use the affirmative (✔) or negative (✗).

1 Can you speak Spanish? (✔)
  Yes, I can .
2 Can your baby sister throw a ball? (✗)
  No, she can't .
3 Can Ana swim? (✔)
  Yes, she can .
4 Can your brother drive a car? (✗)
  No, he can't .
5 Can we run fast? (✗)
  No, we can't .
6 Can you ice-skate? (✔)
  Yes, I can .
7 Can they dance? (✔)
  Yes, they can .
8 Can he drive? (✗)
  No, he can't .

---

can (questions and short answers)

5 Review and controlled practice of *can* (questions and short answers)

- Write the answers.
- Use the affirmative (✔) or negative (✗).
- Check answers.

Extra activity (stronger classes)

Practice *can* (affirmative, negative, questions, and short answers)

- Take turns to ask and answer questions about ability, using *Can you …?*
- Write your partner's answers.
- Take turns to tell the class what your partner can and can't do, e.g. *He can swim. He can't play tennis.*

Further practice
Workbook page W5

Imperatives

> **Take note!**
> * We use the imperative to give instructions.
>   Read the e-mail. Don't read the e-mail.
>   Watch this TV show. Don't watch this TV show.

1 Fill in the blanks with the affirmative or negative imperative form.

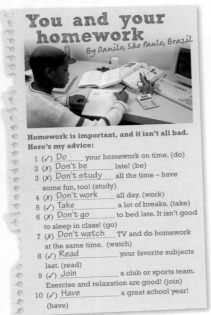

You and your homework
By Danilo, São Paulo, Brazil

Homework is important, and it isn't all bad. Here's my advice:

1 (✓) __Do__ your homework on time. (do)
2 (✗) __Don't be__ late! (be)
3 (✗) __Don't study__ all the time – have some fun, too! (study)
4 (✗) __Don't work__ all day. (work)
5 (✓) __Take__ a lot of breaks. (take)
6 (✗) __Don't go__ to bed late. It isn't good to sleep in class! (go)
7 (✗) __Don't watch__ TV and do homework at the same time. (watch)
8 (✓) __Read__ your favorite subjects last. (read)
9 (✓) __Join__ a club or sports team. Exercise and relaxation are good! (join)
10 (✓) __Have__ a great school year! (have)

Simple present (affirmative and negative)

2 Look at the chart. Fill in the blanks.

Affirmative	Negative
I (1) __get__ up at 7 a.m.	I (2) __don't get up__ at 7 a.m.
He (3) __loves__ math.	He (4) __doesn't love__ math.
We live in Toronto.	We (5) __don't live__ in Toronto.

3 Complete Matt's e-mail with the simple present affirmative form of the verbs in parentheses.

Hi, Rich!
My name's Matt. I (1) __live__ (live) in Toronto, Canada. I (2) __go__ (go) to Central High School. I (3) __speak__ (speak) French and English. Here's what I do on a school day!
I (4) __get up__ (get up) at 7 a.m. and I (5) __have__ (have) breakfast with my family. At 8 a.m. my mom (6) __drives__ (drive) me to school with my brother. School (7) __starts__ (start) at 8:30 a.m. and it (8) __finishes__ (finish) at 3:30 p.m. My favorite subject is art. I love it! I (9) __get__ (get) home at 4 p.m. and I (10) __do__ (do) my homework. On Tuesdays, I (11) __play__ (play) basketball after school. We always (12) __have__ (have) dinner at 6:30 p.m. After dinner, I (13) __send__ (send) e-mails or I (14) __watch__ (watch) TV.
Write soon! Tell me about your school day.
Matt

4 Correct the sentences about Matt.

1 Matt speaks French and Spanish.
  Matt doesn't speak French and Spanish.
  He speaks French and English .
2 Matt gets up at 6:30 a.m.
  Matt doesn't get up at 6:30 a.m.
  He gets up at 7 a.m. .
3 Matt loves math.
  Matt doesn't love math .
  He loves art .
4 Matt's school finishes at 4 p.m.
  Matt's school doesn't finish at 4 p.m.
  It finishes at 3:30 p.m. .
5 Matt has dinner at 5:30 p.m.
  Matt doesn't have dinner at 5:30 p.m.
  He has dinner at 6:30 p.m. .
6 On Tuesdays, Matt plays soccer.
  On Tuesdays, Matt doesn't play soccer .
  He plays basketball .

Workbook p.W6 9

> **Note:**
> * We add -s to the verbs to make the present simple forms for *he / she / it*.
> * If the verb ends in -o, -x, -sh, or -ch, we add -es (*go = goes, relax = relaxes, wash = washes, watch = watches*).
> * Some verbs are irregular, and have their own forms for *he / she / it*, e.g. *have = has*

3 Review and controlled practice of simple present (affirmative)
* Complete the e-mail.
* Check answers.

4 Further practice of simple present (affirmative and negative)
* Correct the sentences: write a negative sentence. Then write an affirmative sentence.
* Check answers.

Extra activity (all classes)
Practice of simple present (he / she / it), affirmative and negative
* Write three sentences about the things you do every day.
* Exchange your sentences with a partner.
* Tell the class something that your partner does or doesn't do, e.g. *He gets up at seven o'clock. He doesn't walk to school.*

| Further practice
Workbook page W6

Imperatives

1 Review and controlled practice of imperatives

> **Take note!**
> * We use the imperative to give instructions.
> * We use the infinitive of the verb for affirmative instructions, e.g. *Be quiet! Read this! Sit!*
> * We use the infinitive of the verb + *Don't* for negative instructions, e.g. *Don't be quiet! Don't read this! Don't sit!*
> * We don't use a subject with imperatives, e.g. *Look at the picture.* (NOT ~~You look at the picture.~~)

* Fill in the blanks.
* Use an affirmative or negative imperative.
* Check answers.

Simple present (affirmative and negative)

2 Grammar chart: simple present (affirmative and negative)
* Look at the chart.
* Fill in the blanks.
* Check answers.

Simple present (questions and short answers)

1 Grammar chart: simple present (questions and short answers)

- Look at the chart.
- Fill in the blanks.
- Check answers.

> **Note:**
> - We make *yes / no* questions in the simple present with *do / does* + subject + verb.
> - The auxiliary verb *do / does* must agree with the subject.
> - The verb is always in the infinitive form, e.g. *Does he like it?* (NOT *Does he likes it?*)
> - In short answers, we use the auxiliary verb *do / does, don't / doesn't*, and NOT the main verb, e.g. *Yes, he does.* (NOT *Yes, he does like.*)

2 Review and controlled practice of simple present (questions and short answers)

- Write the questions and then write the answers in the affirmative (✔) or negative (✗).
- Check answers.

> **Note:**
> - We form simple present *Wh-* questions with question word + *do / does* + subject + verb.
> - We use *What* to ask for information.
> - We use *When* to ask about the time.
> - We use *Where* to ask about a place or position.
> - We use *Why* to ask about a reason for something.
> - We use *How* to ask about the way something is done.

Question words

3 Review and controlled practice of question words

- Look at the answers.
- Write the questions.
- Use the question word in parentheses.
- Check answers.

| Further practice
Workbook   page W6

Welcome

Simple present (questions and short answers)

1 Look at the chart. Fill in the blanks.

Yes / No Questions	Short answers
(1) *Do* you live in Tokyo?	Yes, I do. / No, I (2) *don't*.
(3) *Does* he play basketball?	Yes, he (4) *does*. / No, he doesn't.
Wh- questions	**Answers**
Where (5) *do* you go on the weekends?	I go to the shopping mall.
When (6) *does* he get up?	At 7:30 a.m.

2 Write the questions. Then write the answers in the affirmative (✔) or negative (✗).

1 you / live / Ottawa / ? (✔)
   Do you live in Ottawa ?
   Yes, I do .

2 Mia / study / French / ? (✗)
   Does Mia study French
   ?
   No, she doesn't .

3 your grandparents / come from / Malaysia / ? (✔)
   Do your grandparents come from Malaysia
   ?
   Yes, they do .

4 your brother / play tennis / after school / ? (✗)
   Does your brother play tennis after school
   ?
   No, he doesn't .

5 you / get up / at 7 a.m. on Saturdays / ? (✔)
   Do you get up at 7 a.m. on Saturdays
   ?
   Yes, I do .

6 your best friends / like / rap music / ? (✔)
   Do your best friends like rap music
   ?
   Yes they do .

7 your sister / go to / college / ? (✗)
   Does your sister go to college
   ?
   No, she doesn't .

8 your parents / work / in the city / ? (✗)
   Do your parents work in the city
   ?
   No, they don't .

Question words

3 Look at the answers. Write questions. Use the question word in parentheses.

You: (1) Where do you live
       ? (where)
Katie: I live in Houston, Texas.
You: Cool! (2) What do you do on
       the weekends ? (what)
Katie: On the weekends, I go to the shopping mall with my friends.
You: (3) How do you go to the mall
       ? (how)
Katie: My mom usually drives us to the shopping mall.
You: (4) What do you do in the evenings
       ? (what)
Katie: I usually go to a dance club in the evenings.
You: Great! (5) When do you go to bed
       ? (when)
Katie: I go to bed after the dance club at eleven thirty.

10   → Workbook p.W6

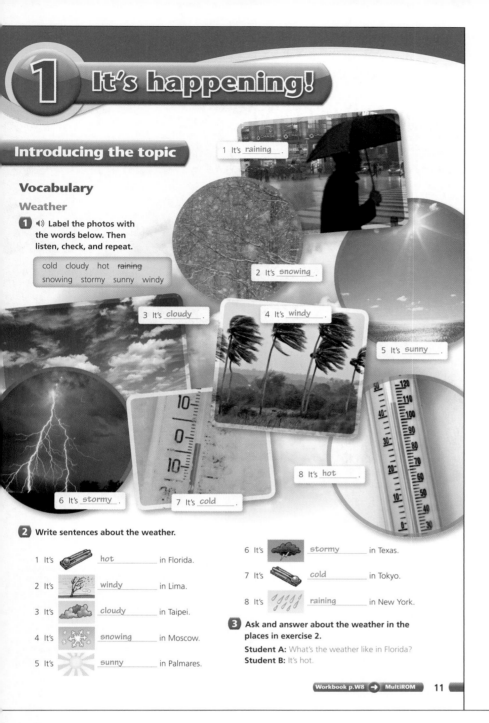

1 It's happening!

Introducing the topic

Vocabulary
Weather

1 🔊 **Label the photos with the words below. Then listen, check, and repeat.**

cold cloudy hot ~~raining~~
snowing stormy sunny windy

1 It's _raining_ .

2 It's _snowing_ .

3 It's _cloudy_ .

4 It's _windy_ .

5 It's _sunny_ .

6 It's _stormy_ .

7 It's _cold_ .

8 It's _hot_ .

2 Write sentences about the weather.

1 It's _hot_ in Florida.

2 It's _windy_ in Lima.

3 It's _cloudy_ in Taipei.

4 It's _snowing_ in Moscow.

5 It's _sunny_ in Palmares.

6 It's _stormy_ in Texas.

7 It's _cold_ in Tokyo.

8 It's _raining_ in New York.

3 Ask and answer about the weather in the places in exercise 2.
Student A: What's the weather like in Florida?
Student B: It's hot.

Workbook p.W8 → MultiROM   11

Unit summary

Vocabulary
Weather: *cold, cloudy, hot, raining, snowing, stormy, sunny, windy*
Everyday activities: *babysit, chat online, do homework, get dressed, post a comment, sleep, send a text message, wait for the bus*

Grammar
Present progressive (affirmative and negative)
Present progressive (questions and short answers)

Skills
Reading: Messages about weather around the world; an article about text messaging; scanning
Listening: Listening and identifying specific information in a conversation
Speaking: Talking about where you are and what you are doing; elision
Writing: Writing an online chat; using capital letters

Cross-curricular
Geography
Computer science

Values and topics
Personal and family relationships
Environmental science

Introducing the topic

Vocabulary

Aim
Present and practice vocabulary to describe weather

Warm-up
Ask students to look at the photos and the vocabulary for weather. Check the meaning with students and give examples. Then ask students to use some of the words to describe that day's weather.

1 Presentation of vocabulary set: words to describe weather 🌐 1.9
- Look at the photos and label them with the words.
- Play the CD.
- Listen, check, and repeat.

2 Vocabulary practice; exposure to adjectives in sentences
- Write the correct weather vocabulary for each place.
- Check answers.

3 Speaking: asking and answering about the weather around the world
- Look at the example dialogue.
- In pairs, ask and answer about the weather in the places in exercise 2.

Extend your vocabulary
It's cool It's foggy It's freezing
It's warm
Workbook page W8

Further practice
Workbook page W8
MultiROM

Exploring the topic

Reading

Aim
Present and practice weather words in four reading texts about different places

1 Matching (first reading) ⊛ 1.10
- Read and listen to the messages.
- Match the texts with the places in the photos.
- Check answers.

2 Detailed comprehension task (second reading)
- Read the messages again and write the places.
- Check answers as a class.

3 Detailed comprehension task (third reading)
- Read the sentences.
- Write M (for Marcelo), J (for Jenni), K (for Kang), or L (for Lola).
- Check answers.

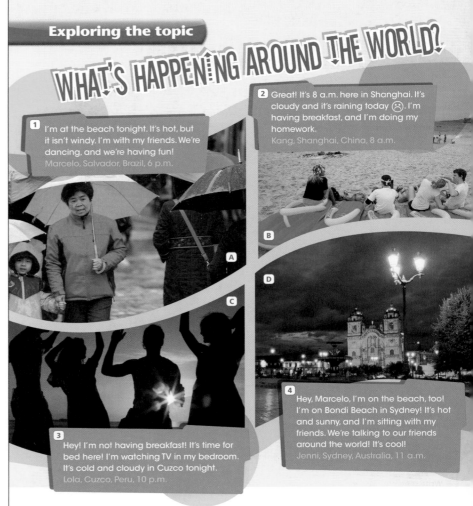

Exploring the topic

WHAT'S HAPPENING AROUND THE WORLD?

1 I'm at the beach tonight. It's hot, but it isn't windy. I'm with my friends. We're dancing, and we're having fun!
Marcelo, Salvador, Brazil, 6 p.m.

2 Great! It's 8 a.m. here in Shanghai. It's cloudy and it's raining today 😞. I'm having breakfast, and I'm doing my homework.
Kang, Shanghai, China, 8 a.m.

3 Hey! I'm not having breakfast! It's time for bed here! I'm watching TV in my bedroom. It's cold and cloudy in Cuzco tonight.
Lola, Cuzco, Peru, 10 p.m.

4 Hey, Marcelo, I'm on the beach, too! I'm on Bondi Beach in Sydney! It's hot and sunny, and I'm sitting with my friends. We're talking to our friends around the world! It's cool!
Jenni, Sydney, Australia, 11 a.m.

Reading

1 🔊 **Read and listen to the messages. Match the texts with the places in the photos.**
1 _C_   2 _A_   3 _D_   4 _B_

2 **Read the messages again. Where is it?**
1 It's hot and sunny. _Bondi Beach_
2 It's cold. _Cuzco_
3 It's cloudy and it's raining. _Shanghai_
4 It's hot and it isn't windy. _Salvador_

3 **Read the sentences. Write M (for Marcelo), J (for Jenni), K (for Kang), or L (for Lola).**
1 I'm dancing with my friends. _M_
2 I'm sitting on the beach with my friends. _J_
3 I'm watching TV. _L_
4 I'm not having breakfast. _L_
5 I'm doing my homework. _K_
6 I'm talking to my friends around the world. _J_

12

Grammar

Present progressive (affirmative and negative)

Talking about things that are happening right now

1 Look at the chart.

Affirmative	
I	**'m** work**ing**.
You	**'re** watch**ing** TV.
He / She / It	**'s** sitt**ing** on the beach.
We	**'re** danc**ing**.
You	**'re** hav**ing** breakfast.
They	**'re** talk**ing**.

Negative	
I	**'m not** work**ing**.
You	**aren't** watch**ing** TV.
He / She / It	**isn't** sitt**ing** on the beach.
We	**aren't** danc**ing**.
You	**aren't** eat**ing** breakfast.
They	**aren't** talk**ing**.

Take note!

Spelling rules for -ing forms
- **Regular: add** *-ing*
  work ➜ working
- **Consonant + -e: e +** *-ing*
  dance ➜ dancing
- **One vowel and one consonant: double the consonant +** *-ing*
  sit ➜ sitting

2 Write sentences. Use the present progressive.

1 I / watch / a movie on TV
   I'm watching a movie on TV .
2 Jude / not do / his homework
   Jude isn't doing his homework .
3 They / dance / on the beach
   They're dancing on the beach .
4 We / not run / in the park
   We aren't running in the park .
5 It / not rain / today
   It isn't raining today .
6 You / listen / to your favorite song
   You're listening to your favorite song .

3 Look at the picture. Write what is happening or isn't happening right now. Use the verbs in parentheses.

Naoki
Danny
Kassie

1 Naoki and Kassie aren't dancing . (dance)
2 Danny and Kassie are playing a game. (play)
3 Kassie isn't running . (run)
4 Naoki isn't talking . (talk)
5 Naoki is watching TV. (watch)
6 Naoki and Danny aren't singing . (sing)

 page 83, puzzle 1A

4 ### Over to you!

Choose a person from page 12. Draw a picture of what the person is doing. Can the class guess who it is?
Student A: It's Marcelo. He's dancing on the beach.
Student B: No, he isn't dancing on the beach.
Student A: Oh, it's Jenni. She's sitting on the beach.

3 Further practice of present progressive (affirmative and negative)

- Look at the picture.
- Write sentences about what is or isn't happening right now.
- Check answers.

PUZZLE PAGE 83
- Fast finishers can do Puzzle 1A on page 83.

ANSWERS
It's raining here today.
My teacher isn't talking now.
My best friend is watching TV.
I'm chatting to my friends online.

Over to you!

4 Personalization; oral practice of present progressive (affirmative and negative)

- Choose a person on page 12.
- Draw a picture of what that person is doing.
- Work in pairs. Show the picture to your partner. Use the present progressive (affirmative and negative) to guess the person and the action.

Further practice
Workbook (page W9)
MultiROM

Grammar

Aims

Present and practice present progressive (affirmative and negative)

Present and practice spelling rules for -ing forms

Talk and write about things that are happening right now

1 Grammar chart: present progressive (affirmative and negative)

- Look at the chart.

Take note!
- We make the present progressive with *be* (+ *not*) + the *-ing* form of the verb.
- We do not use *have* in the progressive form for physical description, e.g. *She has long hair.* (NOT ~~She's having long hair.~~)

Grammar reference (page W7)

2 Controlled practice of present progressive (affirmative and negative)

- Read the sentence skeletons.
- Write sentences.
- Check answers.

Building the topic

Vocabulary

Aims
Present and practice vocabulary for everyday activities
Model present progressive question form

Warm-up
Ask students to write a list of things they do every day. Compare their lists in pairs. How many things are the same?

1 Presentation of vocabulary set: everyday activities 🔊 1.11
- Match the words with the pictures.
- Write the words next to the pictures.
- Play the CD.
- Listen, check, and repeat.

2 Vocabulary practice: exposure to vocabulary for everyday activities 🔊 1.12
- Read the questions and choose the correct answer.
- Play the CD.
- Listen and check.

3 Vocabulary practice and extension
- Write four sentences in the present progressive (affirmative or negative).
- Check answers.

ANSWERS
Students' own answers.

Extend your vocabulary
brush your teeth   comb your hair
get ready for school
say "Goodbye"   wash your face
Workbook page W10

Further practice
Workbook page W10
MultiROM

Building the topic

Vocabulary
Everyday activities

1 🔊 Match the words with the pictures. Then listen, check, and repeat.

babysit   chat online   do homework
get dressed   post a comment   sleep
send a text message   wait for the bus

1 wait for the bus
2 do homework
3 get dressed
4 sleep
5 babysit
6 send a text message
7 chat online
8 post a comment

2 🔊 Write the correct answers under the questions. Then listen and check.

At Fifth Avenue and Main Street
He's sending a text message   No, I'm not
No, I'm not   No, they aren't   She's sleeping
Yes, I am   Yes, she is

Where are you waiting for the bus, Lucas?
1 At Fifth Avenue and Main Street

Are you eating dinner, Poppy?
2 No, I'm not

Are Jack and Emily getting dressed, Carol?
3 No, they aren't

What's your sister doing, Akiko?
4 She's sleeping

Are you babysitting your brother, Marcos?
5 Yes, I am

What is your brother doing, Leina?
6 He's sending a text message

Jun, are you chatting online to Kenta?
7 No, I'm not

Bea, is Paula posting a comment on my blog?
8 Yes, she is

3 Write sentences that are true for you, your friends, and your family.
1 I'm doing my homework .
2 I'm not .
3 My mom / dad / brother / sister is / isn't
4 My best friend is / isn't
5 My

14   Workbook p.W10 → MultiROM

Grammar

Present progressive (questions and short answers)

Asking about what is happening now

1 Look at the chart.

Questions	Short answers
Am I babysitt**ing**?	Yes, I **am**. / No, I'**m not**.
Are you sleep**ing**?	Yes, you **are**. / No, you **aren't**.
Is he / she / it eat**ing**?	Yes, he / she / it **is**. / No, he / she / it **isn't**.
Are we wait**ing**?	Yes, we **are**. / No, we **aren't**.
Are you getting dressed?	Yes, you **are**. / No, you **aren't**.
Are they talk**ing**?	Yes, they **are**. / No, they **aren't**.
Wh- questions	
What are you do**ing**? **Where is** he wait**ing**?	

2 Match the questions with the answers.

1 Are you doing your homework? _d_
2 Where are they waiting for the bus? _f_
3 What is she doing? _e_
4 Are we dancing on the beach? _c_
5 What are you doing? _a_
6 Is he playing soccer in the park? _b_

a I'm posting a comment on your blog.
b Yes, he is.
c Yes, we are.
d No, I'm not.
e She's sending a text message.
f At Fourth Avenue and Tenth Street.

3 Look at the picture. Write the answers for the questions.

1 Are John and Tim watching TV?
   No, they aren't .
2 Are John and Tim playing computer games?
   Yes, they are .
3 Is Ted chatting to his friends online?
   Yes, he is .
4 Is Ted standing in the kitchen?
   No, he isn't .
5 Is Mrs. James cooking?
   Yes, she is .
6 Is Rose sending a text message?
   Yes, she is .

4 Look at the picture again. Write the questions and answers.

1 Mrs. James / eating dinner / ?
   Is Mrs. James eating dinner ?
   No, she isn't .
   She's cooking dinner .
2 John and Tim / do their homework / ?
   Are John and Tim doing their homework ?
   No, they aren't .
   They're playing computer games .
3 Rose / listen to music / ?
   Is Rose listening to music ?
   No, she isn't .
   She's sending a text message .
4 Ted / play soccer / ?
   Is Ted playing soccer ?
   No, he isn't .
   He's chatting to his friends online .

Puzzle page 83, puzzle 1B →

5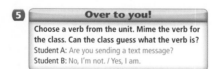
Over to you!
Choose a verb from the unit. Mime the verb for the class. Can the class guess what the verb is?
Student A: Are you sending a text message?
Student B: No, I'm not. / Yes, I am.

Workbook p.W11 → MultiROM   15

Grammar

Aims

Present and practice present progressive (questions and short answers)

Ask and answer questions about things that are happening right now

1 Grammar chart: present progressive (questions and short answers)

• Look at the chart.

Note:
• We make questions with the present progressive by inverting *be* and the pronoun, e.g.
He (pronoun) *is* (verb *to be*) *talking* = *Is* (verb *to be*) he (pronoun) *talking*?

• We do not use the *-ing* form in a short answer, e.g. *Are you working? Yes, I am / No, I'm not.* (NOT ~~Yes, I am working. / No, I'm not working.~~)

• We do not contract *be* in affirmative short answers, e.g. *Yes, I am.* (NOT ~~Yes, I'm.~~)

Grammar reference (page W7)

2 Controlled practice of present progressive (questions and short answers)

• Read questions (1–6).
• Choose answers (a–f).
• Check answers.

3 Further practice of present progressive (questions and short answers)

• Look at the picture.
• Write the answers for the questions.
• Check answers.

4 Further practice of present progressive (questions and short answers)

• Look at the picture again.
• Write the questions and write short answers and the correct answers.
• Check answers.

PUZZLE PAGE 83
• Fast finishers can do Puzzle 1B on page 83.

ANSWERS
Is your mom singing in the yard?
Are you sleeping in your bed?
Is the dog eating your homework?
Students' own answers.

Over to you!

5 Personalization of present progressive (questions and short answers)

• Choose a verb from the unit.
• Mime the verb for the class.
• Take turns to ask questions in the present progressive to guess the verb, and answer using short answers.

Extra activity (all classes)

Practice present progressive (questions and short answers)

• Students mime an action for other students to guess.
• Either give students actions (on a piece of paper, e.g. *swimming, eating*), or ask them to think of their own action to mime.
• Students mime the actions to the class or in groups.
• Other students try to guess the action. Encourage them to use the present progressive in questions and short answers, e.g. *Are you swimming? No, I'm not. / Yes, I am.*

Further practice
Workbook (page W11)
MultiROM

Living English

Reading

🔊 1.13

Aims

Read about language used in text messages

Reading skills: scanning to find specific information

Warm-up

Ask Do you send text messages? Who do you send them to? How often do you send or get text messages?

BACKGROUND INFORMATION

Text messaging (SMS – short message service) is a service on most cell phones which allows people to send short messages to other cell phone users. The first text message was sent in 1992 and the service quickly became popular. In 2009, over 1.5 trillion text messages were sent around the world. The popularity of text messaging has led to a special texting language that is an abbreviated form of normal language. There are many examples in the reading texts.

1 Global comprehension task (first reading)

- Read the article quickly. What is it about?
- What is unusual about the messages?

ANSWER

They are in an abbreviated language called texting.

2 Reading skills: scanning (second reading)

- Read the Reading skills box.

> **Reading skills: scanning**
> - You can read the text quickly to find information.
> - Remind students that it is not necessary to read every word in order to find out the general idea (gist) of a text.

3 Detailed comprehension task (third reading)

- Read the article again quickly and complete the sentences.
- Check answers.

4 Detailed comprehension task (fourth reading)

- Read and listen to the article more carefully.
- Match the text messages to the correct statements (1–5).
- Check answers.

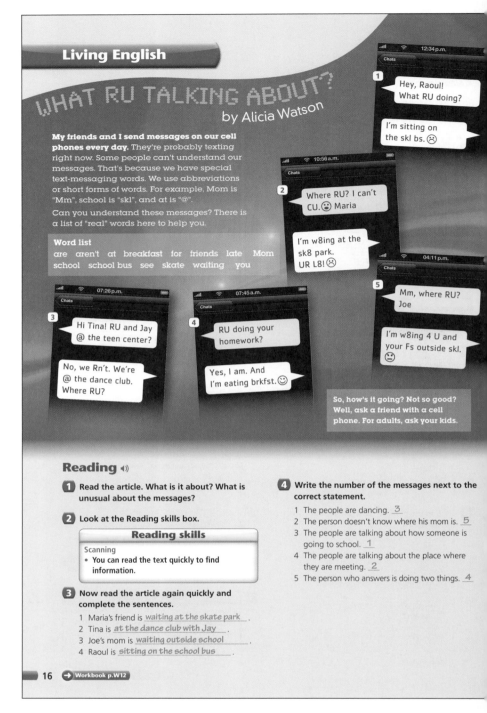

Extra activity (stronger classes)

Exposure to "real" language is motivating and meaningful to students

- Write the following text messages on the board:
  1 RU OK?
  2 RU zzzz?
  3 CU 2moro
  4 Luv U 4eva!
  5 RU sk8tng l8r?
- Students try to write the messages in full.

ANSWERS

1 Are you OK?
2 Are you sleeping?
3 See you tomorrow.
4 Love you forever!
5 Are you skating later?

Further practice

Workbook page W12

Listening

Talking about what you are doing

1 ◀)) **Listen to the phone call. Who is talking?**
 a Abel and Bart
 b Abel and Katie
 c Abel and Rachel

2 ◀)) **Listen again. Circle the correct words.**
 1 Katie is in her bedroom / the living room.
 2 Bart is in the living room / kitchen.
 3 Rachel is in the living room / her bedroom.

3 ◀)) **Listen again. Choose the correct answers.**
 1 Katie is in … .
  a Rio   b California   c Natal
 2 Katie is … .
  a watching a DVD   b watching TV
  c sleeping
 3 Katie says it's … .
  a sunny   b cloudy   c raining
 4 Bart is … .
  a watching the DVD with Katie
  b reading a book   c sleeping
 5 Abel is … .
  a listening to music   b watching TV
  c dancing
 6 Rachel is … .
  a chatting online
  b dancing in the living room
  c dancing in her bedroom

Speaking

Talking about where you are and what you are doing

1 ◀)) **Listen and read.**

Hi, Toni! It's Lena. Where are you?
I'm at the movie theater.
What are you doing?
I'm waiting for Henry and Heather, and I'm talking to you!

Hi, Lena. Where are you?
I'm in my bedroom. I'm reading.
What are you reading?
I'm reading a magazine.

2 ◀)) **Look at the Pronunciation box. Listen to the examples. Then listen again, and repeat.**

> **Pronunciation**
>
> **Elision**
> What are you doing?
> What are you reading?

3 ◀)) **Practice the questions. Then listen and repeat.**
 1 What are you eating?
 2 What are they reading?
 3 What are you doing?
 4 What are you watching?
 5 What are they cooking?

4 **Practice the dialogue in exercise 1.**

5 **Now change the words in blue. Write a new dialogue. Then practice the dialogue in class.**

Listening

Aim

Listen and identify activities people are doing now

1 Global comprehension of the listening task (first listening) ◎ 1.14

- Play the CD.
- Listen and decide which two people are talking.
- Check answers.

Audioscript

Abel: Hey, is that Katie?
Katie: Yes. Who's this?
Abel: Hi Katie, this is Abel! Are you sleeping?
Katie: Oh, hi Abel. No, I'm not. It's six o'clock here in California. What time is it in Natal?
Abel: It's ten o'clock. What are you doing, Katie?
Katie: Well, it's raining at the moment. I'm in my bedroom and I'm watching a DVD.
Abel: What are you watching?
Katie: I'm watching *Kung Fu Panda 2*.
Abel: Boring! What's Bart doing? Is he watching the movie with you?
Katie: No, he's reading a book in the kitchen. What are you doing, Abel?
Abel: I'm listening to music.
Katie: Really? Is Rachel chatting online to her friends?
Abel: No, she isn't. She's dancing in the living room. It's very funny!

2 Detailed comprehension of the listening task (second listening) ◎ 1.14

- Play the CD again.
- Listen again. Circle the correct words.

3 Detailed comprehension of the listening task (third listening) ◎ 1.14

- Play the CD again.
- Choose the correct answers.
- Check answers.

Speaking

Aims

Talk about where you are and what you are doing
Pronunciation: elision

1 First listening ◎ 1.15

- Play the CD.
- Listen and read.

2 Presentation of pronunciation point ◎ 1.16

- Look at the Pronunciation box.
- Play the CD.
- Listen to the examples.

> **Pronunciation: elision**
> - In spoken English we leave out certain sounds in order to make words flow into one another more freely.

- Play the CD again.
- Listen again, and repeat.

3 Pronunciation practice ◎ 1.17

- Practise the questions with elision.
- Play the CD. Listen and repeat.

4 Dialogue practice

- Practice the dialogue in exercise 1 with a partner.
- Listen to students' dialogues. Check that they are using elision.
- Ask stronger students to demonstrate their dialogues out in front of the class.

5 Dialogue personalization and practice

- Change the words in blue and write a new dialogue in pairs.
- Ask students to practice the dialogue in their partners.
- Listen to students' dialogues. Check the elision.
- Ask stronger students to demonstrate their dialogues out in front of the class.

ANSWERS
Students' own answers.

Further practice
MultiROM

Round-up

Writing

Aims

Write an online chat
Writing skills: capital letters

1 Writing skills: capital letters

* Read the Writing skills box.

> **Writing skills: capital letters**
> * We use capital letters for names of people, cities, countries, languages, and nationalities.
> * We also use capitals for names of mountains, seas, and other geographical or historical features, e.g. *the Iguazu Falls, the Atacama desert, the Great Wall of China.*

* Read the online chat and find two names, two cities, and two countries.
* Check answers.

ANSWERS
Names: Tomoko and Sara; Cities: Tokyo and Porto Alegre; Countries: Japan and Brazil

2 Detailed analysis of model writing task

* Complete the chart with information about Tomoko.
* Check answers.

3 Preparation for personalized writing

* Complete the chart with information about you.
* Check that students are completing the chart correctly.

ANSWERS
Students' own answers.

4 Personalized writing

* Follow the model writing text. Use your own information from the chart to change the text.
* Write your online chat.

ANSWERS
Students' own answers.

I can …

Aims

Check understanding of the present progressive (affirmative, negative, questions, and short answers); self-assessment of own progress

---

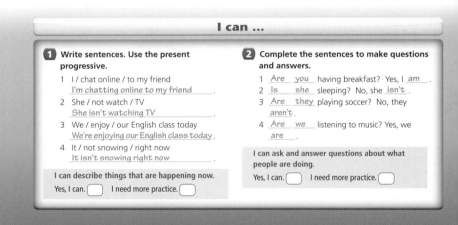

Round-up

Writing

An online chat

1 Look at the Writing skills box.

> **Writing skills**
>
> Capital letters
> * Remember we use capital letters in English for names of people, cities, and countries.

Now read the online chat and find two names, two cities, and two countries.

2 Fill in the chart with information about Tomoko.

		You
Name	Tomoko	
From	Tokyo, Japan	
Weather	sunny	
Doing right now	chatting to friends online, drinking soda	

3 Now fill in the chart with your information.

4 Imagine you are chatting to Tomoko online. Write a reply to her message. Use Sara's reply and the chart to help you.

Chat
Settings | 10:15 p.m.

Tomoko, Tokyo — 10:00 a.m.
Hi, Sara! How are you? It's 10 a.m. here in Tokyo, Japan, and it's sunny today! Hooray! I'm at the shopping mall with my friends. We're in the cybercafé. We're chatting to our friends online, and we're drinking soda. What are you doing?

Sara, Porto Alegre — 10:01 p.m.
Hi, Tomoko! I'm good, thanks. How are you? Well, I'm in Porto Alegre, Brazil, and it's 10 p.m. It's cold here! I'm in my bedroom. I'm watching a movie on TV.

Tomoko, Tokyo — 10:03 a.m.
Oh, OK! Are you watching a good movie?

Sara, Porto Alegre — 10:06 p.m.
I'm watching Spider-Man 3. It's awesome! Do you like the Spider-Man movies?

Tomoko, Tokyo — 10:10 a.m.
Yes, I love them! Enjoy the movie! See you later!

Sara, Porto Alegre — 10:14 p.m.
OK! Bye! Goodnight!

I can …

1 **Write sentences. Use the present progressive.**
1 I / chat online / to my friend
   I'm chatting online to my friend .
2 She / not watch / TV
   She isn't watching TV .
3 We / enjoy / our English class today
   We're enjoying our English class today .
4 It / not snowing / right now
   It isn't snowing right now .

I can describe things that are happening now.
Yes, I can. ☐   I need more practice. ☐

2 **Complete the sentences to make questions and answers.**
1 Are you having breakfast? Yes, I am .
2 Is she sleeping? No, she isn't .
3 Are they playing soccer? No, they aren't .
4 Are we listening to music? Yes, we are .

I can ask and answer questions about what people are doing.
Yes, I can. ☐   I need more practice. ☐

18

---

1 Self-assessment of present progressive (affirmative and negative)

* For items (1–4), students read the sentences and complete them with the correct answers.
* Students check (✓) *Yes, I can.* if they think they understand the vocabulary or grammar well, or check (✓) *I need more practice.* if they think they need more practice.
* If students have chosen *I need more practice.*, encourage them to review these sections and to do more practice.

2 Self-assessment of present progressive (questions and short answers)

* For items (1–4), students read the sentences and complete them with the correct answers.
* Students check (✓) *Yes, I can.* if they think they understand the vocabulary or grammar well, or check (✓) *I need more practice.* if they think they need more practice.
* If students have chosen *I need more practice.*, encourage them to review these sections and to do more practice.

Further practice
Pairwork pages 108–109
Test pages 88–89; 104

2 What's he wearing?

Introducing the topic

Cal — shirt
Denise — 4 top
Melina — 7 glasses
2 pants
5 skirt
6 boots
8 socks
shoes

Vocabulary

Clothes

1 🔊 **Label the pictures with the words below. Then listen and repeat.**

> boots glasses pants ~~shirt~~ shoes skirt
> socks top

2 🔊 **Listen and check (✓) the clothes the people are wearing today.**

Carolina: ☐ sweatpants ✓ skirt
☐ sweatshirt ✓ top
Max: ✓ pants ☐ jeans
☐ T-shirt ✓ shirt
Steve: ☐ sneakers ✓ shoes
☐ glasses ☐ boots
Nicky: ☐ shoes ✓ socks
✓ boots ☐ glasses

3 **Unscramble the letters. Then fill in the blanks.**

1 Milly's wearing a _skirt_ today. (t i k r s)
2 Look at those _boots_ ! They're very old. (s o b o t)
3 My dad always wears _socks_ . (c o s k s)
4 Why are you wearing a _shirt_ today? (r i t s h)
5 My mom's wearing her _glasses_ today. (e s l a s g s)
6 I like your _shoes_ . Are they new? (e s h o s)

4 **Complete the information about your clothes.**

Clothes I wear to school: _____

Clothes I wear on the weekends: _____

Clothes I wear to parties: _____

Workbook p.W14 ➜ MultiROM   **19**

Introducing the topic

Vocabulary

Aim

Present and practice words to describe clothes

Warm-up

Ask *What are you wearing now? What are your favorite clothes?* Encourage students to use a color when appropriate, e.g. *a red shirt.*

1 Presentation of vocabulary set: clothes 🔊 1.18

- Label the pictures with the words in the box.
- Play the CD.
- Listen, check, and repeat.

2 Vocabulary practice; exposure to words for clothes 🔊 1.19

- Play the CD.
- Students listen and check (✓) the correct words to describe what people are wearing. Check answers.

Audioscript

Carolina: I'm Carolina. I usually wear sweatpants and a sweatshirt, but today I'm visiting my grandparents. I'm wearing a red skirt and a white top.
Max: I'm Max and I love my jeans, but today I'm at a party with my family. I'm wearing my gray shirt and black pants.
Steve: I'm Steve. I usually wear sneakers, but I'm wearing my new shoes today. Do you like them?
Nicky: Hello. I'm Nicky. I'm wearing my socks and boots today because it's cold and it's raining.

3 Checking comprehension of vocabulary

- Unscramble the letters and fill in the blanks.
- Check answers.

4 Personalization

- Complete the sentences with information about your own clothes.

ANSWERS
Students' own answers.

Extend your vocabulary

belt gloves hat jacket sandals scarf
sunglasses swimsuit
Workbook   page W14

Further practice
Workbook   page W14
MultiROM

Unit summary

Vocabulary
Clothes: *boots, glasses, pants, shirt, shoes, skirt, socks, top*
Physical descriptions: Eyes: *big, small, blue, (light) brown, green*; Hair: *long, short, straight, wavy, blond, (dark) brown, red*; Other: *a beard, a mustache*

Grammar
Simple present and present progressive
has / have for appearance
have or *be* for physical description

Skills
Reading: A comicbook detective story; using pictures to help understand a text
Listening: Listening and identifying specific information in a description
Speaking: Describing clothes and appearance; *h* sound at the start of words
Writing: Writing a personal blog; word order: position of adjectives

Cross-curricular
Computer science

Values and topics
Citizenship
Multiculturalism
Society
Popular culture
Identity
Crime

Exploring the topic

Reading

Aims

Present and practice clothes vocabulary and present progressive in a comic book detective story

Warm-up

Students look at the picture story. Ask *What are the people's jobs?* (They are detectives.), *Which other famous detectives do you know from books, movies, or TV?*

1 Identifying (first reading) 🎧 1.20

- Play the CD.
- Listen to and read the text.
- Answer the question.
- Check answers.

ANSWER

The suspect's socks are pink.

2 Detailed comprehension task (second reading)

- Read the text again and circle T or F next to the sentences.
- Check answers as a class.

3 Detailed comprehension task (third reading)

- Read the text again and answer the questions.
- Check answers.

Extra activity (all classes)

Review and practice of present progressive (affirmative and negative); clothes

- Students take turns to describe someone in the class using the present progressive and clothes vocabulary.
- Can the other students guess who is being described?

Reading

1 🔊 **Read and listen to the story. What color are the suspect's socks?**

2 **Read again. Circle T (True) or F (False).**

1 Agents Lee and Daniels normally work in an office. **T**/ F
2 Agent Daniels is watching the suspect. **T**/ F
3 The suspect usually walks. T /**F**
4 The suspect never wears jeans. T /**F**
5 The suspect is waiting for a bus. **T**/ F
6 A woman is waiting at the bus stop. **T**/ F

3 **Answer the questions.**

1 Who is Agent Lee talking to?
   She's talking to Agent Daniels
2 Where is the suspect?
   He's on Maple Street
3 What is the suspect carrying?
   He's carrying a briefcase
4 What is the suspect wearing?
   He's wearing gray pants, a white shirt, and pink socks
5 Where is the bus stop?
   It's on the corner of Maple and Tenth
6 What is the woman at the bus stop wearing?
   She's wearing a red skirt, a white top, black glasses, and black boots

20

What's he wearing?

Grammar

Simple present and present progressive

Talking about regular activities and when they happen
Talking about things that are happening right now

1 Look at the chart.

Simple present	Present progressive
Regular activities	**Now**
I (always) **wear** sneakers.	I**'m wearing** shoes (right now).
You (usually) **get up** (at seven o'clock).	You**'re sleeping** (now).
He (normally) **walks**.	He**'s taking** the bus (at the moment).
Do they **work** in an office (every day)?	**Are** they **working** in an office (today)?

2 Circle the correct time word.

1 I (always) / right now wear a school uniform.
2 My mom isn't cooking dinner every day / (at the moment)
3 Tino at the moment / (usually) plays basketball on the weekends.
4 Sam (normally) / right now wears glasses.
5 We start school at 8 a.m. (every day) / now.
6 Sorry, they can't help you. They're doing their homework (right now) / normally.

3 Look at the pictures and read the sentences. Write U (for usually) or RN (for right now).

1 Marcos and Carla normally stay at home. _U_
2 Marcos watches DVDs on Friday evenings. _U_
3 Marcos is dancing with his friends. _RN_
4 They eat snacks at home. _U_
5 They're wearing their best clothes. _RN_
6 Carla calls her friends at night. _U_

Marcos
Carla
A normal Friday evening.

4 Complete the sentences with the simple present or present progressive.

1 Carla and Marcos _don't go out_ on Friday evenings. (not go out)
2 Right now, Carla _is having_ a good time. (have)
3 Marcos normally _wears_ his pajamas at home. (wear)
4 Marcos _is wearing_ his best clothes right now. (wear)
5 Carla and Marcos normally _go_ to bed at ten thirty. (go)
6 At the moment, Marcos and Carla _are staying up_ late with their friends. (stay up)

Puzzle page 83, puzzle 2A

5 ### Over to you!

Think of someone you know. Write two sentences about what they normally do and two sentences about what they are doing right now. Can the class guess who it is?
Student A: She normally works at home. She usually wears jeans and a T-shirt. Right now, she's teaching a math class. She's wearing a skirt and a top today.
Student B: Is she your mother?

HAPPY BIRTHDAY MIGUEL!
Marcos
Carla
It's a special Friday evening tonight!

Workbook p.W15 → MultiROM **21**

PUZZLE PAGE 83

• Fast finishers can do Puzzle 2A on page 83.

ANSWERS
2 listens 3 reads 4 watches 5 play
6 drive 7 sings 8 get up
Mystery word: sleeping

Over to you!

5 Personalization: oral practice of simple present and present progressive

• Think of someone you know.
• Write two sentences about what they normally do and two sentences about what they are doing right now.
• Can the class guess who it is?

Further practice
Workbook page W15
MultiROM

Grammar

Aims

Present and practice simple present and present progressive
Talk about regular activities
Talk about things that are happening right now

1 Grammar chart: Simple present and present progressive

• Look at the chart.

Note:
• We use the simple present for regular activities, habits, and facts.
• We use the present progressive for things that are happening right now.
Grammar reference page W13

2 Review of simple present and present progressive

• Circle the correct time word.
• Check answers.

3 Controlled practice of simple present and present progressive

• Look at the pictures and read the sentences.
• Write U for usually or RN for right now.
• Check answers.

4 Further practice of simple present and present progressive

• Fill in the blanks.
• Check answers.

Building the topic

Vocabulary

Aims

Present and practice vocabulary for physical descriptions

Write physical descriptions

Warm-up

Ask students to close their eyes. Can they remember the color of their partner's eyes? Can they remember the color of your eyes?

Captain Jack Sparrow is a character played by Johnny Depp in the *The Pirates of the Caribbean* movies. The newest movie is *On Stranger Tides* and was released in 2011.

Princess Fiona is a character from the *Shrek* movies, voiced by Cameron Diaz. Princess Fiona marries the ogre Shrek and they have a family of ogre babies.

Jack Driscoll is a character from the movie *King Kong*, and is played by Adrien Brody. Jack Driscoll is a writer and visits the mysterious Skull Island in search of adventure.

Alice is a character from Tim Burton's 2010 *Alice In Wonderland*. Alice is played by Mia Wasikowska.

Howl is a wizard from the Japanese movie *Howl's Moving Castle* by Hayao Miyazaki. Howl is voiced by Takuya Kimura in Japanese and Christian Bale in English.

> **Note:**
> • We use *dark brown*, rather than *black*, to describe eye color.

1 Presentation of vocabulary set: physical descriptions 🔊 1.21

- Look at the faces. Complete labels (1–10) with the words in the box.
- Play the CD.
- Check answers. Then listen, and repeat.

2 Vocabulary practice: exposure to vocabulary for physical descriptions 🔊 1.22

- Play the CD.
- Read and listen to the descriptions.
- Write the correct name on the photos (A–D).
- Listen, repeat, and check answers.

3 Vocabulary practice and extension

- Complete three sentences about people you know.
- Check answers.

Students' own answers.

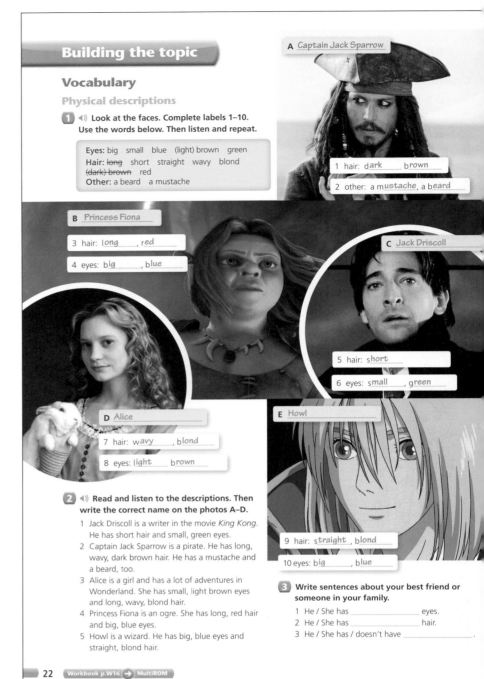

Building the topic

Vocabulary
Physical descriptions

1 🔊 **Look at the faces. Complete labels 1–10. Use the words below. Then listen and repeat.**

> **Eyes:** big small blue (light) brown green
> **Hair:** ~~long~~ short straight wavy blond ~~(dark) brown~~ red
> **Other:** a beard a mustache

A Captain Jack Sparrow
1 hair: dark   brown
2 other: a mustache, a beard

B Princess Fiona
3 hair: long   , red
4 eyes: big   , blue

C Jack Driscoll
5 hair: short
6 eyes: small   , green

D Alice
7 hair: wavy   , blond
8 eyes: light   brown

E Howl
9 hair: straight , blond
10 eyes: big   , blue

2 🔊 **Read and listen to the descriptions. Then write the correct name on the photos A–D.**

1 Jack Driscoll is a writer in the movie *King Kong*. He has short hair and small, green eyes.
2 Captain Jack Sparrow is a pirate. He has long, wavy, dark brown hair. He has a mustache and a beard, too.
3 Alice is a girl and has a lot of adventures in Wonderland. She has small, light brown eyes and long, wavy, blond hair.
4 Princess Fiona is an ogre. She has long, red hair and big, blue eyes.
5 Howl is a wizard. He has big, blue eyes and straight, blond hair.

3 **Write sentences about your best friend or someone in your family.**

1 He / She has _____ eyes.
2 He / She has _____ hair.
3 He / She has / doesn't have _____

22   Workbook p.W16 → MultiROM

Extend your vocabulary

bald good-looking overweight short slim strong tall

Workbook   page W16

Note:
• We use *short* and *tall* to describe height, (NOT ~~low and high~~).

Further practice
Workbook   page W16
MultiROM

Grammar

has / have

Talking about physical appearance

1 Look at the chart.

Affirmative	Negative
I **have** short hair.	I **don't have** short hair.
You **have** wavy hair.	You **don't have** wavy hair.
He / She / It **has** long hair.	He / She / It **doesn't have** long hair.
We **have** blue eyes.	We **don't have** blue eyes.
You **have** big eyes.	You **don't have** big eyes.
They **have** straight hair.	They **don't have** straight hair.
What does he / she look like?	

Take note!

Describing people
* *have* + adjective + noun:
He has blue eyes.
* *be* + adjective:
He is tall.

2 Read the text about Jack and his friends. Fill in the blanks with *has* or *have*. Use the affirmative or negative.

These are my friends. Miguel (1) __has__ short, wavy hair. His sister Tanya (2) __has__ long, straight hair. Miguel and Tanya (3) __have__ blond hair, and they (4) __have__ green eyes. Seth and I (5) __have__ short hair. We (6) __don't have__ blond hair. Seth (7) __has__ brown hair, and I (8) __have__ black hair. We (9) __have__ big, blue eyes.

What's he wearing?

3 Look at the pictures and complete the descriptions. Use the correct form of *be* or *have*.

Colonel Miles Quaritch

Corporal Jake Sully

AVATAR

Neytiri

Grace

1 Corporal Jake Sully __is__ short. He __has__ short, brown hair and small, blue eyes. He __doesn't have__ a beard or a mustache.
2 Neytiri __is__ very tall. She __has__ big, yellow eyes and long, straight, black hair.
3 Grace __is__ tall and slim. She __has__ short, wavy, red hair and dark brown eyes.
4 Colonel Miles Quaritch __is__ very big. He __doesn't have__ long, blond hair. He __has__ short, gray hair and green eyes.

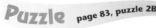 **Puzzle** page 83, puzzle 2B

4
Over to you!

Describe a character from your favorite movie. Use words from the unit.
My favorite movie is *Toy Story*. Woody has short, brown hair and big, brown eyes.

Workbook p.W17 → MultiROM   23

---

2 Controlled practice of *has* / *have* (affirmative and negative)
* Read the text.
* Fill in the blanks with *has* or *have*. Use the affirmative or negative.
* Check answers.

3 Controlled practice of *have* / *has* or *be* (affirmative and negative)
* Look at the pictures.
* Complete the descriptions.
* Check answers.

PUZZLE PAGE 83
* Fast finishers can do Puzzle 2B on page 83.

ANSWERS
Height: short   **Hair:** long wavy
Hair (Color): red   **Eyes:** big
Eyes (Color): blue

Over to you!

4 Personalization of *has* / *is* to describe someone
* Think of a character from your favorite movie.
* Write sentences to describe that character. Use *is* or *has*.

Extra activity (all classes)

Review and practice describing people
* Students take turns to describe someone in the class using *is* or *has*: *She has blue eyes and she's tall.*
* The rest of the class has to see how quickly they can guess who it is.

Further practice
Workbook   page W17
MultiROM

Grammar

Aims

Present and practice *has / have* (affirmative and negative)
Review *be* for physical descriptions
Talk about physical appearance

BACKGROUND INFORMATION

Avatar is a movie directed by James Cameron and follows the story of Corporal Jake Sully (played by Sam Worthington) as he is chosen to use an avatar to study the Na'vi people on the planet of Pandora. He soon becomes a part of the culture with the help of Neytiri (played by Zoë Saldana) and Grace (Sigourney Weaver). Colonel Miles Quaritch (Stephen Lang) tries to destroy the Na'vi people by taking the precious natural resource *unobtanium*

and war breaks out. The movie won three Oscar awards and two more movies are planned.

1 Grammar chart: *has / have*
* Look at the chart.

Note:
* The negative form of *has / have* for possessions and descriptions is *don't / doesn't have*. He doesn't have blond hair. (NOT *He hasn't blond hair.*)
Grammar reference   page W13

Take note!
* We use *be* when we talk about size and height, but *have* when we talk about hair and eyes.
Grammar reference   page W13

Living English

Reading

🎧 1.23

Aims

Present and practice clothes vocabulary and present progressive in a comic book detective story

Reading skills: using pictures

Warm-up

Look at the photos on page 22 or 23. Ask students to choose a person to describe to a partner. Can they guess which person is being described?

1 Reading skills: using pictures; global comprehension task

- Read the Reading skills box.

> **Reading skills: using pictures**
> - Use pictures to help you understand a text.
> - Pictures can help students predict what a text is about, and interpret a text while reading.

2 Global comprehension task (first reading)

- Look at the pictures and read the text quickly. *Where are Daniels and Lee? What are they doing?*
- Check answers.

ANSWERS

They are at a shopping mall.
They are watching the suspect's friend.

3 Detailed comprehension task (second reading)

- Read and listen to the story.
- Match the sentence halves.
- Check answers.

4 Detailed comprehension task (third reading)

- Read the story again and answer the questions.
- Check answers.

Further practice
Workbook (page W18)

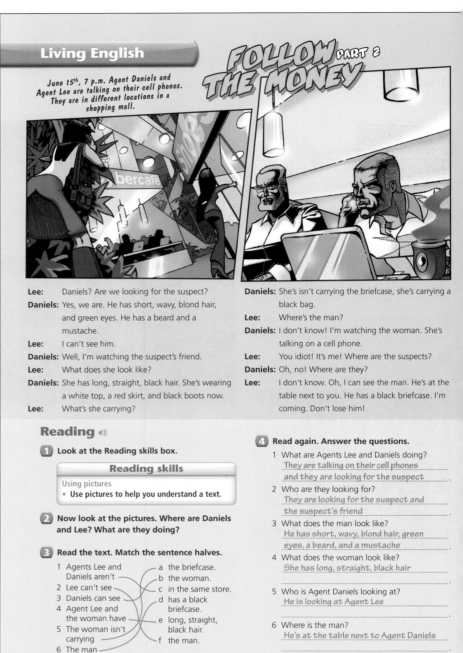

Listening

Clothes and physical descriptions

Kirsten Dunst | Shia LaBeouf

1 ◄)) **Look at the adjectives. Listen to the radio show and check (✓) the adjectives you hear to describe the actors' hair.**

✓ blond	☐ long	☐ straight
✓ brown	✓ red	☐ wavy
☐ dark	☐ short	

2 ◄)) **Listen again. Circle the words you hear.**

Kirsten Dunst
1 Her hair isn't blond / red.
2 She's wearing a black / red skirt with a white T-shirt / top.
3 She's wearing black boots / shoes.
4 She looks awesome / tall.

Shia LaBeouf
1 He has green / blue eyes.
2 He has / doesn't have a beard.
3 He's wearing a white shirt / T-shirt tonight.
4 He's wearing black pants / shoes tonight.

3 **Fill in the blanks with the words below.**

> jeans   long   ~~red~~   T-shirt

1 Kirsten Dunst's hair is red in the *Spider-Man* movies.
2 Her skirt is long.
3 Shia LaBeouf wears jeans in the *Transformers* movies.
4 He usually wears a dirty T-shirt.

Speaking

Describing what you look like and what you are wearing

1 ◄)) **Listen and read.**

Hi! I'm Henry. I'm tall. I have short, brown hair, and big, blue eyes. I usually wear gray sneakers. Today, I'm wearing black shoes.

Hello. I'm Heather. I'm short. I have long, wavy, black hair, and brown eyes. I usually wear jeans. Today, I'm wearing a skirt.

2 ◄)) **Look at the Pronunciation box. Listen to the examples. Then listen again, and repeat.**

> **Pronunciation**
>
> /h/
> • We pronounce the /h/ sound at the start of words in English.
> Hi! I'm Henry.   Hello. I'm Heather.

3 ◄)) **Listen and repeat.**
1 Her pants are blue.
2 His beard is black.
3 He has short, black hair.
4 Henry has brown hair.
5 Heather has black hair.

4 **Practice the dialogue in exercise 1.**

5 **Now change the words in blue. Write a new dialogue. Then practice the dialogue in class.**

→ MultiROM   25

Listening

Aim

Listen to the descriptions of people and identify adjectives

1 Global comprehension of the listening task (first listening) ◉ 1.24
• Play the CD.
• Listen to the radio show and check (✓) the adjectives you hear.
• Check answers.

Audioscript
TV Host: So, I'm here tonight on Broadway for a movie premiere with all the Hollywood stars. OK, who can I see? Well, there's Kirsten Dunst. WOW! Look at her hair! Her hair is red in all the *Spider-Man* movies, but tonight it's blond. She's wearing a long black skirt with a white top, and black shoes. She looks awesome tonight.
Oh, look! There's Shia LaBeouf. He looks amazing. He's very tall and his eyes are green, and he has a beard. He has brown hair. In *Transformers*, he usually wears jeans, a dirty T-shirt, and sneakers. But tonight he's wearing a white shirt and black pants. Look at his red shoes, too! And now we're …

2 Detailed comprehension of the listening task (second listening) ◉ 1.24
• Play the CD again.
• Listen again. Circle the words you hear.
• Check answers.

3 Detailed comprehension of the listening task
• Fill in the blanks with the words in the box.
• Check answers.

Speaking

Aims
Describing what you look like and what you are wearing
Pronunciation: /h/ sound

1 First listening ◉ 1.25
• Play the CD.
• Listen and read.

2 Presentation of pronunciation point ◉ 1.26
• Look at the Pronunciation box.
• Play the CD.
• Listen to the examples.

> **Pronunciation: /h/ sound**
> • We pronounce the /h/ at the start of words in English.
> **Note:**
> • Sometimes the /h/ is silent, as in *hour*.

• Play the CD again.
• Listen again, and repeat.

3 Pronunciation practice ◉ 1.27
• Play the CD.
• Listen and repeat.

4 Dialogue practice
• Practice the dialogue in exercise 1 with a partner.
• Listen to students' dialogues.
• Check the pronunciation of /h/.

5 Dialogue personalization and practice
• Change the words in blue and write a new dialogue in pairs.
• Practice the dialogue with their partners.
• Listen to students' dialogues. Check the pronunciation of /h/.
• Ask stronger students to read their sentences out in front of the class.

ANSWERS
Students' own answers.

| Further practice
| MultiROM

Round-up

Writing

Aims

Write a personal blog

Writing skills: word order: position of adjectives

1 Writing skills: word order: position of adjectives

- Read the Writing skills box.

> **Writing skills: word order: position of adjectives**
> - Adjectives have a specific position in the sentence.
> - *I have short brown hair.* (NOT ~~I have brown short hair.~~)

- Read the text.
- Find and circle the adjectives.
- Check answers.

2 Detailed analysis of model writing task

- Fill in the chart with information about Daniel.
- Check answers.

3 Preparation for personalized writing

- Fill in the chart with information about you.
- Check that students are completing the chart correctly.

ANSWERS
Students' own answers.

4 Personalized writing

- Follow the model writing text. Use your information from the chart to change the text.
- Write your blog.

ANSWERS
Students' own answers.

I can ...

Aims

Check understanding of simple present and present progressive; self-assessment of own progress

1 Self-assessment of simple present and present progressive

- For items (1–4), students read the sentences and choose the correct verbs.
- Students check (✔) *Yes, I can.* if they think they understand the vocabulary or grammar well, or check (✔) *I need more practice.* if they think they need more practice.

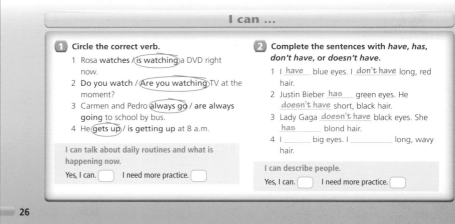

Round-up

Writing

A personal blog

1 Look at the Writing skills box.

> **Writing skills**
> Word order: position of adjectives
> - Adjectives have a specific position in the sentence.
> I have short, brown hair. ✓
> I have ~~brown, short~~ hair.

Now read the text. Find and circle the adjectives.

2 Fill in the chart with information about Daniel.

	Daniel	You
Name	Daniel Garcia	
Age	14	
Eyes	big, brown	
Hair	short, brown	
Clothes	favorite T-shirt, jeans, red cap	
School routine	classes start at 8:30 a.m.	
Doing at the moment	writing blog and listening to music	

3 Fill in the chart with information about you.

4 Write your blog. Use Daniel's blog and the chart to help you.

All about me!

Hi! Welcome to my blog! My name is Daniel Garcia. I'm fourteen years old, and I live in Boston, Massachusetts. I have short, brown hair, and big, brown eyes. Today, I'm wearing my favorite T-shirt, my jeans, and my red cap!

During the week, I get up at 7 a.m. every day. After breakfast, I walk to the bus stop with my friends. The school bus always arrives at 7:45 a.m. My classes start at 8:30 a.m. I sometimes play basketball after school.

I'm in my bedroom right now. I'm writing my blog, and I'm listening to music. Post a comment soon!
Bye!

I can ...

1 **Circle the correct verb.**
1 Rosa watches / **is watching** a DVD right now.
2 Do you watch / **Are you watching** TV at the moment?
3 Carmen and Pedro **always go** / are always going to school by bus.
4 He **gets up** / is getting up at 8 a.m.

I can talk about daily routines and what is happening now.
Yes, I can. [ ] I need more practice. [ ]

2 **Complete the sentences with *have, has, don't have,* or *doesn't have.***
1 I _have_ blue eyes. I _don't have_ long, red hair.
2 Justin Bieber _has_ green eyes. He _doesn't have_ short, black hair.
3 Lady Gaga _doesn't have_ black eyes. She _has_ blond hair.
4 I _____ big eyes. I _____ long, wavy hair.

I can describe people.
Yes, I can. [ ] I need more practice. [ ]

26

- If students have chosen *I need more practice.*, encourage them to review these sections and to do more practice.

2 Self-assessment of *has / have* for physical appearance

- For items (1–4), students read the sentences and complete them with the correct answers.
- Students check (✔) *Yes, I can.* if they think they understand the vocabulary or grammar well, or check (✔) *I need more practice.* if they think they need more practice.
- If students have chosen *I need more practice.*, encourage them to review these sections and to do more practice.

Further practice

Pairwork pages 110–111
Test pages 90–91; 104

Review

Vocabulary

Weather

1 What's the weather like? Unscramble the words.

1 It's snowing . (g w n s i n o)
2 It's hot . (t o h)
3 It's cloudy . (d u l y o c)
4 It's windy . (d i w n y)
5 It's sunny . (n y u n s)
6 It's stormy . (m o r y s t)
7 It's raining . (n i a r i g n)

Everyday activities

2 Look at the pictures. Write the activities.

1 babysit

2 do homework

3 get dressed

4 sleep

5 wait for a bus

6 chat online

7 post a comment

8 send a text message

Clothes

3 Label the pictures.

1 shirt
2 pants
3 socks
4 shoes
5 glasses
6 top
7 skirt
8 boots

Physical appearance

4 Write the opposites.

1 blond hair black hair
2 straight hair wavy hair
3 short hair long hair
4 tall man short man
5 small mustache big mustache
6 big eyes small eyes

Grammar

Present progressive (affirmative and negative)

1 Fill in the blanks. Use the present progressive affirmative and negative.

Celia   Ryan   Boyd   Max   Tina

1 Celia 's watching TV.
2 Ryan 's listening to music.
3 Boyd isn't doing his homework.
  He 's sending a text message.
4 Max is in the living room. He isn't reading
  a book. He 's reading a newspaper.
5 Tina is in the kitchen. She isn't having
  breakfast. She 's drinking coffee.

Vocabulary

Aim

Present and practice words for weather, everyday activities, clothes, and physical appearance

1 Review of vocabulary set: weather

- Unscramble the weather words.
- Check answers.

2 Review of vocabulary set: everyday activities

- Look at the pictures.
- Write the activities.
- Check answers.

3 Review of vocabulary set: clothes

- Label the pictures.
- Check answers.

4 Review of vocabulary set: physical appearance

- Write the opposites.
- Check answers.

Grammar

1 Review of present progressive (affirmative and negative)

- Fill in the blanks.
- Check answers.

Unit summary

Vocabulary
Weather
Everyday activities
Clothes
Physical appearance

Grammar
Present progressive (affirmative and negative)
Present progressive (questions)
Simple present and present progressive
has / have

Study skills
Recording vocabulary

Project
Writing a description based on a photo

2 Review of present progressive (questions)

- Write questions about the people in exercise 1 on page 27.
- Check answers.

3 Review of simple present and present progressive

- Label the columns.
- Check answers.

4 Review of simple present and present progressive

- Write sentences.
- Check answers.

5 Review of *has / have*

- Fill in the blanks.
- Look at the pictures and write the names.
- Check answers.

Study skills

Recording vocabulary

It is important to encourage students to record vocabulary so that they have their own personal descriptions of language that they can easily understand.

1 Recording vocabulary: appearance

- Read through and look at the example with the students.
- Write the word *long* on the board.
- Invite students to suggest pictures, example sentences, or opposites which will help them remember the word.
- Make a "model" notebook entry on the board.
- Students start an appearance section in their notebooks, and list the words.
- Students can compare lists and ways of recording the new vocabulary in pairs.

| Further practice
| MultiROM

Project 1 page 84

Aims

Read a description of a (fictitious) TV host
Invent information about a person
Write a description of a person

1 Reading

- Look at the photo and read the text.
- Match the headings with the paragraphs.
- Check answers.

ANSWERS
2 Appearance 3 Hobbies 4 Family

A Review

Present progressive (questions)

2 Write questions about the people in exercise 1 on page 27.

1 Boyd and Ryan / sleep / ?
   Are Boyd and Ryan sleeping ?
2 Ryan / sing / ?
   Is Ryan singing ?
3 what / Boyd / send / ?
   What is Boyd sending ?
4 what / Celia / do / ?
   What is Celia doing ?
5 Max / watch TV / ?
   Is Max watching TV ?
6 where / Tina / drink coffee / ?
   Where is Tina drinking coffee ?

Simple present and present progressive

3 Label the two columns: *simple present* or *present progressive*.

(1) simple present	(2) present progressive
usually	now
normally	right now
every day	at the moment

4 Write sentences. Use the simple present or present progressive.

1 Julio / go / to school / every day
   Julio goes to school every day .
2 he / usually / wear / sweatpants
   He usually wears sweatpants .
3 at the moment / he / wear / jeans and a T-shirt
   At the moment, he's wearing jeans and a T-shirt .
4 right now / he / on a school trip / with his art club
   Right now, he's on a school trip with his art club .
5 right now / Julio / reading about / the pictures
   Right now, Julio is reading about the pictures .
6 now / they / walk into the art gallery
   Now they're walking into the art gallery .

28 ⟶ MultiROM

has / have

5 Fill in the blanks with *have, has, don't have,* or *doesn't have*. Then label the pictures: *Julie* or *Lara*.

Lara   Julie

1 Julie and Lara have straight hair.
2 Lara has long hair.
3 She has dark brown hair.
4 Julie doesn't have long hair.
5 She has blond hair.
6 Julie and Lara don't have green eyes.
7 Julie doesn't have big eyes.

Study skills

Recording vocabulary
In your notebook, make a vocabulary section by topic. Write a new word. Then draw a picture, write an example sentence, or write opposites.

1 Start an appearance section in your notebook. Use the words below.

big long short small straight
wavy

long   big
short   small

---

2 Preparation for writing (first task)

- Find a photo of someone to write about. (Choose a photo – not a famous person – on the Internet, in magazines, or newspapers.)

3 Preparation for writing (second task)

- Invent information about the person in your photo. Include: name, age, nationality, job, appearance, hobbies, family.

ANSWERS
Students' own answers.

4 Writing

- Follow the model text.
- Write a description of the person in your photo.

ANSWERS
Students' own answers.

Project extension

- If you have the facilities, ask students to post their profiles onto your class or school website. If students have found their own photos, they could also upload them with their profiles.
- Encourage other students to log on to the website, and to read and compare the profiles.

3 Have some more

Vocabulary

Food

1 🔊 **Listen and repeat.**

> apples   bananas   eggs   French fries
> hamburgers   mangoes   pizzas   potatoes
> sausages   strawberries   tomatoes

Take note!

Plural nouns
- **Regular: add -s**
  apple ➜ apples
- **Ending in a vowel: add -es**
  mango ➜ mangoes
- **Ending in -y: -ÿ, add -ies**
  strawberry ➜ strawberries

2 🔊 **Fill in the blanks with food words from exercise 1. Then listen and check.**

1 A: Oh yuck! What are those? They look like fingers.
   B: Don't be silly! They're _sausages_ .

2 A: I'm making a fruit salad. Are there any apples?
   B: Yes, there are. There are bananas, mangoes, and _strawberries_ , too.

3 A: I'm making an omelet. Are there any _eggs_ ?
   B: Yes, there are.

4 A: Let's go to the Italian restaurant.
   B: Great idea! We can order _pizzas_ .

5 A: I'm making French fries. Are there any _potatoes_ ?
   B: Yes, there are.

6 A: Do you like fast food restaurants?
   B: I love them! I always have _hamburgers_ and French fries.

3 **Ask and answer about the food in exercise 1.**

Student A: Do you like eggs?
Student B: Yuck! No, I don't. Do you like apples?
Student A: Yes, I do. I love apples.

Workbook p.W20 ➜ MultiROM   29

Unit summary

Vocabulary
Food: *apples, bananas, eggs, French fries, hamburgers, mangoes, pizza, potatoes, sausages, strawberries, tomatoes*

Food and drink: *bread, cheese, coffee, ketchup, milk, oil, pasta, rice, salad, salt, soda, water*

Grammar
there is / there are + countable nouns

uncountable nouns (affirmative, negative, and questions)

Skills
Reading: Fun food facts, a text about healthy eating habits; using questions to help understand the gist of a text

Listening: Listening and identifying specific information in a radio show

Speaking: Requesting food and drink in a restaurant; weak form of *some*

Writing: Writing a report about a favorite meal

Cross-curricular
Science: biology

Values and topics
Environment

Health

Food science

Introducing the topic

Vocabulary

Aim
Present and practice words for food

Warm-up
Ask students what their favorite foods are. Do they have any unusual tastes? Write new vocabulary on the board.

1 Presentation of vocabulary set: food 🔊 1.28
- Play the CD. Listen and repeat.

> ### Take note!
> Model the pronunciation of the plural forms -es (/s/ NOT /es/) and -ies /ɪz/.

2 Vocabulary practice; exposure to words for food 🔊 1.29
- Students fill in the blanks.
- Play the CD.
- Listen and check.
- Check answers.

3 Personalization
- In pairs, students ask and answer about the food in exercise 1.

ANSWERS
Students' own answers.

> ### Extend your vocabulary
> cakes   cookies   muffin   pear
> watermelon
> **Workbook**   page W20

Extra activity (stronger classes)
Further practice of food vocabulary
- Students work in pairs, small groups, or as a whole class.
- One student starts the game by saying a food item starting with the first letter of the alphabet: *apple.*
- The next student has to repeat that item, and add another with the second (and third, etc.) letters of the alphabet: *apple, banana, carrot,* etc.
- The game continues until someone a) forgets an item in the alphabetical list, or b) can't think of an item to add.

▌ Further practice
Workbook   page W20
MultiROM

Exploring the topic

Reading

Aim

Present and practice food vocabulary through fun facts

BACKGROUND INFORMATION

The number of **calories** in an item of food or drink is a measure of the energy in that substance. Our bodies need a certain number of calories from food for moving, thinking, breathing, and every other bodily function.

1 Identifying (first reading) 🎧 1.30

- Play the CD.
- Listen to and read the article.
- Answer the question.
- Check answers.

ANSWER

The tomato is a fruit.

2 Detailed comprehension task (second reading)

- Read the article again.
- Match the numbers and facts.
- Check answers as a class.

3 Detailed comprehension task (third reading)

- Read the article again.
- Correct the false statements.
- Check answers.

Exploring the topic

FUN FOOD FACTS!

Watch your diet!
The average American eats three hamburgers with French fries every week. That's 159 fast food meals every year!

Oops!
There is one fruit that thinks it's a vegetable! It's the tomato! There are more than 10,000 kinds of tomatoes in the world.

King of fruits
The mango is called the king of fruits. There are 500 different kinds of mangoes! There are two important vitamins in mangoes: vitamin A and vitamin C.

Inside or outside?
There are about 200 seeds on every strawberry. BUT strawberries are the only fruit with seeds on the outside!

Pizza galore
In the U.S., there are more than 61,000 pizza restaurants! Every year, Americans eat more than three billion pizzas. That's 10 kilos of pizza per person!

How many?
There are 110 calories in a 22-gram potato. Potatoes originally come from the Andes mountains.

Reading

1 🔊 Read and listen to the article. Is the tomato a fruit or a vegetable?

2 Read again. Match the numbers with the facts.

1 10,000 _f_
2 200 _e_
3 500 _c_
4 2 _a_
5 10 _d_
6 110 _b_

a important vitamins in a mango
b calories in a 22-gram potato
c kinds of mangoes
d kilos of pizza that Americans eat every year
e the number of seeds on a strawberry
f kinds of tomatoes in the world

3 Correct the false statements.

1 The tomato is a ~~vegetable~~.
  fruit

2 Americans eat 159 fast food meals every ~~week~~.
  year

3 The strawberry has seeds ~~inside and~~ outside.
  on the

4 There ~~aren't any~~ vitamins in mangoes.
  are two important

5 There are ~~three billion~~ pizza restaurants in the U.S.
  _61,000_

6 Potatoes are originally from the ~~Rocky~~ mountains.
  Andes

30

Grammar

there is / there are + **countable nouns**

Talking about things that we can count

1 Look at the chart.

Singular	Plural
There **is a** banana.	There **are some** bananas.
	There **are four** bananas.
There **isn't an** apple.	There **aren't any** hamburgers.
Is there a pizza?	**Are there any** tomatoes?
Yes, **there is.** / No, **there isn't.**	Yes, **there are.** / No, **there aren't.**

Take note!

a / an / some / any
- *a* + singular noun starting with a consonant sound
- *an* + singular noun starting with a vowel sound
- *some* + plural noun (affirmative)
- *any* + plural noun (negative, questions)

2 Circle the correct word.

1 There is *(an)* / some apple on the table.
2 Are there an / *(any)* mangoes?
3 There are *(some)* / any eggs in the refrigerator.
4 There is *(a)* / an potato under the table!
5 There aren't *(any)* / some strawberries at the store.
6 Is there *(a)* / an tomato in this recipe?

3 Look at the picture. Fill in the blanks.

1 There _are some_ strawberries.
2 There _is a_ mango.
3 There _are some_ potatoes.
4 There _isn't a_ banana.
5 There _are some_ tomatoes.
6 There _aren't any_ sausages.

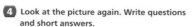

Have some more 3

4 Look at the picture again. Write questions and short answers.

1 _Are there any sausages_ ? (sausages)
  No, there aren't .
2 _Are there any tomatoes_ ? (tomatoes)
  Yes, there are .
3 _Is there a mango_ ? (mango)
  Yes, there is .
4 _Is there a pizza_ ? (pizza)
  No, there isn't .
5 _Are there any hamburgers_ ? (hamburgers)
  No, there aren't .
6 _Is there a woman_ ? (woman)
  Yes, there is .

 Puzzle page 85, puzzle 3A

5 **Over to you!**

Look around the classroom for one minute. Then close your eyes and tell the class about the things that are or aren't in the classroom.

Student A: There are some desks.
Teacher: That's true.
Student A: There is a map.
Teacher: That isn't true.
Student B: There aren't any dogs.
Teacher: That's true!

Workbook p.W21 MultiROM   **31**

Grammar

Aims

Present and practice *there is / there are* + countable nouns (affirmative, negative, interrogative, short answers)

Talk about things that we can count

1 Grammar chart: *there is / there are* with singular and plural countable nouns

- Look at the chart.

Take note!
- We make short answers with the singular or plural form of the verb *be* (*Yes, there is.* / *No, there aren't.*)

- We do not contract the verb *be* in short answers, e.g. *Yes, there is.* (NOT *Yes, there's.*)

Grammar reference page W19

2 Controlled practice of *a, an, some,* or *any* with countable nouns

- Circle the correct word.
- Check answers.

3 Controlled practice of *there is / there are* (affirmative) and countable nouns

- Look at the picture. Fill in the blanks.
- Check answers.

4 Controlled practice of *there is / there are* (questions and short answers)

- Look at the picture again.
- Write questions and short answers, using *Is there …? / Are there …?*
- Check answers.

PUZZLE PAGE 85
- Fast finishers can do Puzzle 3A on page 85.

ANSWER

pizzas 6   eggs 10   tomatoes 7
mangoes 3   potatoes 8
strawberries 5   apples 2
Total: 41

Over to you!

5 Personalization: oral practice of *there is / there are* and countable nouns

- Students look around the classroom and memorize what they can see.
- They close their eyes and take turns to tell the class about objects that are or aren't in the classroom.

Extra activity (all classes)

Further practice of *there is / there are* with countable nouns

- Collect a number of items from students and arrange them in front of the class. Make sure students are familiar with the vocabulary, e.g. one or more of the following: erasers, pencils, pens, rulers, notebooks, pencil cases, etc.
- Give students a few minutes to study the collection. Tell them that they are going to play a memory game, so they have to memorize the number of items in the display.
- Cover or remove the items from view and see how many students can remember exactly what the items were. They should use *there is / there are* to describe them: *There is a pencil case. There are two erasers,* etc.

Further practice
Workbook   page W21
MultiROM

Building the topic

Vocabulary

Aims
Present and practice vocabulary for food and drink

Write about favorite food and drink

Warm-up
Ask students *What's your favorite food and drink – for breakfast, lunch, and dinner? What food and drink do you hate?*

1 Presentation of vocabulary set: food and drink ⊙ 1.31
- Match the words and the pictures.
- Play the CD.
- Listen, check, and repeat.

2 Vocabulary practice: exposure to vocabulary for food and drink ⊙ 1.32
- Play the CD.
- Listen and fill in the blanks.
- Check answers.

3 Vocabulary practice and extension
- Fill in the blanks for you.
- Compare with a partner.
- Ask students to tell the class about themselves and their partner: *My favorite food is pasta. My partner's favorite food is pizza.*
- Check answers.

ANSWERS
Students' own answers.

Extend your vocabulary

fruit juice orange salad sandwich smoothie soup

Workbook page W22

Further practice
Workbook page W22
MultiROM

Building the topic

Vocabulary
Food and drink

1 ◀) Match the pictures with the words below. Then listen, check, and repeat.

bread cheese coffee ketchup milk oil
pasta rice salad salt soda water

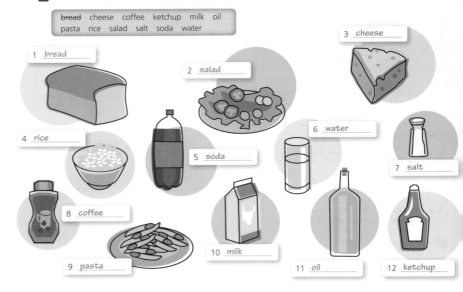

1 bread 2 salad 3 cheese 4 rice 5 soda 6 water 7 salt 8 coffee 9 pasta 10 milk 11 oil 12 ketchup

2 ◀) Listen and fill in the blanks with food and drink words.

1 I don't put any ketchup on French fries. I put it on bread.

2 We like eating apples, but we always put some salt on them.

5 Cheese is old milk.

For breakfast, I eat some rice with salad, and strawberries.

I drink a cup of coffee every morning to wake me up!

I love eating pasta with some cheese and sausage on top.

3 Fill in the blanks for you. Compare with a partner.
Favorite food: _____ _____
Favorite drink: _____ _____

32 Workbook p.W22 ➔ MultiROM

Grammar

Uncountable nouns

Talking about things that we can't count

1 Look at the chart.

Affirmative	I want **some** coffee.
Negative	There isn't **any** coffee.
Questions	Do you have **any** coffee?

Take note!

Uncountable nouns
- With uncountable nouns, we can't say a number and we don't use an article. Uncountable nouns always take a singular verb.
  Cheese is disgusting. I don't like coffee.

2 Look at the nouns in blue. Write C (for countable) or U (for uncountable).

1 Give me some milk, please. _U_
2 I eat an apple every day. _C_
3 There isn't any salt on my French fries. _U_
4 There is some bread in the bag. _U_
5 Ketchup is good on French fries. _U_
6 Do you want a hamburger for lunch? _C_
7 I don't eat bananas. _C_
8 I normally have coffee for breakfast. _U_

3 Look at the picture. Fill in the blanks with the correct form of *be* and *some, any, a,* or *an.*

1 There _is some_ rice.
2 There _isn't any_ oil.
3 There _is a_ tomato.
4 There _aren't any_ bananas.
5 There _is some_ soda.
6 There _are some_ strawberries.
7 There _isn't any_ cheese.
8 There _aren't any_ potatoes.

4 Look at the picture again. Write true sentences about the nouns in parentheses.

1 _There is some milk_ . (milk)
2 _There isn't any ketchup_ . (ketchup)
3 _There aren't any mangoes_ . (mangoes)
4 _There is a tomato_ . (tomato)
5 _There is some salt_ . (salt)
6 _There aren't any sausages_ . (sausages)
7 _There are some eggs_ . (eggs)
8 _There isn't any pasta_ . (pasta)

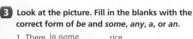 **Puzzle** page 85, puzzle 3B →

5

Over to you!

Think of a sentence with *there is, there are,* and *a, an, some,* or *any.* Change *a / an* and *some* or *any* to "Engage". Tell the class the sentence. Can the class guess the original word?
Student A: There isn't Engage coffee.
Student B: There isn't some coffee.
Student A: No.
Student C: There isn't any coffee.
Student A: Yes. Your turn.

Grammar

Aims

Present and practice uncountable nouns (affirmative, negative, interrogative, and short answers)
Review *some, any*
Review *there is / there are*
Talk about things that we can't count

1 Grammar chart: Uncountable nouns (affirmative, negative, and questions)

- Look at the chart.

Take note!

- Uncountable nouns only have a singular form. They don't have a plural, e.g. *cheese, milk, bread.*

- With uncountable nouns, we always use a singular verb, e.g. *There is some milk.* (NOT ~~There are some milk.~~)
- We don't use a number or an article with uncountable nouns, e.g. *There isn't any bread.* (NOT ~~There isn't two breads.~~)

Grammar reference page W19

2 Review and controlled practice of countable and uncountable nouns

- Write C or U next to the sentences.
- Check answers.

3 Controlled practice of *be* with countable and uncountable nouns, and review of *some, any, a,* or *an.*

- Look at the picture.

- Fill in the blanks.
- Check answers.

4 Further practice of countable and uncountable nouns

- Look at the picture and write sentences.
- Check answers.

PUZZLE PAGE 85

- Fast finishers can do Puzzle 3B on page 85.

ANSWER
Do you play soccer?
Students' own answers.

Over to you!

5 Personalization; oral practice of countable and uncountable nouns with *a, an some, a, any*

- Think of a sentence with *there is, there are,* and *a, an, some,* or *any* about a food or drink item.
- Say the sentence to the class, changing *some, a, any,* or *an* to "Engage".
- Can the class guess which word should be there instead?

Extra activity (all classes)

Review and practice countable and uncountable nouns (questions and short answers)

- Ask students to write a list of at least ten items of food and drink to take on a picnic.
- In pairs, students ask each other questions to find out what is on the list, e.g. *Is there any pizza? (Yes, there is.) Are there any apples? (Yes, there are.)*, etc.
- When both students in a pair have had a turn to ask questions, have them compare their lists to see what they both want to take to the picnic.

Further practice
Workbook page W21
MultiROM

Living English

Reading

🔘 1.33

Aims

Present and practice some food and drink vocabulary in a text about healthy eating habits

Reading skills: reading questions first

Warm-up

Ask students if they eat healthily or not. What kind of healthy foods do they eat? What unhealthy foods do they enjoy eating?

BACKGROUND INFORMATION

Fast food is food which is prepared and served quickly in fast food restaurants. The history of modern fast food started in the U.S. in 1921, when a restaurant called White Castle started selling hamburgers very cheaply. White Castle still has fast food restaurants all over the U.S.

Super size portions are offered at some fast food restaurants. They are much bigger than normal size meals.

1 Global comprehension task (first reading)

- Read the article and choose the best title.
- Check answers.

2 Reading skills: reading questions first

- Read the Reading skills box.

> **Reading skills: reading questions first**
> - Reading questions first makes students "active" readers and helps them find the information more quickly.

3 Detailed comprehension task (second reading)

- Read and listen to the sentences in exercise 3.
- Read the article again.
- Check (✓) or cross (✗) the sentences.
- Check answers.

| **Further practice**
| Workbook   page W24

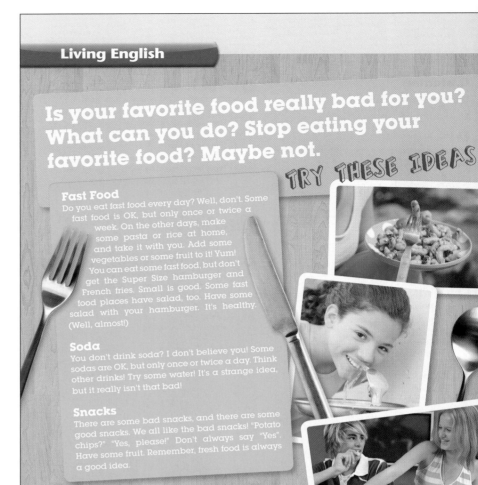

Living English

Is your favorite food really bad for you? What can you do? Stop eating your favorite food? Maybe not.

TRY THESE IDEAS

Fast Food
Do you eat fast food every day? Well, don't. Some fast food is OK, but only once or twice a week. On the other days, make some pasta or rice at home, and take it with you. Add some vegetables or some fruit to it! Yum! You can eat some fast food, but don't get the Super Size hamburger and French fries. Small is good. Some fast food places have salad, too. Have some salad with your hamburger. It's healthy. (Well, almost!)

Soda
You don't drink soda? I don't believe you! Some sodas are OK, but only once or twice a day. Think other drinks! Try some water! It's a strange idea, but it really isn't that bad!

Snacks
There are some bad snacks, and there are some good snacks. We all like the bad snacks! "Potato chips?" "Yes, please!" Don't always say "Yes". Have some fruit. Remember, fresh food is always a good idea.

Reading ◀))

1 **Read the article. What is the best title for the article?**
a Never Eat This Food!
ⓑ Healthy Eating – Your Way!
c Junk Food Is Healthy!

2 **Look at the Reading skills box.**

Reading skills
Reading questions first
• **Read the questions for a reading text first, before you start reading for detail.**

3 **Read the sentences below. Then read the article again. Check (✓) the things the writer says. Put an X (✗) by the things she doesn't say.**

1 Don't eat any fast food.　　　　　　　　　　　✗
2 Pasta and rice can be good.　　　　　　　　　✓
3 Eat fast food salad, but don't eat hamburgers.　✗
4 Drink two liters of water every day.　　　　　✗
5 All snacks are bad.　　　　　　　　　　　　　✗
6 Fresh food is good for you.　　　　　　　　　✓

34 ➔ **Workbook p.W24**

Listening
Favorite food

1 🔊 **Listen to the radio show. Where is the radio show host?**

a Florida   (b) Texas   c Tokyo

2 🔊 **Listen again. Check (✓) the food and drink Brad and Angela like.**

Brad

Angela

3 **Fill in the blanks with the words below. Then ask and answer with a partner.**

| favorite   food   ~~name~~   school |

1 What's your _name_ ?
2 What's your favorite _food_ ?
3 How often do you eat your _favorite_ food?
4 What food do you like to eat after _school_ ?

Speaking
Making requests

1 🔊 **Listen and read.**

2 🔊 **Look at the Pronunciation box. Listen to the examples. Then listen again, and repeat.**

Pronunciation

Weak form of *some*
• In sentences, *some* is pronounced with the weak /ə/ sound.

/səm/
Can I have some Swiss cheese?
And here's some ketchup!

3 🔊 **Practice the sentences. Then listen and repeat.**

1 Here's some salt.
2 Can I have some water?
3 There are some strawberries in the refrigerator.

4 **Practice the dialogue in exercise 1.**

5 **Now change the words in blue. Write a new dialogue. Then practice the dialogue in class.**

→ **MultiROM**   **35**

Listening

Aim

Listen to people talking about their favorite food

1 Global comprehension of the listening task (first listening) 💿 1.34

• Play the CD. Listen and answer the question. Check answers.

Audioscript

Interviewer: Hello from Texas! Today we're out and about and we're asking people about their favorite food.
Hey! Excuse me! Can we ask you about your favorite food, please?
Brad: Sure!
Interviewer: OK. First, what's your name?
Brad: I'm Brad.

Interviewer: OK, Brad. What's your favorite food?
Brad: Mmm, that's difficult. I guess it's hamburgers and French fries.
Interviewer: OK. How often do you eat your favorite food?
Brad: Once a week.
Interviewer: And your favorite drink?
Brad: Soda! You can't have hamburgers and French fries and no soda!
Interviewer: OK, thanks! … And now, Angela. What food do you like to eat after school?
Angela: Well, I love potato chips and I usually have some when I get home from school with a glass of milk.
Interviewer: Potato chips and milk. That's interesting! Weird even!
Angela: Not weird, it's delicious!
Interviewer: OK, thanks! Next week, we'll be in …

---

2 Detailed comprehension of the listening task (second listening) 💿 1.34

• Listen again. Check (✓) the food and drink Brad and Angela like.
• Check answers.

3 Detailed comprehension of the listening task

• Fill in the blanks with the words.
• Ask and answer with a partner.
• Ask students to tell the class something about their partner.

Speaking

Aims

Make requests for food and drink in a restaurant
Pronunciation: weak form of *some*

1 First listening 💿 1.35

• Play the CD.
• Listen and read.

2 Presentation of pronunciation point 💿 1.36

• Look at the Pronunciation box.
• Play the CD.
• Listen to the examples.

Pronunciation: weak form of *some*

• In sentences, *some* is pronounced with the weak form /ə/

• Listen again, and repeat.

3 Pronunciation practice 💿 1.37

• Practice the sentences with your partner.
• Play the CD. Listen and repeat.

4 Dialogue practice

• Practice the dialogue in exercise 1 with a partner.
• Listen to students' dialogues. Make sure they are pronouncing *some* in its weak form.

5 Dialogue personalization and practice

• Change the words in blue and write a new dialogue in pairs.
• Practice the dialogue with their partners.
• Listen to students' dialogues. Make sure they are pronouncing *some* in its weak form.
• Ask stronger students to read their new dialogues out in front of the class.

ANSWERS
Students' own answers.

▌ Further practice
MultiROM

Round-up

Writing

Aim

Write a report about a favorite meal

1 Global comprehension of model writing text

- Read the report quickly and say what it is about.
- Check answers.

ANSWER

The report is about Alex's favorite meal: Thanksgiving dinner.

2 Detailed analysis of model writing task

- Fill in the chart with information about Alex.
- Check answers.

3 Preparation for personalized writing

- Fill in the chart with information about you.
- Check that students are completing the chart correctly.

ANSWERS

Students' own answers.

4 Personalized writing

- Follow the model writing text. Use your own information from the chart to change the text.
- Write your report.

ANSWERS

Students' own answers.

I can ...

Aims

Check understanding of *there is / there are*, countable nouns, and uncountable nouns; self-assessment of own progress

1 Self-assessment of *there is / there are* and countable nouns

- For items (1–4), students read the sentences and complete them with the correct answers.
- Students check (✓) *Yes, I can.* if they think they understand the vocabulary or grammar well, or check (✓) *I need more practice.* if they think they need more practice.
- If students have chosen *I need more practice.*, encourage them to review these sections and to do more practice.

2 Self-assessment of uncountable nouns

- For items (1–4), students read the sentences and complete them with the correct answers.

Round-up

Writing

A report about a favorite meal

1 Read the report. What is it about?

My favorite meal

My name is Alex, and I'm from Detroit, Michigan, in the U.S. My favorite meal is Thanksgiving dinner. Thanksgiving is an American celebration at the end of November. We always cook in the morning. Then a lot of people come to our house: my grandparents, aunts, uncles, cousins, and friends. We all eat together in the afternoon. We always have a big turkey. We also have corn, carrots, potatoes, and bread. Then we have pumpkin pie, apple pie, and ice cream. Pumpkin pie is my favorite food!

2 Fill in the chart with the information about Alex's favorite meal.

	Alex	You
Name	Alex	
From	Detroit, Michigan, in the U.S.	
Favorite meal	Thanksgiving dinner	
When	at the end of November	
What they do	cook in the morning; a lot of people come to our house: my grandparents, aunts, uncles, cousins, and friends; we all eat together in the afternoon	
Food	a big turkey, corn, carrots, potatoes, bread, pumpkin pie, apple pie, and ice cream	
Favorite food	pumpkin pie	

3 Now fill in the chart with information about your favorite special meal.

4 Write a report about your favorite meal. Use Alex's report and the chart to help you.

I can ...

1 Circle the correct word.

1 Is there a /(an) apple on the table?
2 There (isn't)/aren't any pizza.
3 Are there (any)/ some hamburgers?
4 Is there any /(a) banana in the refrigerator?

I can talk about things we can count.
Yes, I can. ☐   I need more practice. ☐

2 Complete the sentences with *some* or *any*.

1 There is _some_ rice.
2 There isn't _any_ coffee.
3 Do you have _any_ bread?
4 There is _some_ cheese.

I can talk about things we can't count.
Yes, I can. ☐   I need more practice. ☐

36

- Students check (✓) *Yes, I can.* if they think they understand the vocabulary or grammar well, or check (✓) *I need more practice.* if they think they need more practice.

- If students have chosen *I need more practice.*, encourage them to review these sections and to do more practice.

Further practice

Pairwork pages 112–113
Test pages 92–93; 105

4 Consumer world

Introducing the topic

furniture | 2 time | 3 baggage | 4 travel | 5 food | 6 traffic | 7 music | 8 money

Vocabulary

Noun categories

1 🔊 **Match the words with the photos. Then listen, check, and repeat.**

> baggage   food   ~~furniture~~   money   music
> time   traffic   travel

2 **Match the words 1–8 with the related words in exercise 1.**

1 songs — music
2 bags — baggage
3 dollars — money
4 hours — time
5 vacations — travel
6 cars — traffic
7 meals — food
8 tables and chairs — furniture

3 **Fill in the blanks with words from exercise 1.**

1 I need some new furniture for my bedroom. I want a new desk and a chair.
2 Those sneakers are expensive. You don't have any money to buy them.
3 My favorite food is French fries with some cheese and ketchup.
4 It's quiet. There isn't much traffic on the highway today.
5 How much baggage can we take on the airplane? We have three bags.
6 Hurry up! We don't have much time . The movie starts in five minutes.

4 **Fill in the blanks with your own answers.**

My favorite food: _____
Furniture in my room: _____
Music on my MP3 player: _____
_____
Travel with my family: _____
Money in my bag: _____

Workbook p.W26 → MultiROM   **37**

Unit summary

Vocabulary
Noun categories: *baggage, food, furniture, money, music, time, traffic, travel*

Possessions: *backpack, belt, bracelet, earrings, ID card, key, key ring, sunglasses*

Grammar
How much …? / How many …? + quantifiers

Whose …? + possessive pronouns

Skills
Reading: Advertisements for products, a quiz about teenage spending habits

Listening: Listening and identifying specific information in advertisements

Speaking: Asking for things in a store; intonation in questions

Writing: Writing a consumer profile: using paragraphs

Cross-curricular
Math

Values and topics
The environment
Consumerism
Advertisements

Introducing the topic

Vocabulary

Aim
Present and practice words for noun categories

Warm-up
Ask students whether they watch advertisements on TV, or look at them in magazines. Which advertisements do they like or dislike? Why?

1 Presentation of vocabulary set: noun categories 🔊 1.38
- Match the words with the photos.
- Play the CD.
- Listen, check, and repeat.

2 Vocabulary practice; exposure to noun categories
- Match the words (1–8) with the noun categories in exercise 1.
- Check answers.

3 Vocabulary practice and extension
- Fill in the blanks with the words from exercise 1.
- Check answers.

4 Personalization
- Fill in the blanks with your own answers.

ANSWERS
Students' own answers.

Extend your vocabulary
billboard department store road sign
skyscraper sidewalk stop light
Workbook page W26

Extra activity (stronger classes)
Further practice of noun categories
- Students think of two more words to write in each category in exercise 1, e.g. *sofa, bed (furniture); plane, train (travel)*.
- Students compare answers in pairs or groups and add the words to their vocabulary notebooks.

Further practice
Workbook page W26
MultiROM

Exploring the topic

Reading

Aim
Present and practice noun categories through advertisements

1 Identifying (first reading) ⊙ 1.39
- Play the CD.
- Listen to and read the advertisements.
- Check (✔) the things in the advertisements.
- Check answers.

2 Detailed comprehension task (second reading)
- Read the advertisements again.
- Match the sentence halves.
- Check answers as a class.

3 Detailed comprehension task (third reading)
- Read the advertisements again.
- Write the numbers next to the matching comments.
- Check answers.

Exploring the topic

How many songs do you have on your MP3 player? Only 1000?

Buy the new 160 GB MP4 player and you can have 40,000 songs or 25,000 photos. You can have videos, movies, music, and more!

DO YOU SPEND A LOT OF TIME ON YOUR CELL PHONE EACH DAY? COME TO **PHONESRUS**.

This week's special offer: ten hours' talk time a month for only $50. That's a lot of time, and it isn't much money.

How much baggage do you really need for your trip?

Check our new website. There are a lot of different suitcases!

www.flexibag.com

IS THERE A LOT OF TRAFFIC IN YOUR CITY?

WE HAVE THE SOLUTION AT CITY BIKES!

TV chef Gordon Blue says "Eat some healthy food a few times a day."

Reading

1 ◄)) Read and listen to the advertisements. Check (✓) the things you can see in the advertisements.

computer	☐	CDs	☐
cell phone	☑	healthy food	☑
suitcase	☑	TVs	☐
bikes	☑	music	☐

2 Read the advertisements again. Match the sentence halves.

1 How many songs
2 Do you spend
3 How much
4 Is there
5 Eat some healthy food

a a few times a day.
b a lot of traffic in your city?
c do you have on your MP3 player?
d baggage do you really need for your trip?
e a lot of time on your cell phone each day?

3 Read again. Write the number of the correct advertisement for each comment below.

1 "There are a lot of cars in my city. What can I do?" _4_
2 "I don't want to eat a lot of fast food. I want to cook healthy meals." _5_
3 "I love listening to music. My MP3 player only has 500 songs and it doesn't have many videos." _1_
4 "I spend a lot of time on my cell phone. It's expensive and I don't have much money." _2_
5 "I need a new bag for my next vacation." _3_

38

Grammar

How much ...? / How many ...? + quantifiers

Asking about the quantities of things

1 Look at the chart.

Countable	Uncountable
How many cars **are** there?	**How much** traffic **is** there?
There **are none**.	There**'s none**.
There **aren't any** (cars).	There **isn't any** (traffic).
There **are a few** (cars).	There**'s a little** (traffic).
There **aren't many** (cars).	There **isn't much** (traffic).
There **are a lot** (**of** cars).	There**'s a lot** (**of** traffic).

2 Write C (for countable) or U (for uncountable).

1 baggage _U_
2 bags _C_
3 cars _C_
4 chairs _C_
5 dollars _C_
6 furniture _U_
7 food _U_
8 hours _C_
9 meals _C_
10 money _U_
11 music _U_
12 songs _C_
13 tables _C_
14 time _U_
15 traffic _U_
16 vacations _C_

3 Circle the correct word.

1 I have some new **furniture** / chair in my bedroom.
2 My sister talks on the phone for two **time** / **hours** every day.
3 There aren't many **cars** / traffic in the city today.
4 There isn't much **food** / meals in the refrigerator.
5 I love these three music / **songs**.
6 We don't have much **money** / dollars to go to the mall.

4 Fill in the blanks with *How much* or *How many.*

1 _How much_ traffic is there in Future City?
2 _How many_ women are waiting at the bus stop?
3 _How much_ baggage do the people have?
4 _How much_ money is there in the street?
5 _How many_ men are carrying a bag?

5 Look at the picture of Future City. Complete the answers to the questions in exercise 4 with *a little, a few,* or *a lot of.*

1 There's _a little_ traffic.
2 There are _a few_ women waiting at the bus stop.
3 The people have _a little_ baggage.
4 There's _a lot of_ money in the street.
5 There are _a few_ men carrying a bag.

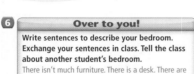

Puzzle page 85, puzzle 4A →

6

Over to you!

Write sentences to describe your bedroom. Exchange your sentences in class. Tell the class about another student's bedroom.

There isn't much furniture. There is a desk. There are two chairs. There are a lot of computer games.

Grammar

Aims

Present and practice *How much ...? / How many ...? +* quantifiers (*a few, a little, a lot of*)

Review of countable and uncountable nouns

Describe things in your bedroom

1 Grammar chart: *How much ...? / How many ...?* with countable and uncountable nouns

- Look at the chart.

Note:

- To indicate zero quantity, we use a singular verb with uncountable nouns (*There isn't any. / There's none.*), and a plural verb with countable nouns (*There aren't any. / There are none.*).

- To talk about small quantities, we use *a little / not much* for uncountable nouns (*There is a little water. There isn't much time.*) and *a few / not many* for countable nouns (*There are a few apples. There aren't many people.*).

- To talk about large quantities, we use *a lot of* for all nouns.

Grammar reference   page W25

Consumer world 4

2 Controlled practice of countable and uncountable nouns; review of noun categories

- Write C or U.
- Check answers.

3 Review of noun categories

- Circle the correct words.
- Check answers.

4 Controlled practice of *How much ...? / How many ...?*

- Fill in the blanks.
- Check answers.

5 Controlled practice of quantifiers (*a little, a few, a lot of*)

- Look at the picture.
- Write answers, using *a little, a few,* or *a lot of.*
- Check answers.

PUZZLE PAGE 85

- Fast finishers can do Puzzle 4A on page 85.

ANSWERS

1 weeks   2 minutes   3 baggage
4 clothes
Secret sentences:
1 Time is money.
2 Travel light.

Over to you!

6 Personalization; oral practice of *there is / there are* and quantifiers

- Students write sentences to describe their bedrooms.
- They exchange their sentences and tell the class about another student's bedroom.

Extra activity (stronger classes)

Further practice of quantifiers with countable and uncountable nouns

- Students make as many sentences as they can about things in the classroom, using *There is / There are, a little, a few,* and *a lot of.*

- Students read out their sentences. Which pair has the most sentences?

- Alternatively, say a word. Students look around the classroom before they respond: *There is / are a little / a few / a lot of ... in the classroom. / There isn't / aren't any ... in the classroom.*

Further practice
Workbook   page W27
MultiROM

Building the topic

Vocabulary

Aims

Present and practice vocabulary for personal possessions

Write about personal possessions

Warm-up

If possible, show students real examples of some of the key vocabulary (*keys, ID card, sunglasses,* etc.) and elicit or teach the words for these objects. Ask students which of the objects they have in their school bags.

1 Presentation of vocabulary set: possessions ⊚ 1.40

- Look at the picture.
- Fill in the blanks with the words in the box.
- Play the CD.
- Listen, check, and repeat.

2 Vocabulary practice: exposure to vocabulary for possessions ⊚ 1.41

- Play the CD.
- Listen and check (✔) the possessions.
- Check answers.

Audioscript

1 **Anna:** Hi! My name's Anna. I have a yellow belt. I'm with my friend Maria and this blue belt is hers.

2 **Talbass:** Hey! I'm Talbass. I have some red sunglasses. They're cool. My friend Jim doesn't have any sunglasses.

3 **Stefan:** Hello! I'm Stefan. My friend Paul has a New York Yankees key ring. It's blue and white. This LA Lakers key ring is mine. It's purple and yellow.

4 **May:** Hi! My name's May. I have a red bracelet. My friend Nora has a bracelet, too. Hers is brown.

5 **Julia:** Hello! I'm Julia. I have pink earrings. Look at Sara's earrings! Hers are green.

6 **Ken:** Hey! I'm Ken. My brother's backpack is black. Mine is gray.

3 Vocabulary practice and extension

- Fill in the blanks.
- Check answers.

4 Personalization: vocabulary practice

- Write sentences with the words in exercise 1.
- Compare with a partner.
- Ask students to tell the class about themselves and their partner: *I have a black and white backpack. My partner's backpack is gray.*

Building the topic

Vocabulary

Personal possessions

1 ◀)) Look at the picture. Fill in the blanks with the words in the box. Then listen, check, and repeat.

> ~~backpack~~ belt bracelet earrings
> ID card key key ring sunglasses

1 Whose _backpack_ is this? It's his.
2 Whose _belt_ is this? It's hers.
3 Whose _bracelet_ is this? It's hers.
4 Whose _key ring_ is this? It's his.
5 Whose _sunglasses_ are these? They're his.
6 Whose _key_ is this? It's his.
7 Whose _ID card_ is this? It's his.
8 Whose _earrings_ are these? They're hers.

2 ◀)) Listen and check (✔) the correct possessions.

Name	Possession		
1 Anna	belt ✔	belt ☐	
2 Talbass	sunglasses ✔	sunglasses ☐	
3 Stefan	key ring ☐	key ring ✔	
4 May	bracelet ✔	belt ☐	
5 Julia	earrings ✔	earrings ☐	
6 Ken	backpack ☐	backpack ✔	

3 Fill in the blanks with words in exercise 1.

1 My brother has an _earring_ in one ear.
2 Where are my _sunglasses_? It's very sunny today.
3 Look! I'm wearing my new _bracelet_ on my wrist today.
4 Where's my _ID card_? I can't travel without it.
5 Your _backpack_ looks heavy. What's in it?
6 Is this _key ring_ yours? It has a dog on it.
7 You need a _belt_ with those pants!
8 Whose _key_ is this? Is it for your house?

4 Write sentences about you. Use the words in exercise 1. Compare with a partner.

I have a blue belt. I don't have any sunglasses.

40 Workbook p.W28 → MultiROM

ANSWERS
Students' own answers.

> **Extend your vocabulary**
>
> calculators coins sunblock wallet
> watch water bottle
>
> **Workbook** page W28

Further practice
Workbook page W28
MultiROM

Grammar

Whose ...? + possessive pronouns

Talking about people's possessions

1 Look at the chart.

Possessive adjectives	Possessive pronouns
Whose key is this? (singular)	
It's my key.	It's **mine**.
It's your key.	It's **yours**.
It's his / her key.	It's **his / hers**.
It's our key.	It's **ours**.
It's your key.	It's **yours**.
It's their key.	It's **theirs**.
Whose keys are these? (plural)	
They're my keys.	They're **mine**.

2 Circle the correct word.

1 Whose backpack is this? It's (mine) / my.
2 Whose radio is this? It's her / (hers).
3 Whose CD is this? It's (yours) / your.
4 Whose books are those? They're (his) / he's.
5 Whose keys are these? They're (theirs) / their.
6 Whose key ring is this? It's (mine) / my.
7 Whose MP3 players are these?
 They're our / (ours).

3 Rewrite the sentences with the correct possessive pronouns.

1 Whose backpack is this? It's my backpack.
 It's mine .
2 Whose earrings are these? They're your earrings.
 They're yours .
3 Whose chairs are these? They're our chairs.
 They're ours .
4 Whose soccer ball is this? It's his soccer ball.
 It's his .
5 Whose computer is this? It's their computer.
 It's theirs .
6 Whose keys are these? They're her keys.
 They're hers .

Consumer world 4

4 Complete the questions and answers.

1 _Whose_ soccer ball _is_ this?
 It's Lionel's soccer ball.
 It's his .

2 _Whose_ pants _are_ these?
 They're Andy's pants.
 They're his .

3 _Whose_ pencil _is_ this?
 It's her pencil. _It's hers_ .

4 _Whose_ shoes _are_ these?
 They're your shoes.
 They're yours .

5 _Whose_ cell phones _are_ these?
 They're our cell phones.
 They're ours .

6 _Whose_ T-shirt _is_ this?
 It's Bob's T-shirt.
 It's his .

7 _Whose_ sneakers _are_ these?
 They're our sneakers.
 They're ours .

Puzzle page 85, puzzle 4B ➔

5 **Over to you!**

Play a game. In groups of four, put three of your possessions on the desk. Ask and answer questions about the things on the desk.
Student A: Whose pencil is this?
Student B: It's hers. Whose books are these?
Student C: They're his.

---

4 Further practice of *Whose ...? +* possessive pronouns

- Complete the questions and answers.
- Check answers.

PUZZLE PAGE 85

- Fast finishers can do Puzzle 4B on page 85.

ANSWERS
Jody: earrings, bracelet, belt, sunglasses
Hiro: backpack, key, key ring, ID card

Over to you!

5 Personalization; oral practice of *Whose ...? +* possessive pronouns

- Students play a game in groups of four.
- They put three of their possessions on the desk, then ask and answer questions to find out who each item belongs to.

Extra activity (all classes)

Review and practice *Whose ...? +* possessive pronouns

- Ask students to write a favorite possession on a piece of paper. Encourage them to describe the item using adjectives, e.g. *a blue and silver MP3 player; a small gold key ring.*
- Collect all the papers and hand them out randomly.
- Students take turns to ask questions to find out who owns the object on their paper: *Whose blue and silver MP3 player is this?* (*It's mine.*)
- The object of the game is to "get back" your own item.

Further practice
Workbook page W29
MultiROM

Grammar

Aims

Present and practice *Whose ...? +* possessive pronouns
Review possessive adjectives
Review *be*, singular and plural
Talk about people's possessions

1 Grammar chart: *Whose ...? +* possessive pronouns

- Look at the chart.

Note:

- We use *Whose ...?* to ask who something belongs to.
- With uncountable or singular nouns, we always use a singular verb, e.g. *Whose backpack is this? Whose money is this?*

- With countable or plural nouns, we always use a plural verb, e.g. *Whose keys are these?*
- We can use possessive pronouns instead of nouns when the noun is obvious from the context, e.g. *Whose CD is this? It's mine.* (= *It's my CD.*).

Grammar reference page W25

2 Review and controlled practice of *Whose ...? +* possessive pronouns

- Circle the correct word.
- Check answers.

3 Controlled practice of possessive pronouns

- Rewrite the sentences.
- Check answers.

Living English

Reading

🔊 1.42

Aim

Present and practice *How much …? / How many …?* with quantifiers and noun categories, in a quiz about teenage spending habits

Warm-up

Ask *How many of you have a cell phone? How many text messages do you send a day? What do you like to spend your money on? How much money do you spend at the shopping mall when you go shopping? Do you read magazines? What kind of things do you like reading about?*

BACKGROUND INFORMATION

Teenagers and cell phones: in a study conducted online in July 2008 among a nationally representative sample of 2,089 teenagers (age 13–19) across the U.S. who have cell phones, it was found that four out of five teens (17 million) carry a wireless device such as a cell phone. More than 1 billion text messages were sent each day, and 42% of teens said they could text blindfolded. The survey was carried out by CTIA and Harris Interactive.

1 Global comprehension task (first reading)

- Read the quiz.
- Match the headings with the questions.
- Check answers.

2 Detailed comprehension task (second reading)

- Read the quiz again and mark your answers.
- Check your answers at the bottom of the quiz.
- Compare answers with a partner.

3 Detailed comprehension task (third reading)

- Read the sentences and circle T or F.
- Check answers.

Further practice
Workbook page W30

Living English

HOW MUCH DO YOU REALLY KNOW ABOUT YOURSELF AND YOUR CONSUMER HABITS? ANSWER THESE QUESTIONS AND FIND OUT.

Teen Trivia Quiz

1 A lot of teenagers have cell phones. How many teenagers have a cell phone?
   a 50%   b 75%   c 95%

2 How many text messages do teenage girls send and receive each day?
   a 20   b 100   c 60

3 How many text messages do teenage boys send and receive each day?
   a 30   b 50   c 60

4 Teenagers go shopping at least once a week to the shopping mall. How much money do they spend each week?
   a $100   b $47   c $60

5 What do boys like buying with their money?
   a computer games and electronic gadgets
   b books and CDs
   c DVDs and books

6 Girls don't buy the same things as boys. What are their favorite things to buy?
   a books and clothes
   b pens, pencils, notebooks
   c clothes, jewelry (bracelets, earrings), make-up

7 Teenagers also buy a lot of magazines. What do they like reading in them?
   a the advertisements, because they like to find out about new products
   b the articles about celebrities, because they like to know what's happening
   c the articles about clothes, because they want to know what's in fashion

1b 2c 3a 4b 5a 6c 7a

Reading 🔊

1 Read the quiz. Match the headings with the questions.
   a Cell phones 1
   b Magazines 7
   c Money 4
   d Shopping 5 6
   e Text messages 2 3

2 Read again. Mark your answers. Check your answers at the bottom of the quiz.

3 Read the sentences. Circle T (True) or F (False).

1 More than half of American teenagers have a cell phone. (T)/ F
2 Teenage girls send and receive more texts than boys each day. (T)/ F
3 Teenagers go shopping three times a week. T /(F)
4 Boys prefer to buy DVDs and books. T /(F)
5 Girls prefer to buy jewelry and make up. (T)/ F
6 Teenagers don't look at the advertisements in a magazine. T /(F)

42 → Workbook p.W30

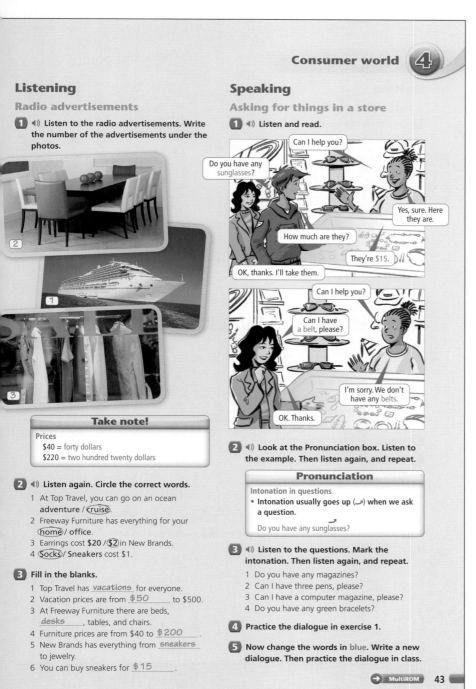

2 Detailed comprehension of the listening task (second listening) 🔊 1.43

- Play the CD again.
- Listen again. Circle the correct words.
- Check answers.

3 Detailed comprehension of the listening task

- Fill in the blanks.
- Check answers.

Speaking

Aims

Ask for things in a store
Pronunciation: intonation in questions

1 First listening 🔊 1.44

- Play the CD.
- Listen and read.

2 Presentation of pronunciation point 🔊 1.45

- Look at the Pronunciation box.
- Play the CD.
- Listen to the example.

> **Pronunciation: intonation in questions**
> - Intonation usually rises when we ask a question.

- Play the CD again.
- Listen again, and repeat.

3 Pronunciation practice 🔊 1.46

- Play the CD.
- Mark the intonation on the questions.
- Play the CD again.
- Listen again, and repeat.

4 Dialogue practice

- Practice the dialogue in exercise 1 with a partner.

5 Personalization

- Change the words in blue and write a new dialogue in pairs.
- Listen to students' dialogues. Make sure they are using the correct rising intonation on questions.
- Ask stronger students to read their new dialogues out in front of the class.

ANSWERS
Students' own answers.

Extra activity (stronger classes)

Review and practice of vocabulary

- Students work in pairs and write a short advertisement, including the price, for an item they own, e.g. a pair of shoes, a watch, a belt, a cell phone.

Further practice
MultiROM

Listening

Aim

Listen to radio advertisements and find specific information

1 Global comprehension of the listening task (first listening) 🔊 1.43

- Play the CD.
- Listen and write the number of the advertisements under the photos.
- Check answers.

Audioscript

1 At Top Travel we have vacations for everyone. An ocean cruise, a city break, a rainforest adventure. Come and see for yourself. Our prices are great, too! From $50 to $500.

2 At Freeway Furniture there's everything for your home. There are beds, desks, tables, and chairs! Prices are from $40 to $200. And you can have it all in your home tomorrow!

3 How often do you buy new clothes? How much do you pay? Come to New Brands today. We have everything from sneakers to jewelry. You can buy sneakers for $15, earrings for $2, socks for $1, and much, much more!

> **Take note!**
> - We say *forty dollars* ($40); *two hundred twenty dollars* ($220), *one dollar and nine cents* ($1.09) or *a / one dollar nine; two dollars twenty-five (cents)* ($2.25).

Round-up

Writing

Aims
Write a consumer profile
Writing skills: using paragraphs

1 Writing skills: using paragraphs
- Read the Writing skills box.

> **Writing skills: using paragraphs**
> - Paragraphs divide a piece of writing into subjects. A paragraph is one or more sentences about the same subject.
> - Each paragraph will have one or two key sentences which contain the main points about that subject.

- Read the consumer profile.
- Choose a heading for each paragraph, and write it in the gap.
- Check answers.

2 Detailed analysis of model writing task
- Fill in the chart with information about Jana.
- Check answers.

3 Preparation for personalized writing
- Fill in the chart with information about you.
- Check that students are completing the chart correctly.

ANSWERS
Students' own answers.

4 Personalized writing
- Follow the model writing text. Use your own information from the chart to change the text.
- Write your consumer profile.

ANSWERS
Students' own answers.

I can ...

Aims
Check understanding of *How much ...?* / *How many ...?* and quantifiers, and *Whose ...?* and possessive adjectives; self-assessment of own progress

1 Self-assessment of *How much ...?* / *How many ...?* and quantifiers
- For items (1–4), students read the sentences and complete them with the correct answers.

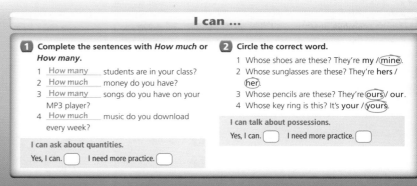

Round-up

Writing
A consumer profile

1 Look at the Writing skills box.

> **Writing skills**
>
> **Using paragraphs**
> - Paragraphs divide a piece of writing into subjects. A paragraph is one or more sentences about the same subject.

Now read Jana's consumer profile. Choose a heading for each paragraph. Write the headings in the gaps.

a What I buy
b When I go shopping
c Where I shop

2 Fill in the chart with information from the consumer profile about Jana.

	Jana	You
Places I shop	in the mall, online, store near her house	
Things I buy	clothes, earrings, books, music, and magazines	
When I shop	shopping mall – once a month; online – every two or three months	

3 Now add your information to the chart.

4 Write your consumer profile. Use the text and the chart to help you.

I can ...

1 Complete the sentences with *How much* or *How many*.

1 How many students are in your class?
2 How much money do you have?
3 How many songs do you have on your MP3 player?
4 How much music do you download every week?

I can ask about quantities.
Yes, I can. ☐   I need more practice. ☐

2 Circle the correct word.

1 Whose shoes are these? They're my / (mine).
2 Whose sunglasses are these? They're hers / (her).
3 Whose pencils are these? They're (ours) / our.
4 Whose key ring is this? It's your / (yours).

I can talk about possessions.
Yes, I can. ☐   I need more practice. ☐

Consumer profile
Jana

1 *Where I shop*
I usually go shopping in the mall, but sometimes I buy things online. I never buy clothes online.

2 *What I buy*
I like clothes, and I buy a lot of clothes. I LOVE earrings! I usually buy my clothes and new earrings at the shopping mall. I like music and books, and I buy a lot of books and music on the Internet. I buy magazines from the store near my house, too.

3 *When I go shopping*
I go to the shopping mall downtown once a month with my friends. I surf the Internet every day, but I only buy things online every two or three months.

44

- Students check (✓) *Yes, I can.* if they think they understand the vocabulary or grammar well, or check (✓) *I need more practice.* if they think they need more practice.
- If students have chosen *I need more practice.*, encourage them to review these sections and to do more practice.

2 Self-assessment of *Whose ...?* and possessive adjectives
- For items (1–4), students read the sentences and choose the correct answers.
- Students check (✓) *Yes, I can.* if they think they understand the vocabulary or grammar well, or check (✓) *I need more practice.* if they think they need more practice.

- If students have chosen *I need more practice.*, encourage them to review these sections and to do more practice.

Further practice
Pairwork pages 114–115
Test pages 94–95, 105

B Review

Vocabulary

Food

1 Circle six food words in the word snake.

bananasd feggsh pizzasi strawberriesk sausagesm nmangoes

Food and drink

2 You are shopping. Look at your list. Check (✓) the things you buy.

- ✓ apples
- ☐ tomatoes
- ✓ bread
- ✓ pasta
- ☐ salad
- ✓ orange juice
- ☐ water
- ✓ oil
- ✓ milk
- ☐ potatoes
- ✓ ketchup
- ☐ bananas

Noun categories

3 Match the categories with the nouns.

1 money — h dollars
2 baggage — b bags
3 music — g songs
4 furniture — a chairs and tables
5 time — f hours
6 traffic — d cars
7 food — c meals
8 travel — e vacations

Personal possessions

4 Complete the possessions. Use *a*, *e*, *i*, *o*, or *u*.

1 k e y r i n g
2 b e l t
3 k e y
4 b a ckp a ck
5 s u ngl a ss e s
6 br a c e l e t
7 e a rr i ngs
8 I D c a rd

Grammar

there is / there are + countable nouns

1 Look at the pictures. Fill in the blanks with *a*, *an*, *some*, or *any*.

1 There's **an** apple on the table.

2 There aren't **any** bananas.

3 There are **some** pizzas in the refrigerator.

4 There aren't **any** French fries, but there is **a** hamburger.

5 There are **some** eggs.

6 There isn't **any** milk.

Unit summary

Vocabulary
Food
Food and drink
Noun categories
Possessions

Grammar
there is / there are + countable nouns
Uncountable nouns
How much ...? / How many ...? + quantifiers
Whose...? + possessive pronouns

Study skills
Using a dictionary

Project 2
Writing a description of diet and eating habits

Vocabulary

Aim

Present and practice words for food, food and drink, noun categories, and personal possessions

1 Review of vocabulary set: food
- Circle the food words.
- Check answers.

2 Review of vocabulary set: food and drink
- Look at the pictures.
- Check (✓) the things in the list.
- Check answers.

3 Review of vocabulary set: noun categories
- Match the two columns.
- Check answers.

4 Review of vocabulary set: personal possessions
- Complete the words with the vowels.
- Check answers.

Grammar

1 Review of *there is / there are* and countable nouns
- Fill in the blanks.
- Check answers.

2 Review of uncountable nouns

- Look at the picture and write sentences.
- Check answers.

3 Review of *How much ...? / How many ...?* and quantifiers

- Complete the questions and answers.
- Check answers.

4 Review of *Whose ...?* and possessive pronouns

- Write questions and answers to complete the dialogues.
- Check answers.

Study skills

Using a dictionary

Dictionaries can help students in many ways. Students can find the meanings of new words; check spelling; give confidence with reading; help students become independent learners.

1 Dictionary skills: classifying words

- Read through the instructions with the students.
- Remind them what a noun (n), verb (v), or adjective (adj) is: elicit examples and write them on the board.
- Students complete the task, using their dictionaries.
- Compare answers in pairs before a whole class check.

2 Dictionary skills: translation

- Students look back at the words in exercise 1.
- Translate the words into your own language.
- Compare answers in pairs before a whole class check.

Further practice
MultiROM

Project 2 `page 86`

Aims

Read an interview with someone about his diet

Interview a classmate about their diet

Write a profile of your classmate's diet

1 Reading

- Read the interview.
- Fill in the blanks.
- Check answers.

ANSWERS

What snacks do you have?
What kinds of food do you normally eat?
Do you eat in restaurants?
What diet do you have?

Review

Uncountable nouns

2 Look at the picture. Write sentences with *there is*, *there isn't*, *some*, and *any*, and the words in parentheses.

1 There is some oil   . (oil)
2 There isn't any pasta   . (pasta)
3 There is some salt   . (salt)
4 There isn't any bread   . (bread)
5 There is some cheese   . (cheese)
6 There is some rice   . (rice)

How much ...? / How many ...? + quantifiers

3 Complete the questions and answers.

1 How much   traffic is there   ? (a lot)
  There's a lot of traffic   .
2 How many   bags are there   ? (a few)
  There are a few bags   .
3 How much   food is there   ? (a little)
  There is a little food   .
4 How many   people are there   ? (not many)
  There aren't many people   .
5 How much   furniture is there   ? (a little)
  There is a little furniture   .
6 How many   chairs are there   ? (not any)
  There aren't any chairs   .

Whose ...? + possessive pronouns

4 Complete the dialogues.

1 It's my backpack.
  A: Whose backpack is this   ?
  B: It's mine   .
2 They're your books.
  A: Whose books are these   ?
  B: They're yours   .
3 It's her bracelet.
  A: Whose bracelet is this   ?
  B: It's hers   .
4 It's his ID card.
  A: Whose ID card is this   ?
  B: It's his   .
5 They're our keys.
  A: Whose keys are these   ?
  B: They're ours   .
6 It's their basketball.
  A: Whose basketball is this   ?
  B: It's theirs   .

Study skills

Using a dictionary

When you look up a word in a dictionary, think about the type of word. Are you looking for a noun (n), verb (v), or adjective (adj)?

1 The words below have two meanings. Look them up in your dictionary. Write n (for noun), v (for verb), or adj (for adjective) for each word.

1 fish   (n)   and   (v)
2 book   (n)   and   (v)
3 light   (v)   and   (adj)
4 cool   (adj) and   (v)
5 drink   (n)   and   (v)
6 water   (n)   and   (v)

2 Translate the words into your own language.

---

2 Preparation for writing (first task)

- Use the questions in the model interview.
- Interview a classmate about their diet.
- Write notes about their answers.

ANSWERS

Students' own answers.

3 Preparation for writing (second task)

- Find or draw a picture to illustrate your classmate's diet. (Use the Internet, magazines, or newspapers.)

4 Writing

- Follow the model text.
- Write a profile of your classmate and their diet.

ANSWERS

Students' own answers.

5 Presentation

- Put your profile in a class magazine for other students to read.
- Read other students' profiles.

ANSWERS

Students' own answers.

Project extension

- If you have the facilities, ask students to record their interviews using a digital camera. The video files could then be uploaded to the Internet.
- You could ask students to share their partners' profiles on a class or school website. Encourage other students to log on to the website, and to read and compare the profiles.

5 A good idea?

Introducing the topic

_____ to a party

3 _get_ a tattoo

2 _have_ a sleepover

4 _borrow_ some money

7 _buy_ a dog

drive the car

6 _stay out_ late

8 _dye_ my hair

Vocabulary

Requests

1 🔊 Look at the photos. Fill in the blanks with the verbs below. Then listen, check, and repeat.

> borrow buy drive dye get ~~go~~ have
> stay out

2 Circle the correct verb.

1 Can we (have) / get a sleepover this weekend?
2 Can I (dye) / get my hair green?
3 Can we (buy) / drive a dog tomorrow?
4 Can I (get) / borrow a tattoo on my leg?
5 Can we (go) / stay out to a party on Saturday?
6 Can I borrow / (drive) the new car to the beach?
7 Can we (stay out) / get late tonight?
8 Can we go / (borrow) some money?

3 Read the requests in exercise 2 again. What would your parents say? Choose a reply below. Write the number of the request next to the reply. Then compare with a partner.

a Sure you can. ____ ____ ____
b I'll think about it. ____ ____ ____
c Absolutely not! No way! ____ ____ ____

Vocabulary

Verbs for requests: *borrow, buy, drive, dye, get, go, have, stay out*

Places to go: *amusement park, coffee shop, library, museum, park, shopping mall, skating rink, swimming pool*

Grammar

can (permission)

Suggestions

Skills

Reading: a story about a sleepover; reading about teenage problems in a story and letters in a teen magazine; looking for key words and phrases

Listening: Listening and identifying specific information in a conversation

Speaking: Making suggestions; responding to suggestions

Writing: Writing an e-mail to a friend

Cross-curricular

Geography

Values and topics

Respect: respecting that others are different

Personal and family relationships

Introducing the topic

Vocabulary

Aim

Present and practice verbs for requests

Warm-up

Ask students what they like doing in their free time. Ask which things they need their parents' permission for.

1 Presentation of vocabulary set: verbs for requests 🌐 2.2

- Look at the photos. Fill in the blanks.
- Play the CD.
- Listen, check, and repeat.

2 Vocabulary practice; exposure to verbs for requests

- Circle the correct words.
- Check answers.

3 Personalization

- Read the requests in exercise 2.
- Choose the reply your parents would give.
- Write the number of the request next to the reply.
- Compare answers with a partner.

ANSWERS
Students' own answers.

Extend your vocabulary

go clubbing go fishing go shopping
go skiing go snowboarding
go swimming
Workbook page W32

Further practice
Workbook page W32
MultiROM

Exploring the topic

Reading

Aim
Present and practice requests through a story about a teenager and his parents

Pre-reading task
Look at the pictures. What do you think the story is about?

1 Identifying (first reading) 🔊 2.3
- Play the CD.
- Read and listen to the story.
- Answer the question.
- Check answers.

2 Detailed comprehension task (second reading)
- Read the story again.
- Write the names.
- Check answers as a class.

3 Detailed comprehension task (third reading)
- Read the story again.
- Complete the sentences.
- Check answers.

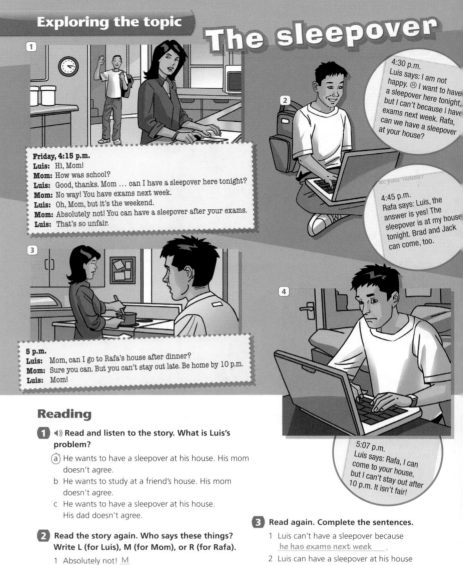

Exploring the topic

The sleepover

1

Friday, 4:15 p.m.
Luis: Hi, Mom!
Mom: How was school?
Luis: Good, thanks. Mom … can I have a sleepover here tonight?
Mom: No way! You have exams next week.
Luis: Oh, Mom, but it's the weekend.
Mom: Absolutely not! You can have a sleepover after your exams.
Luis: That's so unfair.

3

5 p.m.
Luis: Mom, can I go to Rafa's house after dinner?
Mom: Sure you can. But you can't stay out late. Be home by 10 p.m.
Luis: Mom!

2

4:30 p.m.
Luis says: I am not happy. ☹ I want to have a sleepover here tonight, but I can't because I have exams next week. Rafa, can we have a sleepover at your house?

4:45 p.m.
Rafa says: Luis, the answer is yes! The sleepover is at my house tonight. Brad and Jack can come, too.

4

5:07 p.m.
Luis says: Rafa, I can come to your house, but I can't stay out after 10 p.m. It isn't fair!

Reading

1 🔊 Read and listen to the story. What is Luis's problem?

(a) He wants to have a sleepover at his house. His mom doesn't agree.

b He wants to study at a friend's house. His mom doesn't agree.

c He wants to have a sleepover at his house. His dad doesn't agree.

2 Read the story again. Who says these things? Write L (for Luis), M (for Mom), or R (for Rafa).

1 Absolutely not! M
2 Can I have a sleepover here tonight? L
3 The sleepover is at my house tonight. R
4 You can't stay out late. M
5 Can I go to Rafa's house tonight after dinner? L
6 Be home by 10 p.m. M

3 Read again. Complete the sentences.

1 Luis can't have a sleepover because
   he has exams next week .
2 Luis can have a sleepover at his house
   after his exams .
3 The sleepover is at Rafa's house.
4 Brad and Jack can come , too.
5 Luis can't stay out after
   10 p.m. .

48

Grammar

can (permission)

Asking for permission

1 Look at the chart.

Questions	Answers
Can I **go** to Rob's party?	Sure you can.
Can we **have** a sleepover?	I'll think about it.
Can we **buy** a dog?	Sorry, you can't.
Can my friend **dye** her hair?	Absolutely not! No way!

2 Match the questions and answers.

Questions
1 Can I buy this jacket? _e_
2 Can Jake sleep over tonight? _d_
3 Can we stay out until midnight? _a_
4 Can I borrow your math book? _c_
5 Can Jane eat dinner with us? _b_
6 Can I dye my hair? _f_

Answers
a Absolutely not! Be home at ten o'clock.
b I'll think about it, but there isn't much food in the house.
c Sorry, you can't. I'm doing my homework now.
d Sure he can, but ask his parents first.
e No, you can't. It's very expensive.
f No way! Green hair isn't cool!

3 Look at the picture. Write the children's questions. Then complete the mother's answers.

1 _Can I have a glass of soda_ ?
  Sure you can, but don't drop it!
2 _Can I listen to music_ ?
  Sure _you can_ , but use your headphones.
3 _Can I go swimming_ ?
  Absolutely _not_ ! It's cold outside.
4 Can we have a party?
  No _way_ ! It's a lot of work.
5 _Can we play computer games_ ?
  I'll _think about_ it.
6 _Can we eat this cake now_ ?
  Sorry, _you can't_ . It's for dessert.

A good idea?

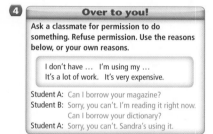

Puzzle page 87, puzzle 5A →

4

Over to you!

Ask a classmate for permission to do something. Refuse permission. Use the reasons below, or your own reasons.

> I don't have … I'm using my …
> It's a lot of work. It's very expensive.

Student A: Can I borrow your magazine?
Student B: Sorry, you can't. I'm reading it right now. Can I borrow your dictionary?
Student A: Sorry, you can't. Sandra's using it.

 Workbook p.W33 → MultiROM **49**

5 Does your dad drive you to school?
6 Can I borrow your new computer game?
7 Where did you buy your goldfish?

Over to you!

4 Personalization; oral practice of making and refusing requests for permission

- Students work in pairs.
- They take turns to ask for and refuse permission to do the things listed.
- Ask several pairs to demonstrate their conversations to the class.

Extra activity (all classes)

Further practice of *can* for permission

- Write the verb *borrow* on the board. Add different nouns to make phrases, or ask students to suggest nouns, e.g. *your pencil / your bike / some money / your new jacket / your homework / your MP3 player / your cell phone / your dictionary*, etc.
- Students take turns to ask for permission and respond to requests.

Further practice
Workbook page W33
MultiROM

Grammar

Aims

Present and practice *can* (permission)
Ask for permission

1 Grammar chart: *can* (permission – questions and answers)

- Look at the chart.

Note:
- We use *can* to ask for permission.
- We use different responses to indicate more or less strength of feeling: *Sure you can* (certain, positive), *I'll think about it* (less certain), *No, you can't* (certain, negative), *Absolutely not* (certain, very strong negative).

Grammar reference page W31

2 Controlled practice of *can* (permission – questions and answers)

- Match the questions and answers.
- Check answers.

3 Further practice of *can* (permission – questions and answers)

- Look at the picture.
- Write questions and answers.
- Check answers.

PUZZLE PAGE 87
- Fast finishers can do Puzzle 5A on page 87.

ANSWERS
2 Do you go to a dance club on Fridays?
3 Does Dan wear his jacket every day?
4 Do you want to dye your hair blue?

Unit 5 49

Building the topic

Vocabulary

Aims
Present and practice vocabulary for places to go
Write about places to go

Warm-up
Look at the pictures. Ask students *Which of the places in the pictures do you go to on the weekends. What do you do there? What is your favorite place to go to?*

1 Presentation of vocabulary set: places to go 2.4
- Look at the pictures.
- Complete the dialogues with the places in the box.
- Play the CD.
- Listen, check, and repeat.

2 Vocabulary practice: exposure to vocabulary for places to go 2.5
- Play the CD.
- Read and listen.
- Listen again, and repeat the suggestions in blue.
- Check answers.

3 Vocabulary practice and extension
- Write about places you like to go.
- Compare with a partner.
- Check answers.

ANSWERS
Students' own answers.

Extend your vocabulary
crazy great hate love not bad OK
stand terrible
Workbook   page W34

Further practice
Workbook   page W34
MultiROM

Building the topic

Vocabulary
Places to go

1 🔊 Look at the pictures. Complete the dialogues below with the places. Then listen, check, and repeat.

amusement park   coffee shop   library
museum   park   shopping mall   skating rink
swimming pool

2 🔊 Read and listen to the dialogues. Then listen again, and repeat the suggestions in blue.

3 What places do you like to go to? Compare with a partner.
After school: _____
On the weekends: _____
On vacation: _____

1
Anna: OK, guys. What are we doing today?
Bruno: Let's go to the skating rink.
Eva: No. Skating is boring.

2
Anna: What about going to the amusement park?
Eva: No way! The rides are scary, and it's expensive.

3
David: Why don't we go to the shopping mall?
Bruno: I don't think so! I hate shopping.

4
David: Let's go to the park and play baseball.
Bruno: No, thanks. I'm tired.

5
Bruno: Let's go to the museum. There's a good exhibit about the Incas.
Anna: No, let's not. I was there last week.

6
Anna: Why don't we go to the library? There's a storyteller there today.
David: No, that's boring.

7
Anna: I know! What about going to the swimming pool?
David: Let's not. There are a lot of people there on Saturdays.

8
Eva: Why don't we go the coffee shop? Then we can have some coffee and talk about our plans.
David: That's a good idea! Let's go.

50   Workbook p.W34 → MultiROM

Grammar

Suggestions

Making suggestions

1 Look at the chart.

Suggestions	Positive responses	Negative responses
Let's go out.	OK.	I don't think so.
What about going out?	That's a good idea.	Let's not.
Why don't we go out?	Great!	No way!

2 Circle the correct form of the verb.

1 What about watch / (watching) a DVD?
2 Let's (eat) / eating in a fast food restaurant.
3 Why don't we having / (have) a party?
4 What about invite / (inviting) Cara over?

3 Look at the pictures. Fill in the blanks with the correct form of the suggestions below.

cook some food   ~~go swimming~~
have a sleepover   play soccer in the park
study for the test

1 What about _going swimming_ ?

2 Let's _have a sleepover_ .

3 Why don't we _cook some food_ ?

A good idea? **A good idea?**

4 What about _playing soccer in the park_ ?

5 Let's _study for the test_ .

4 Write suggestions with *Let's ...*, *What about ...?*, and *Why don't we ...?* Use each suggestion once. Then write the responses.

buy some new clothes   do our homework
go to the coffee shop   ~~watch TV~~

1 _What about watching TV_ ?
  Let's not .
2 _____ ?
  _____ .
3 _____ ?
  _____ .
4 _____ ?
  _____ .

Puzzle page 87, puzzle 5B →

5 **Over to you!**

What do you want to do this evening? Make suggestions. Use the ideas below.

get a pizza   go to a movie
go to the skating rink   play video games
watch a DVD

Student A: Let's get a pizza.
Student B: Let's not.
Student C: What about a hamburger?
Student D: That's a good idea!

Workbook p.W35 → MultiROM   **51**

Grammar

Aims

Present and practice *Let's ... / What about ...? / Why don't we ...?* for suggestions
Make and respond to suggestions

1 Grammar chart: suggestions and responses (positive and negative)

- Look at the chart.

Note:
- We use *Let's ...* and *Why don't we ...?* + verb to make suggestions, e.g. *Let's go to the movies. / Why don't we play tennis?*
- We use *What about ...?* + *-ing* form to make suggestions, e.g. *What about playing tennis?*

- Although we can respond to suggestions with *Yes* or *No*, it's more polite to use one of the suggested positive or negative responses in the chart.

Grammar reference   page W31

2 Review and controlled practice of verb or *-ing* form after suggestions

- Circle the correct word.
- Check answers.

3 Controlled practice of suggestions

- Look at the pictures and fill in the blanks.
- Check answers.

---

4 Further practice of making and responding to suggestions

- Write suggestions and responses. Use your own ideas.
- Compare suggestions and responses in pairs.

ANSWERS
Students' own answers.

PUZZLE PAGE 87

- Fast finishers can do Puzzle 5B on page 87.

ANSWERS
1 skating rink
2 shopping mall
3 coffee shop
4 amusement park
5 swimming pool
Mystery word: museum

Over to you!

5 Personalization; oral practice of making and responding to suggestions

- Students work in pairs.
- They take turns to make and respond to suggestions, using the ideas given.
- Ask some pairs to demonstrate their conversations to the class.

Extra activity (stronger classes)

Review and practice of making and responding to suggestions

- Draw a blank "week-to-view" diary page on the board and ask students to copy it in their notebooks.
- Ask students to write six time activities on different days, morning, afternoon, or evening, e.g. (*Wednesday morning: play tennis; Friday evening: go out for dinner*).
- Students work in pairs, making a suggestion about a place to go together.
- The object of the activity is to find a time when they are both free, and an activity they both want to do.

Further practice
Workbook   page W35
MultiROM

Unit 5   51 **Unit 5   51**

Living English

Reading

🎵 2.6

Aims

Present and practice suggestions in the context of a teenage magazine problem page

Reading skills: looking for key words and phrases

Warm-up

Ask students what they do when they have a problem. Who do they talk to? Do they ever read problem pages in magazines or on the Internet?

1 Global comprehension task (first reading)

- Read the problem page and answer the question.
- Check answers.

2 Reading skills: looking for key words and phrases

- Read the Reading skills box.

Reading skills: looking for key words and phrases

- Looking for key words and phrases in the text helps students to read the text more quickly and find the comprehension answers more quickly and accurately.

---

3 Detailed comprehension task (second reading)

- Read and listen to the problem page again and circle T or F next to the sentences.
- Compare answers with a partner.
- Check answers with the class.

Further practice
Workbook page W36

Living English

teen trouble

Are you a teenager with a problem? Marcia Clark answers your questions.

Dear Marcia,
I'm fourteen years old. I love basketball, and I'm a good player. The problem is that my grades at school aren't very good – and now I can't play on the school basketball team. My parents want me to study for my school exams, and not play basketball all the time. Do you have any advice?
Gregg
San Luis Obispo, California

Dear Gregg,
Think about it. Good grades equal a place on the basketball team. Why don't you study now? Before long, you're a basketball player AND a good student!
Marcia

Dear Marcia,
I'm a fifteen-year-old girl. I met a really cute boy. He's seventeen. He asked me out, but my parents aren't happy because of my age, and I can't date until I'm sixteen. I really like this boy! My parents don't know him. What can I do?
Ariana
Birmingham, Alabama

Dear Marcia,
I'm sixteen. I'm a good student, and I'm very responsible. The problem? I want a tattoo, but my parents hate them, and I can't get one. I don't understand their problem. All my friends have tattoos. What's your advice?
Madison
Salt Lake City, Utah

Dear Madison,
Why don't you think about it some more? Tattoos are cool right now – but do you really want a picture on your body for the rest of your life? Sixteen is probably too young to decide things like that.
Marcia

Dear Ariana,
What about going out in a group? Why not invite some of your friends and some of his friends? Go to the movies, or the coffee shop. Then you can be together, have fun, and please your parents.
(P.S. Your parents are right. 15 + 17 = trouble!)
Marcia

Reading 🔊

1 Read the problem page. Where can you find a text like this?

a in a sports magazine
b in a teen magazine
c in a school book

2 Look at the Reading skills box.

Reading skills

Looking for key words and phrases
- **When you answer comprehension questions, find the word or the phrase in the text that tells you the answer.**

---

3 Read again. Circle T (True) or F (False).

1 Gregg is a very good student. T / **F**
2 Gregg is on the basketball team now. T / **F**
3 Marcia's solution is for Gregg to study more. **T** / F
4 Ariana's parents don't know the seventeen-year-old boy. **T** / F
5 Marcia thinks a group activity is a good idea. **T** / F
6 Marcia thinks Ariana's parents are right. **T** / F
7 Madison is angry with her friends. T / **F**
8 Marcia thinks tattoos are a good idea. T / **F**

52 → **Workbook p.W36**

Listening

Talking about what to do on the weekend

1 🔊 **Listen to the students. What does Tom suggest they do?**

a study for the exams
b have a party *(circled)*
c go to the movies

2 🔊 **Listen again. Circle the correct word.**

1 Lola thinks Tom's idea is great / **boring**.
2 Andi wants to go to the **amusement park** / park.
3 Lola likes / **doesn't like** the rides.
4 Tom suggests going to the **skating rink** / movies.
5 Andi thinks that's a **good** / bad idea.
6 Lola wants to borrow money from Andi / **Tom**.

3 🔊 **Listen again. Fill in the blanks with the correct words.**

1 Let's have a _party_ !
2 Why don't we go to the _amusement park_ ?
3 What about going to the _skating rink_ ?
4 Let's do _that_ !

Speaking

Making suggestions

1 🔊 **Listen and read.**

Why don't we play soccer?

I don't think so.

OK. What about going to the swimming pool?

That's a good idea. I love swimming.

I have a good idea! Let's watch TV.

Let's not.

Why not?

Because it's eleven o'clock. I want to go to bed.

Oh, OK.

2 🔊 **Look at the Pronunciation box. Listen to the examples. Then listen again, and repeat.**

Pronunciation

Responding to suggestions
• Our voice goes up (↗) on positive responses, and down (↘) on negative responses.

Positive ↗	Negative ↘
That's a good idea!	I don't think so.
	Let's not. ↘

3 🔊 **Listen to the suggestions and responses. Write P for a positive response and N for a negative response.**

1 _N_   2 _P_   3 _N_   4 _N_

4 **Practice the dialogue in exercise 1.**

5 **Now change the words in blue. Write a new dialogue. Then practice the dialogue in class.**

➜ MultiROM   53

Listening

Aim

Listen to conversations and find specific information

1 Global comprehension of the listening task (first listening) 🎧 2.7

• Play the CD. Listen and choose the correct answer. Check answers.

Audioscript

Tom: So, no school, no more exams. Let's have a party!
Lola: No, Tom. That's boring. We always have a party after the exams.
Andi: Well, why don't we go to the amusement park?
Lola: I don't think so. I don't like the rides. They're scary and it's expensive.

Tom: OK. What about going to the skating rink and then to a fast food restaurant?
Andi: Now that's a good idea. Let's do that!
Lola: No way! I can't skate and I don't have any money. Why don't we just go and eat? Tom, can I borrow some money from you?
Tom: Oh, Lola, not again …!

2 Detailed comprehension of the listening task (second listening) 🎧 2.7

• Play the CD again. Listen again. Circle the correct word. Check answers.

3 Detailed comprehension of the listening task (third listening) 🎧 2.7

• Play the CD again.
• Listen again and fill in the blanks.
• Check answers.

Speaking

Aims

Making suggestions
Pronunciation: responding to suggestions (with rising or falling intonation)

1 First listening 🎧 2.8

• Play the CD. Listen and read.

2 Presentation of pronunciation point 🎧 2.9

• Look at the Pronunciation box.
• Play the CD.
• Listen to the examples.

> **Pronunciation: responding to suggestions**
> • Using appropriate intonation helps students sound more natural, and encourages people to listen. Our voice goes up on positive responses, and down on negative responses.

• Play the CD again.
• Listen again, and repeat.

3 Pronunciation practice 🎧 2.10

• Play the CD.
• Write P for positive or N for negative.
• Check answers.

Audioscript

1 **Girl:** Why don't we go to the coffee shop?
   Boy: I don't think so. I don't have any money.
2 **Boy:** What about going to see a movie?
   Girl: Yeah, that's a good idea. What's playing?
3 **Boy:** Let's go to the skating rink.
   Boy: But there are always a lot of people there. Let's not.
4 **Boy:** Why don't we stay home and play computer games?
   Girl: No way. That's boring!

4 Dialogue practice

• Practice the dialogue in exercise 1.
• Listen to students' dialogues. Make sure they are using the correct rising intonation on questions.

5 Dialogue personalization and practice

• Change the words in blue and write a new dialogue in pairs.
• Practice the dialogue with their partners.
• Listen to students' dialogues. Make sure they are using the correct intonation.
• Ask stronger students to read their new dialogues out in front of the class.

ANSWERS
Students' own answers.

Further practice
MultiROM

Round-up

Writing

Aim
Write an e-mail to a friend

1 Global comprehension of model writing text
- Read the e-mail quickly.
- What is it about?
- Check answer.

ANSWER
The e-mail is about suggestions for things to do when Holly comes to stay.

2 Detailed analysis of model writing task
- Fill in the chart with information about April.
- Check answers.

3 Preparation for personalized writing
- Fill in the chart with information about things to do in or near your city.
- Check that students are completing the chart correctly.

ANSWERS
Students' own answers.

4 Personalized writing
- Follow the model writing text. Use your own information from the chart to change the text.
- Write your e-mail.

ANSWERS
Students' own answers.

I can ...

Aims
Check understanding of *can* (permission) and suggestions; self-assessment of own progress

1 Self-assessment of *can* (permission)
- For items (1–4), students read the sentences and match them with the correct responses (a–d).
- Students check (✓) *Yes, I can.* if they think they understand the vocabulary or grammar well, or check (✓) *I need more practice.* if they think they need more practice.
- If students have chosen *I need more practice.*, encourage them to review these sections and to do more practice.

2 Self-assessment of suggestions
- For items (1–4), students read the sentences and choose the correct answers.

Round-up

Writing

An e-mail to a friend

1 Read April's e-mail to her friend Holly. What is it about?

2 Fill in the chart with the information about April.

April	
Suggestions	Reasons
take bus to Chicago	not far; a lot to do
go ice-skating on the lake	lots of kids go there; it's really fun
go to see grandparents	they live in Vermont – it's an amazing place
You	
Suggestions	Reasons

3 Now fill in the chart with suggestions and reasons to do things in or near your city.

4 Write an e-mail to a friend making your suggestions and giving reasons. Use the text and the chart to help you.

○ ○ ○   Winter vacation

Hi, Holly
It's great that you're coming to stay with us for the winter vacation. I'm really looking forward to it!
When you're here, let's take the bus into Chicago for a day. It isn't far, and there's a lot to do. And why don't we go ice-skating on the lake near here? Lots of kids go there, and it's really fun. Then what about going to see my grandparents? They live in Vermont. It's an amazing place.
See you soon!
April

I can ...

1 Match the sentence halves.
1 Can I go shopping with Claudia? _d_
2 Can Luke sleep over tonight? _a_
3 Can Beatriz come for lunch tomorrow? _b_
4 Can I borrow your English book? _c_

a No way! You have school tomorrow.
b Sorry. We're having lunch with your aunt.
c Sorry, but I'm reading it.
d Sure you can.

I can ask for permission.
Yes, I can. ☐   I need more practice. ☐

2 Circle the correct verb.
1 Why don't we (go) / going out?
2 What about have / (having) pizza for dinner?
3 Let's (play) / playing soccer in the park.
4 Why don't we (do) / doing our homework now?

I can make suggestions.
Yes, I can. ☐   I need more practice. ☐

54

- Students check (✓) *Yes, I can.* if they think they understand the vocabulary or grammar well, or check (✓) *I need more practice.* if they think they need more practice.
- If students have chosen *I need more practice.*, encourage them to review these sections and to do more practice.

Further practice
Pairwork pages 116–117
Test pages 96–97; 106

6 One of a kind

Introducing the topic

Pablo Picasso was an **artist**.

2 Christian Dior was a **fashion designer**.

3 Jimi Hendrix was a **musician**.

4 Newman Darby was an **inventor**.

John F. Kennedy was a **politician**.

6 Frank Lloyd Wright was an **architect**.

7 Albert Einstein was a **scientist**.

8 Agatha Christie was a **writer**.

Vocabulary

Jobs

1 🔊 **Look at the photos. Write the jobs. Then listen and check.**

> architect ~~artist~~ fashion designer inventor
> musician politician scientist writer

2 **Fill in the blanks with the words in exercise 1.**

1 I study physics and I make important discoveries about science. I'm a **scientist**.
2 He plays the guitar and he writes songs. He's a **musician**.
3 I write books. I'm a **writer**.
4 My dad invents things. He's an **inventor**.

5 She designs houses and museums. She's an **architect**.
6 I work in politics. I'm a **politician**.
7 My aunt paints and draws pictures. She's an **artist**.
8 His mom designs clothes and she makes perfumes. She's a **fashion designer**.

3 **Complete the sentences with your favorite person. Compare with a partner.**

1 _Salvador Dalí_ is my favorite artist.
2 _____ is my favorite fashion designer.
3 _____ is my favorite musician.
4 _____ is my favorite writer.

Workbook p.W38 ➔ MultiROM 55

Unit summary

Vocabulary

Jobs: *architect, artist, fashion designer, inventor, musician, politician, scientist, writer*

Adjectives of opinion: *awesome, awful, boring, delicious, disgusting, fantastic, interesting, terrible*

Grammar
was / were
Ordinal numbers

Skills

Reading: an article about famous people; an article about famous firsts; using headings

Listening: Listening and identifying specific information in a history talk

Speaking: Giving personal information; *th* sound in ordinal numbers

Writing: Writing a biography of a famous person; dates and time expressions

Cross-curricular
History
Sport
Science
Math

Values and topics
Multiculturalism
Human achievement

Introducing the topic

Vocabulary

Aim
Present and practice vocabulary for jobs

Warm-up
Ask students to look at the photos. Ask them if they know any of the people, or why they are famous.

BACKGROUND INFORMATION
Pablo Picasso (1881–1973) was a Spanish artist.

Christian Dior (1905–1957) was a French fashion designer.

Jimi Hendrix (1942–1970) was an American musician. He was one of the greatest electric guitarists that ever lived.

Newman Darby (born 1928) is an inventor, famous for designing and building sailing boats.

John F. Kennedy (1917–1963) was the 35th President of the U.S.A., when he was assassinated.

Frank Lloyd Wright (1867–1959) was an American architect. He is regarded by many as the greatest American architect of all time.

Albert Einstein (1879–1955) was a German scientist. He is called the "father of modern physics".

Agatha Christie (1890–1976) was a British writer. She wrote detective novels.

1 Presentation of vocabulary set: jobs 🔊 2.11

- Look at the photos and write the jobs.
- Play the CD. Listen and check.

2 Vocabulary practice; exposure to vocabulary for jobs

- Fill in the blanks. Check answers.

3 Personalization

- Complete the sentences with your favorite person.
- Compare answers with a partner.

ANSWERS
Students' own answers.

Extend your vocabulary
baseball player composer explorer
movie director queen racing driver
Workbook page W38

Further practice
Workbook page W38
MultiROM

Exploring the topic

Reading

Aim
Present and practice jobs vocabulary through a text about famous people

Pre-reading task
Look at the pictures. Do you know any of the people?

Martin Luther King (1929–1968) was a minister and a leader of the American civil rights movement.

Frida Kahlo (1907–1954) was a Mexican painter.

Coco Chanel (1883–1971) was a French fashion designer, famous for starting the design label named after her.

Ian Fleming (1908–1964) was a British writer, famous for his James Bond character.

1 Matching (first reading) 🎧 2.12
- Play the CD.
- Read and listen to the biographies.
- Match the people and the jobs.
- Check answers.

2 Detailed comprehension task (second reading)
- Read the biographies again.
- Complete the chart.
- Check answers as a class.

3 Detailed comprehension task (third reading)
- Read the biographies again.
- Write the name of the person.
- Check answers.

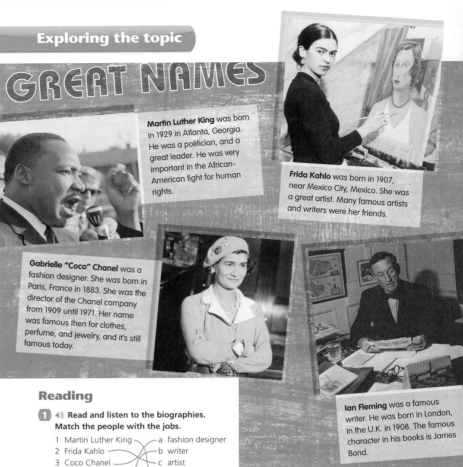

Exploring the topic

GREAT NAMES

Martin Luther King was born in 1929 in Atlanta, Georgia. He was a politician, and a great leader. He was very important in the African-American fight for human rights.

Frida Kahlo was born in 1907, near Mexico City, Mexico. She was a great artist. Many famous artists and writers were her friends.

Gabrielle "Coco" Chanel was a fashion designer. She was born in Paris, France in 1883. She was the director of the Chanel company from 1909 until 1971. Her name was famous then for clothes, perfume, and jewelry, and it's still famous today.

Ian Fleming was a famous writer. He was born in London, in the U.K. in 1908. The famous character in his books is James Bond.

Reading

1 🔊 **Read and listen to the biographies. Match the people with the jobs.**

1 Martin Luther King — a fashion designer
2 Frida Kahlo — b writer
3 Coco Chanel — c artist
4 Ian Fleming — d politician

2 Read the biographies again. Complete the chart with information in the text.

Name	Born	When?
Martin Luther King	Atlanta, Georgia	1929
Frida Kahlo	Mexico City, Mexico	1907
Coco Chanel	Paris, France	1883
Ian Fleming	London, the U.K.	1908

3 Read again. Write the name of the person.

1 She was born in Mexico.
   Frida Kahlo
2 He was a famous leader.
   Martin Luther King
3 She was French.
   Coco Chanel
4 He was British.
   Ian Fleming
5 She was the friend of writers and artists.
   Frida Kahlo

56

Grammar

was / were

Talking about the past

1 Look at the chart.

Affirmative	Negative
I **was** a musician.	I **wasn't** a musician.
You **were** an inventor.	You **weren't** an inventor.
He / She / It **was** in my class.	He / She / It **wasn't** in my class.
We **were** artists.	We **weren't** artists.
You **were** inventors.	You **weren't** inventors.
They **were** writers.	They **weren't** writers.

2 Look at the timeline of Pelé's professional life. Complete the sentences with the correct negative or affirmative form of *be*.

1940	born in Três Corações, Brazil
1958	World Cup, Sweden
1962	World Cup, Chile
1970	World Cup, Mexico
1975–1977	New York, the U.S.

1 Pelé ___wasn't___ born in the U.S.
2 In 1958, Pelé and the Brazilian national team ___were___ in Sweden.
3 In 1962, Pelé ___was___ in the World Cup in Chile.
4 Pelé and the Brazilian team ___weren't___ in Chile for the World Cup in 1970.
5 Pelé ___was___ in the United States from 1975–1977.
6 Pelé ___wasn't___ in the World Cup in 2010.

3 Look at the chart.

Questions	Short answers
Was I a musician?	Yes, I **was**. / No, I **wasn't**.
Were you an inventor?	Yes, you **were**. / No, you **weren't**.
Was he / she / it in my class?	Yes, he / she / it **was**. / No, he / she / it **wasn't**.
Were we artists?	Yes, we **were**. / No, we **weren't**.
Were you inventors?	Yes, you **were**. / No, you **weren't**.
Were they artists?	Yes, they **were**. / No, they **weren't**.
Were they writers?	Yes, they **were**. / No, they **weren't**.

4 Write questions and answers about Althea Gibson.

1927 born in Clarendon County, South Carolina, the U.S.	**1956** first African-American Grand Slam champion	**1956, 1957, 1958** winner of five Grand Slam titles

1 born / in the U.S. / in 1927 / ?
   Was she born in the U.S. in 1927 ___?
   Yes, she was ___.
2 first African-American Grand Slam Champion / in 1956 / ?
   Was she the first African-American Grand Slam Champion in 1956 ___?
   Yes, she was ___.
3 winner of Grand Slam title / in 1954 / ?
   Was she the winner of a Grand Slam title in 1954 ___?
   No, she wasn't ___.

 *Puzzle* page 87, puzzle 6A →

5 **Over to you!**

Think of a famous person. Give three clues to the class. Can the class guess the person?
Student A: She was born in 1907. She was an artist. She was Mexican.
Student B: Was she Frida Kahlo?
Student A: Yes, she was. It's your turn.

Grammar

Aims

Present and practice *was / were* (affirmative and negative, questions, and short answers)

Talk about the past

BACKGROUND INFORMATION

Edison "Edson" Arantes do Nascimento, best known by his nickname **Pelé** (born 1940) is a former Brazilian footballer. In his career, Pelé won three World Cups playing for Brazil, and holds a record of scoring 1,281 goals in 1,363 matches.

Althea Gibson (1927–2003) was an American tennis player. She was the first African-American woman to win the Grand Slam title, in 1956.

1 Grammar chart: *was / were* (affirmative and negative)

• Look at the chart.

Note:
• The affirmative past tense of *be* is *was* (singular) and *were* (plural).
• The negative past tense of *be* is *was not* (*wasn't*) in the singular or *were not* (*weren't*) in the plural.

Grammar reference page W37

2 Controlled practice of *was / were* (affirmative and negative)

• Look at the timeline.
• Fill in the blanks.
• Check answers.

3 Grammar chart: *was / were* (questions and short answers)

• Look at the chart.

Note:
• We make questions with *was* or *were* in the past simple, by changing the position of the verb and subject: *He was here.* = *Was he here?*

Grammar reference page W37

4 Controlled practice of *was / were* (questions and short answers)

• Write questions and answers about Althea Gibson.
• Check answers.

PUZZLE PAGE 87

Fast finishers can do Puzzle 6A on page 87.

ANSWER

Gianni Versace was an Italian fashion designer.

Over to you!

5 Personalization; oral practice of *was / were* (affirmative, questions, and short answers)

• Students work in pairs.
• They take turns to make sentences / ask and answer questions about a famous person on the page.

Extra activity (all classes)

Further practice of *was / were* (affirmative, questions, and short answers)

• Students play a game guessing true or false facts about other students.
• Students write five sentences – three true and two false – using *was / were*, e.g. *I was born in 1994. My grandfather was a famous actor.*
• In pairs, students read out their sentences to each other and guess which are true and which are false.

Further practice
Workbook page W39
MultiROM

Unit 6   57

Building the topic

Vocabulary

Aims
Present and practice vocabulary for adjectives of opinion
Talk about opinions

Warm-up
Ask students *What are your favorite memories of the past? Why are they favorite memories? How do you record your memories – do you keep a journal, or write about them in a notebook?*

BACKGROUND INFORMATION

The **Tower of London** is a building in central London, which, in its history, has been used as a royal palace, a private zoo, and a prison. It was built in 1078 and is the home of the Crown Jewels – a collection of crowns and other royal jewelry. It is one of London's most famous tourist attractions.

1 Presentation of vocabulary set: adjectives of opinion ⊚ 2.13
- Read the words in the box.
- Translate them in your own language.
- Play the CD.
- Listen and repeat.

2 Vocabulary practice: exposure to adjectives of opinion
- Look at the photos.
- Complete the comments with the adjectives in exercise 1.
- Check answers.

3 Vocabulary practice and extension
- Circle the correct word.
- Check answers.

4 Vocabulary practice: personalization
- Look at the situations.
- Give your opinion. Use a word from exercise 1.
- Compare with a partner.

ANSWERS
Students' own answers.

Extend your vocabulary

disappointing exciting exhausting
romantic scary surprising

Workbook page W40

Building the topic

Vocabulary
Adjectives of opinion

1 ◀)) Look at the adjectives in the box. What do they mean in your language? Listen and repeat.

> awesome awful ~~boring~~ delicious
> disgusting fantastic interesting terrible

2 Look at the photos, and complete the comments with an adjective from exercise 1.

Here I am on my fourth visit to the Tower of London. It was SO (1) _boring_ . ZZZZ! (Damon, London)
Comment: I love the Tower of London. It's really (2) _interesting_ . ☺ (Jin-woo, Seoul)

This is a picture of me on my last school trip. It was (5) _awful_ . (Stefano, 8th grade)
Comment: That isn't true! I was there. The trip was (6) _awesome_ , but the weather wasn't! ☹ (Grace, 8th grade)

I'm eating snails for the first time on vacation in Paris. Mmm, (3) _delicious_ (Evan, Stockholm)
Comment: That's gross! Snails are (4) _disgusting_ ! I ha them. ☺ (Eduardo, Mexico City)

Here I am on the Train of Terror for the second time. It was (7) _fantastic_ ! (Casper, Miami)
Comment: No, it wasn't. It was (8) _terrible_ ! (Your sister, Miami)

3 Circle the correct word.
1 The food at the party was (delicious)/ boring.
2 Yuck! This pasta is (disgusting)/ fantastic.
3 I love the Shrek movies. They're (awesome)/ awful.
4 This is a (fantastic)/ terrible book. It's a really good story.
5 The art museum is a very (interesting)/ delicious building.
6 Look at those shoes! They look (terrible)/ disgusting.
7 My mom thinks science fiction movies are delicious /(boring).
8 Don't read this magazine article. It's (awful)/ awesome!

4 Look at the situations below. Give your opinion. Compare with a partner.
1 You are eating snails for the first time.
2 You don't like your best friend's new boots.
3 You hate shopping. Your friends want to go to the mall.
4 You are reading a new book. You aren't enjoying it.

58   Workbook p.W40 ➔ MultiROM

Extra activity (stronger classes)
Review and practice adjectives of opinion
- Write the following on the board: *eating pizza, drinking cold milk, swimming on a hot day, doing lots of homework, running a race, going on vacation, watching a love story movie, getting zero in a test, watching a horror movie.*
- Ask students to write a sentence with an adjective of opinion for each one, e.g. *It's … (boring / fantastic / exhausting).*
- Students compare answers in pairs.

Further practice
Workbook   page W40
MultiROM

Grammar

Ordinal numbers

Talking about the order of things

1 Look at the chart.

Cardinal and ordinal numbers			
1 one	1st first	11 eleven	11th eleventh
2 two	2nd second	12 twelve	12th twelfth
3 three	3rd third	13 thirteen	13th thirteenth
4 four	4th fourth	14 fourteen	14th fourteenth
5 five	5th fifth	15 fifteen	15th fifteenth
6 six	6th sixth	16 sixteen	16th sixteenth
7 seven	7th seventh	17 seventeen	17th seventeenth
8 eight	8th eighth	18 eighteen	18th eighteenth
9 nine	9th ninth	19 nineteen	19th nineteenth
10 ten	10th tenth	20 twenty	20th twentieth
		30 thirty	30th thirtieth
		40 forty	40th fortieth
		100 a hundred	100th hundredth

Take note!

Cardinal and ordinal numbers
21 = twenty-one 21st = twenty-first
22 = twenty-two 22nd = twenty-second
• **Last** means *final*.
   It was my last day at my old school.

2 Write the numbers in words.

1 25th twenty-fifth
2 89th eighty-ninth
3 76th seventy-sixth
4 63rd sixty-third
5 90th nintieth
6 47th forty-seventh
7 58th fifty-eighth
8 31st thirty-first
9 22nd twenty-second

3 Circle the correct word.

1 It was his second / two birthday.
2 He is thirty-two / thirty-second years old.
3 She wasn't the winner, she was in three / third place.
4 It was her twelve / twelfth birthday.
5 There are six / sixth people in my family.
6 He was the first / one man in space.
7 I was in Greece when I was two / second years old.
8 This is the fourth / four floor.

4 Look at the picture. Write what position the people are in.

1 Sally and Joe are eighth and ninth in line.
2 Abdul is third in line.
3 Maggie is fourteenth in line.
4 Max is seventh in line.
5 Cath and Adam are twelfth and thirteenth in line.
6 Lori is first in line.

 **Puzzle** page 87, puzzle 6B

5 **Over to you!**

Put the sports in order from most popular (first) to least popular (seventh) for your class. Read your order to the class. Who agrees with your order?

baseball basketball car racing golf
ice hockey tennis soccer

Student A: I think soccer is first, baseball is second, basketball is third, ...
Student B: I don't agree. I think basketball is first and soccer is second.

---

4 Further practice of ordinal numbers

• Look at the picture and write the positions of the people.
• Compare answers in pairs.
• Check answers as a class.

PUZZLE PAGE 87

Fast finishers can do Puzzle 6B on page 87.

ANSWERS
1 terrible
2 fantastic
3 boring
4 interesting

Over to you!

5 Personalization; written practice of ordinal numbers and adjectives of opinion

• Students number the order of the sports from 1 (most liked) to 7 (least liked).
• They take turns to read out their order, using ordinal numbers as in the example.
• Find out how many students have the same sporting likes and dislikes.

Further practice
Workbook page W41
MultiROM

Grammar

Aims

Present and practice ordinal numbers 1–100

Rank sports in order of popularity

1 Grammar chart: cardinal and ordinal numbers

• Look at the chart.

Take note!

• We use ordinal numbers to talk about the order of things.
• Most ordinal numbers are made by adding *th* to the number, with the exceptions of *one* (*first*), *two* (*second*), *three* (*third*), *five* (*fifth*), *eight* (*eighth*), *twelve* (*twelfth*).

• We use ordinal numbers in dates, e.g. *June fifth* (NOT *June five*.)
• We often use *last* to mean *final*, and *second last* to mean *penultimate*.

Grammar reference page W37

2 Review and controlled practice of ordinal numbers

• Write the numbers in words.
• Check answers.

3 Further controlled practice of ordinal numbers

• Circle the correct word.
• Check answers.

Living English

Reading

🔊 2.14

Aims

Present and practice *was / were* and ordinal numbers in texts about famous people

Reading skills: using headings to help you understand what a section of text is about

Warm-up

Books closed. Ask students if they know the following information:

the first man in space (*Yuri Gagarin*)

the first man to walk on the moon (*Neil Armstrong*)

when the first successful airplane flight was (*1903*) and who the pilots were (*the Wright brothers*)

the first woman to fly across the Atlantic Ocean alone (*Amelia Earhart*)

Pre-reading task

Look at the title and the photos. Do you recognize any of the people? Compare with a partner.

BACKGROUND INFORMATION

Usain Bolt is a Jamaican sprinter. He was born in 1986. He is the Olympic champion in the 100 m, 200 m, and 4 x100 m relay races.

Danica Patrick is an American racing driver. She was born in 1982. The "Indy (Indianapolis) 500" is a 500-mile car race held annually in Indiana, in the U.S. The event started in 1911.

Svetlana Savitskaya is a Russian cosmonaut. She was born in 1948.

Yuri Gagarin (1934–1968) was a Russian cosmonaut and the first man in space.

Orville (1871–1948) and **Wilbur** (1867–1912) **Wright** were American brothers.

Amelia Earhart (1897–1937) was an American aviator. She went missing during a flight in 1937, and was declared legally dead two years later.

1 Global comprehension task

- Look at the title of the article and the photos.
- Ask students if they recognize any of the people. What were they famous for?
- Check answers.

2 Reading skills: using headings; global comprehension task (first reading)

- Read the Reading skills box.

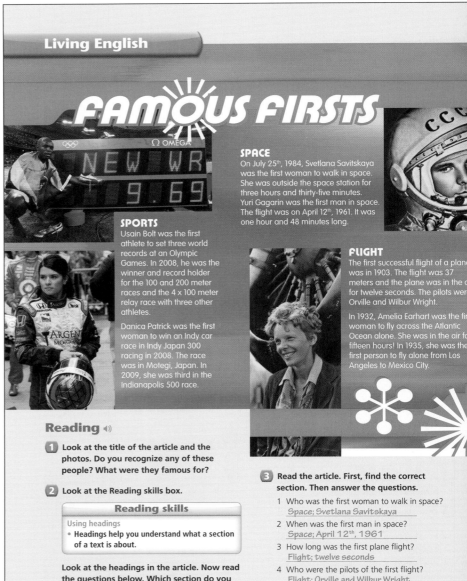

Living English

FAMOUS FIRSTS

SPACE
On July 25th, 1984, Svetlana Savitskaya was the first woman to walk in space. She was outside the space station for three hours and thirty-five minutes. Yuri Gagarin was the first man in space. The flight was on April 12th, 1961. It was one hour and 48 minutes long.

SPORTS
Usain Bolt was the first athlete to set three world records at an Olympic Games. In 2008, he was the winner and record holder for the 100 and 200 meter races and the 4 x 100 meter relay race with three other athletes.

Danica Patrick was the first woman to win an Indy car race in Indy Japan 300 racing in 2008. The race was in Motegi, Japan. In 2009, she was third in the Indianapolis 500 race.

FLIGHT
The first successful flight of a plane was in 1903. The flight was 37 meters and the plane was in the [ ] for twelve seconds. The pilots were [ ] Orville and Wilbur Wright.

In 1932, Amelia Earhart was the fir[ ] woman to fly across the Atlantic Ocean alone. She was in the air fo[ ] fifteen hours! In 1935, she was the first person to fly alone from Los Angeles to Mexico City.

Reading 🔊

1 **Look at the title of the article and the photos. Do you recognize any of these people? What were they famous for?**

2 **Look at the Reading skills box.**

Reading skills

Using headings
- Headings help you understand what a section of a text is about.

Look at the headings in the article. Now read the questions below. Which section do you need to read to find the information?

1 Who was the first man in space? *Space*
2 Who was the first athlete to set three world records at an Olympic Games? *Sports*
3 When was the first flight? *Flight*

3 **Read the article. First, find the correct section. Then answer the questions.**

1 Who was the first woman to walk in space?
   Space; Svetlana Savitskaya
2 When was the first man in space?
   Space; April 12th, 1961
3 How long was the first plane flight?
   Flight; twelve seconds
4 Who were the pilots of the first flight?
   Flight; Orville and Wilbur Wright
5 How long was the first flight by a woman across the Atlantic?
   Flight; fifteen hours
6 When was the first solo flight from Los Angeles to Mexico City?
   Flight;1935

60 ➜ Workbook p.W42

Reading skills: using headings

- Headings are brief summaries of the contents of a paragraph or section of text.
- Reading the headings before reading the text will help you understand what each section of text is about.

- Look at the headings.
- Read the questions.
- Write the section where you can find the information.
- Check answers.

3 Detailed comprehension task (second reading)

- Read and listen to the article again and answer the questions.
- Compare answers with a partner.
- Check answers with the class.

Further practice
Workbook page W42

Listening
Famous politicians

Barack Obama

Nelson Mandela

1 🔊 **Guess the answers to these questions. Then listen to the radio show and check.**

1 What is the connection between these two men?
   a sport   b politics   c flight
2 What do they both have?
   a an Olympic medal
   b a wife named Michelle
   c a Nobel Peace Prize

2 🔊 **Listen again. Circle the correct answer.**

1 Nelson Mandela was born on July 18th / 8th.
2 The first elections for black South African people were in 1994 / 1993.
3 Mandela was president for five / fifteen years.
4 Barack Obama was born in Hawaii / Houston.
5 He was born on August 14th / 4th.
6 He is the 40th / 44th president of the U.S.

3 🔊 **Listen again. Fill in the blanks with the correct year.**

1 Nelson Mandela was born in 1918 .
2 Nelson Mandela was president until 1999 .
3 Barack Obama was born in 1961 .
4 Barack Obama was the winner of the Nobel Peace Prize in 2009 .

Speaking
Giving personal information

1 🔊 **Listen and read.**

Where were you born, Lena?

I was born in Chicago.

When's your birthday?

November 30th. I'm fifteen years old.

Where were you born, Toni?

I was born in Brasília.

When's your birthday?

March 15th. I'm sixteen years old.

2 🔊 **Look at the Pronunciation box. Listen to the examples. Then listen again, and repeat.**

Pronunciation

th sound
• Most ordinal numbers end in the "*th*" sound.
November thirtieth
March fifteenth

3 🔊 **Listen. Circle the number you hear. Then listen again, and repeat.**

1 twelve / twelfth
2 sixty-six / sixty-sixth
3 twenty / twentieth
4 hundred / hundredth
5 four / fourth

4 **Practice the dialogue in exercise 1.**

5 **Now change the words in blue. Write a new dialogue. Then practice the dialogue in class.**

Workbook p.22   →   MultiROM   **61**

Listening

Aim
Listen to a history radio show and find specific information

1 Global comprehension of the listening task (first listening) 🔊 2.15
• Read the questions and guess the answers.
• Play the CD.
• Listen and check.

Audioscript
Radio show host: Today on *The History Show* we continue to look at famous firsts. We're looking at two famous politicians and their fantastic achievements in the world of politics.
Let's look at Nelson Mandela first. He was born on July 18th, 1918. He was the first black African president of South Africa. There were elections in South Africa in 1994. These were the first elections for black South Africans. After those elections, he was the president. He was president of South Africa until 1999. That's five years! In 1993, he was the winner of the Nobel Peace Prize. Even today, people say he was a brilliant politician.
Barack Obama is the first African-American president of the U.S. He was born on August 4th, 1961 in Hawaii, and he is the 44th U.S. president. He is also the first U.S. president born in Hawaii. Before he was president, he was a lawyer. In 2009, he was the winner of the Nobel Peace Prize. What an achievement!
So, there you are: two amazing and very interesting politicians! On next week's programme …

---

2 Detailed comprehension of the listening task (second listening) 🔊 2.15
• Play the CD again.
• Listen again. Circle the correct answer.
• Check answers.

3 Detailed comprehension of the listening task (third listening) 🔊 2.15
• Play the CD again.
• Listen again and fill in the blanks.
• Check answers.

Speaking

Aims
Giving personal information
Pronunciation: *th* sound

1 First listening 🔊 2.16
• Play the CD.
• Listen and read.

2 Presentation of pronunciation point 🔊 2.17
• Look at the Pronunciation box.
• Play the CD.
• Listen to the examples.

Pronunciation: *th* sound
• In many languages, the *th* sound doesn't exist, and some students will need help making the sound.

• Play the CD again.
• Listen again, and repeat.

3 Pronunciation practice 🔊 2.18
• Play the CD.
• Circle the number you hear.
• Play the CD again.
• Listen again, and repeat.

4 Dialogue practice
• Practice the dialogue in exercise 1 with a partner.
• Listen to students' dialogues. Monitor their pronunciation of *th*.

5 Dialogue personalization and practice
• Change the words in blue and write a new dialogue in pairs.
• Practice the dialogue with their partners.
• Listen to students' dialogues. Monitor their pronunciation of *th*.

ANSWERS
Students' own answers.

Further practice
MultiROM

Round-up

Writing

Aims

Write a biography of a famous person
Writing skills: dates and time expressions

Andy Warhol (1928–1987) was an American artist. He is considered by many to be the greatest American pop artist of all time.

1 Writing skills: dates and time expressions

- Read the Writing skills box.

> **Writing skills: dates and time expressions**
> - Use dates and time expressions to make the order of events clear.
> - We say *on July 2nd*, but *in July*, and *in 1980*.

- Read the biography.
- Circle the dates and times.
- Check answers.

2 Detailed analysis of model writing task

- Fill in the chart with information about Andy Warhol.
- Check answers.

3 Preparation for personalized writing

- Make notes about a famous person you like.
- Use the chart for ideas.
- Check that students are completing the notes correctly.

Students' own answers.

4 Personalized writing

- Follow the model writing text and the chart. Use your own notes to write about a famous person you like.
- Write your biography.

Students' own answers.

I can ...

Aims

Check understanding of *was / were* and ordinal numbers; self-assessment of own progress

1 Self-assessment of *was / were*

- For items (1–4), students read the sentences and complete them with the correct answers.

Round-up

Writing

A biography of a famous person

1. Look at the Writing skills box.

> **Writing skills**
> Dates and time expressions
> - We use dates and time expressions to make the order of events clear.
>   Dates: on July 2nd, in 1980
>   Time expressions: When he / she was two years old

Now read the biography. Circle the dates and time expressions.

2. Fill in the chart with information about Andy Warhol.

Date and time	Event
on August 6th, 1928	was born
today	still popular
in 1952, when he was 24 years old	his first solo exhibition
in 1955	his first exhibition with other artists
in 1963	price of painting was $100 million
Today	two museums

3. Now make notes about a famous person you like.

4. Write the biography of the person in exercise 3. Use the text and chart to help you.

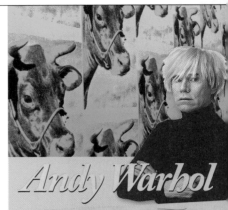

Andy Warhol

Andy Warhol was born on August 6th, 1928 in Pittsburgh, Pennsylvania, in the U.S. His mom and dad were from Slovakia and he was their third child. Warhol was a famous artist. His art is "pop art" and it is still very popular today.

Warhol was an art student at the Carnegie Institute of Technology in Pittsburgh. His first solo exhibition was in the Hugo Gallery in New York City. This was in 1952 when he was 24 years old. In 1955, his first exhibition with other artists was in the Museum of Modern Art in New York.

His paintings are pictures of popular people and things: Marilyn Monroe's face, Elvis Presley's face, soda cans, and food cans. In 1963, the price of his painting *Eight Elvises* was $100 million.

Today, there are two Andy Warhol Museums: one in Pennsylvania, and one in Slovakia.

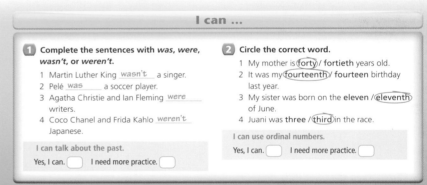

I can ...

1. Complete the sentences with *was, were, wasn't,* or *weren't*.
   1. Martin Luther King _wasn't_ a singer.
   2. Pelé _was_ a soccer player.
   3. Agatha Christie and Ian Fleming _were_ writers.
   4. Coco Chanel and Frida Kahlo _weren't_ Japanese.

   I can talk about the past.
   Yes, I can. ☐ I need more practice. ☐

2. Circle the correct word.
   1. My mother is *forty* / fortieth years old.
   2. It was my *fourteenth* / fourteen birthday last year.
   3. My sister was born on the eleven / *eleventh* of June.
   4. Juani was three / *third* in the race.

   I can use ordinal numbers.
   Yes, I can. ☐ I need more practice. ☐

- Students check (✔) *Yes, I can.* if they think they understand the vocabulary or grammar well, or check (✔) *I need more practice.* if they think they need more practice.
- If students have chosen *I need more practice.*, encourage them to review these sections and to do more practice.

2 Self-assessment of ordinal numbers

- For items (1–4), students read the sentences and complete them with the correct answers.
- Students check (✔) *Yes, I can.* if they think they understand the vocabulary or grammar well, or check (✔) *I need more practice.* if they think they need more practice.

- If students have chosen *I need more practice.*, encourage them to review these sections and to do more practice.

Further practice
Pairwork pages 118–119
Test pages 98–99; 106

Review

Vocabulary

Requests

1 Match the verbs with the expressions.

1 borrow ——— a a new cell phone
2 buy ——— b a sleepover
3 drive ——— c a tattoo
4 dye ——— d some money from somebody
5 get ——— e my hair
6 have ——— f the car

Places to go

2 Look at the pictures. Write the places.

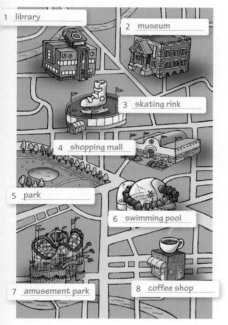

1 library
2 museum
3 skating rink
4 shopping mall
5 park
6 swimming pool
7 amusement park
8 coffee shop

Jobs

3 Fill in the blanks with the jobs.

1 An inventor invents things.
2 An artist paints pictures.
3 A designer designs clothes.
4 A politician works in politics.
5 An architect designs buildings.
6 A writer writes books.
7 A scientist discovers new things about science.
8 A musician can play, sing, and write music.

Adjectives of opinion

4 Replace the words in blue with the opposite words below.

awesome delicious ~~fantastic~~ interesting

1 Those shoes look terrible. fantastic
2 Mmm! That pizza smells disgusting. delicious
3 This book is very boring. interesting
4 The new James Bond movie is awful. awesome

Grammar

can (requests and permission)

1 Complete the questions. Use *can*.

1 Can I stay out late? (I / stay out)
2 Can Juan have dinner with us? (Juan / have)
3 Can we buy a new TV? (we / buy)
4 Can I dye my hair blue? (I / dye)
5 Can Luis and Abel play in my room? (Luis and Abel / play)
6 Can I drive your new car? (I / drive)

Unit summary

Vocabulary
Requests
Places to go
Jobs
Adjectives of opinion

Grammar
can (requests and permission)
Suggestions
was / were
Ordinal numbers

Study skills
Learning from your mistakes

Project
Writing about your hero

Vocabulary

Aim

Present and practice vocabulary for requests, places to go, jobs, adjectives of opinion

1 Review of vocabulary set: requests

- Match the verbs with the expressions.
- Check answers.

2 Review of vocabulary set: places to go

- Look at the pictures.
- Write the places.
- Check answers.

3 Review of vocabulary set: jobs

- Fill in the blanks.
- Check answers.

4 Review of vocabulary set: adjectives of opinion

- Write the opposites.
- Check answers.

Grammar

1 Review of *can* (requests and permission)

- Complete the questions.
- Check answers.

2 Review of suggestions

- Circle the correct word.
- Check answers.

3 Review of *was / were*

- Fill in the blanks.
- Check answers.

4 Review of ordinal numbers

- Look at the schedule for the soccer team.
- Write the dates in words.
- Check answers.

Study skills

Learning from your mistakes

It is very important to make students aware of their most common mistakes as they can learn a lot from their mistakes.

1 Error correction: awareness

- Read through the instructions with the students.
- Elicit or write the mistakes students often make on the board: spelling, grammar, word order, and using the wrong word.
- Go through the examples and ask students to correct the mistakes in each one.
- Ask them to identify and label the mistake – spelling, grammar, word order, or using the wrong word.

2 Error correction: self-assessment

- Ask students to find similar mistakes in their own recent homework and to correct them.
- Students evaluate their own work, based on how many corrections they had to make (i.e. a low mark for a low number of errors in a section).

| Further practice
MultiROM

Project 3 page 88

Aims

Read a profile of a famous person
Research and write about your hero
Give a presentation about a hero

BACKGROUND INFORMATION

Alexander McQueen was a British fashion designer who worked as chief designer Givenchy, and later started his own label, Alexander McQueen. He won four British Designer of the Year awards (1996, 1997, 2001, 2003) and was well known for his lavish, unconventional, often shocking runway shows. His designs were popular with many celebrities. He died in 2010.

Review

Suggestions

2 Circle the correct word.

1 Let's **go** / going to a movie tonight.
2 What about **have** / **having** a party for Kerry?
3 Why don't we **go** / going to the coffee shop?
4 What about **watch** / **watching** a DVD tonight?
5 Let's **eat** / eating in a fast food restaurant tonight!
6 Why don't we **drive** / driving to the new shopping mall tomorrow?

was / were

3 Fill in the blanks in the conversation about Jia's vacation. Use the correct form of the simple past of *be*: affirmative, negative, or question.

Jannie: Where (1) were ____ you last week, Jia?
Jia: I (2) was ____ in China with my family. It (3) was ____ really cool!
Jannie: (4) Were ____ you in Beijing?
Jia: No, we (5) weren't ____ . We (6) were ____ in Harbin most of the time. It (7) was ____ really interesting, but the weather (8) wasn't ____ very good. In fact, it (9) was ____ terrible!

Ordinal numbers

4 Look at the schedule for the soccer team *Henry's Heroes*. Then write the dates in words.

Soccer tour: April / May

Country / Stadium	Date
Brazil, Maracanã	April 17th
Uruguay, Centenario	April 19th
Mexico, Jalisco	April 21st
Argentina, El Monumental	April 22nd
Colombia, Estadio Metropolitano	April 30th
Peru, Estadio Universidad San Marco	May 3rd

1 On April seventeenth ____ , he was in Brazil.
2 On April nineteenth ____ , he was in Uruguay.
3 On May third ____ , he was in Peru.
4 On April twenty-first ____ , he was in Mexico.
5 On April thirtieth ____ , he was in Colombia.
6 On April twenty-second ____ , he was in Argentina.

Study skills

Learning from your mistakes
You can learn from your mistakes. Find the problem and try again!

1 Correct the mistakes below. Then label them: *grammar, spelling, wrong word, or word order.*

spelling : I really lik this song! like
grammar : Let's going to the mall. go
word order : I can have a sleepover, please? Can I
wrong word : I wait to the library every day after school. go

2 Look at the corrections on a piece of homework. Rewrite the parts that have problems. Now give yourself a score on a scale of 1–10.
Grammar: ____ / 10   Spelling: ____ / 10
Word order: ____ / 10   Wrong word: ____ / 10

---

1 Reading

- Read the profile.
- Match the headings to the paragraphs.
- Check answers.

ANSWERS
2 Family   3 School and college
4 Career

2 Preparation for writing (first task)

- Work in pairs. Make a list of people you admire – think of writers, musicians, artists, designers, world leaders, inventors.
- Use the ideas in exercise 2, or your own.
- Choose someone to write about.
- Ask: *What do you know about this person? Why is he / she your hero? What more can you find out about the person?*

ANSWERS
Students' own answers.

3 Preparation for writing (second task)

- Use the headings in exercise 1.
- Write notes about your hero under each heading.

ANSWERS
Students' own answers.

4 Writing and presentation

- Write about your hero.
- Add photos if you can.
- Talk about your hero to the class.

ANSWERS
Students' own answers.

Project extension

- If you have the facilities, ask students to post their profiles of their heroes onto your class or school website.

---

7 The sounds of music

Introducing the topic

Louis Armstrong
jazz

2 Dizzee Rascal
rap

3 Demi Lovato
pop

4 Bob Marley
reggae

Estelle
soul

6 André Rieu
classical

7 Kings of Leon
rock

8 Sheryl Crow
country

Vocabulary

Kinds of music

1 🔊 **Label the photos with the words below. Then listen, check, and repeat.**

> classical country ~~jazz~~ pop rap reggae
> rock soul

2 🔊 **Listen and fill in the blanks with the kinds of music you hear.**

1 I listen to rock music on my MP3 player every day.
2 My grandfather was from New Orleans. He loved jazz music.
3 Kana watched the pop music awards on TV last night.

4 We were at a classical music concert last night. It was fantastic.
5 I listened to country music for the first time yesterday.
6 My best friend loves soul music.
7 "What kind of music is that?"
   "It's reggae music."
8 I played a rap song for my parents yesterday. They hated it!

3 **Write sentences about the music that you like and don't like. Give a reason.**

I like jazz music. It's awesome.
I don't like classical music. It's boring.

Workbook p.W44 ➡ MultiROM   **65**

Unit summary

Vocabulary
Kinds of music: *classical, country, jazz, pop, rap, reggae, rock, soul*
Musical instruments: *bass, drums, guitar, keyboard, piano, saxophone, trumpet, violin*

Grammar
Simple past regular verbs (affirmative)
Simple past irregular verbs (affirmative)

Skills
Reading: Reading a text about different kinds of music and musicians; a text about *Habbo*, a virtual world; getting the general idea
Listening: Listening and identifying specific information in a conversation
Speaking: Talking about activities in the past; past tense *-ed* endings
Writing: Writing a profile of your favorite band

Cross-curricular
Music
Computer science

Values and topics
Multiculturalism
Popular culture
Famous people
Human achievement

Introducing the topic

Vocabulary

Aim
Present and practice vocabulary for kinds of music

Warm-up
Ask students to look at the photos. Ask what kinds of music they like, and whether they know any of the bands and musicians in the photos.

BACKGROUND INFORMATION

Louis Armstrong (1901–1971) was an American jazz trumpeter and singer.
Dizzee Rascal (born 1985) is a British rapper.

Demi Lovato (born 1992) is an American pop singer and actress.
Bob Marley (1945–1981) was a Jamaican singer-songwriter and musician. He is best known for his reggae music..
Estelle (born 1980) is a British soul singer, most famous for her song *American Boy*.
André Rieu (born 1949) is a Dutch violinist, conductor, and composer.
Kings of Leon are an American rock band.
Sheryl Crow (born 1962) is an American country singer.

1 Presentation of vocabulary set: kinds of music 💿 2.19
• Label the photos with the words from the box.
• Play the CD.
• Listen, check, and repeat.

2 Vocabulary practice; exposure to vocabulary for kinds of music 💿 2.20
• Play the CD.
• Fill in the blanks. Check answers.

3 Personalization
• Write sentences about the music that you like and don't like. Give a reason. Compare with a partner.

ANSWERS
Students' own answers.

Extend your vocabulary
folk grunge hip-hop rock and roll
Workbook page W44

Further practice
Workbook page W44
MultiROM

Exploring the topic

Reading

Aims

Present and practice vocabulary for kinds of music through texts about famous musicians

Pre-reading task

Look at the photos. Do you know any of the people?

The Rolling Stones are a British rock band.

U2 are an Irish rock band (lead singer Bono), formed in 1976.

Aretha Franklin is an American singer, born in 1942. She is known as "the Queen of Soul".

Alicia Keys is an American singer, born in 1981.

Jay-Z is an American rapper, born in 1969.

Eminem is an American rapper and record producer, born in 1972.

The Fatback Band is an American funk and disco band, which was very popular in the 1970s and 1980s, and is attributed for creating rap music.

1 Identifying (first reading) 🔊 2.21

- Play the CD.
- Read and listen to the article.
- Complete the chart.
- Check answers.

2 Detailed comprehension task (second reading)

- Read the article again.
- Match the sentence halves.
- Check answers as a class.

3 Detailed comprehension task (third reading)

- Read the article again.
- Circle T or F next to the sentences.
- Correct the false sentences.
- Check answers.

Exploring the topic

MUSIC PAST AND PRESENT

ROCK

In 1962, Mick Jagger and three others formed The Rolling Stones. They changed the sounds of the pop bands of the early 1960s and created rock music. They were the first famous rock band.

Bands like U2 helped to create the sounds of modern rock music. They tried new sounds with hard rock music from the 1960s and created modern rock.

RAP

Eminem is a famous rapper, but rap started when Eminem was very young. The Fatback Band recorded the first rap song in 1979, when Eminem was seven years old! He released his seventh album *Recovery* in 2010. It topped the charts in many countries.

Reading

1 🔊 **Read and listen to the article. Complete the chart.**

Music style	Modern band / singer	Legendary band / singer
rock	U2	The Rolling Stones
rap	Eminem	The Fatback Band
soul	Alicia Keys	Aretha Franklin

2 Read again. Match the sentence halves.

1 The Rolling Stones became _d_
2 U2 helped _f_
3 Rap started _a_
4 Eminem was seven years old _c_
5 Alicia Keys performed _e_
6 Aretha Franklin was _b_

a in 1979.
b "The Queen of Soul".
c when rap started.
d the first famous rock band.
e a soul and rap song.
f to create a new kind of rock music.

SOUL

"The Queen of Soul" was Aretha Franklin. She influenced many of today's soul singers.

Alicia Keys is a soul singer, but sometimes she mixes different kinds of music with soul. For example, she performed *Empire State of Mind* with Jay-Z. It was a mix of soul and rap.

3 Are the sentences True or False? Correct the false sentences.

1 The Rolling Stones was a pop band in the 1960s. T /(F)
   The Rolling Stones was a rock band in the 1960s

2 The Rolling Stones created rock music from pop music. (T)/ F

3 Eminem recorded the first rap song. T /(F)
   The Fatback Band recorded the first rap song

4 Alicia Keys used rock and pop music in her song with Jay-Z. T /(F)
   Alicia Keys used soul and rap in her song with Jay-Z

66

Grammar

Simple past regular verbs (affirmative)

Talking about actions in the past

1 Look at the chart.

Affirmative		
I	**formed**	a band.
You	**tried**	new sounds.
He / She / It	**topped**	the chart in 1979.
We	**started**	playing together.
You	**performed**	a soul song.
They	**created**	a new kind of rock music.

Take note!

Spelling rules for simple past regular verbs
- + -*ed*
  play ➜ played
- + -*d*
  arrive ➜ arrived
- **Double consonant** + -*ed*
  stop ➜ stopped
- **Consonant** + -*y*: changes to -*i* + -*ed*
  try ➜ tried

---

2 Complete the sentences with the simple past of the verbs in parentheses.

1 They ___listened___ to the radio last night. (listen)
2 The concert ___finished___ at midnight. (finish)
3 Marcus ___visited___ Asia in 2009. (visit)
4 Sarah ___studied___ in Los Angeles. (study)
5 We ___played___ soccer in the park yesterday. (play)
6 The train ___stopped___ for two hours. (stop)

3 Look at the pictures and write what happened to Keira and Harry yesterday. Use the verbs below.

arrive   chat   ~~drop~~   help   try   watch

1 Keira ___dropped___ her books.
2 They ___chatted___ online last night.

3 They ___arrived___ late for class.

4 Keira ___tried___ to cheat on an exam.

5 Harry ___helped___ his brother with his homework.

6 Keira and her boyfriend ___watched___ a movie.

Take note!

Past time expressions
in 1968   yesterday
100 years ago   last year

---

4 Write true sentences about you.

1 start school
  ___I started school seven years ago___.

2 learn to swim

3 listen to music

4 watch TV

5 stay out

Puzzle page 89, puzzle 7A ➜

5 **Over to you!**

Write a sentence in the simple past, using the ideas in exercise 4. The sentence can be true or false. Say the sentence to the class. Does the class think the sentence is true or false?
Student A: I started school in 2002.
Student B: That isn't true. You started school in 2003.

Workbook p.W45 ➜ MultiROM   **67**

Take note!
- We use certain past time expressions to talk about when actions happened.
- We use *in* + *year*, e.g. *We moved in 1996.*
- We use (number of) *minutes / hours / days / weeks / months / years + ago*, e.g. *We moved ten years ago.*
- We use *yesterday* to refer to the previous day.
- We use *last* + *week / month / year*, e.g. *I visited my aunt last month.*

Grammar reference   page W43

---

4 Further practice of simple past regular verbs (affirmative)

- Write true sentences about you.
- Compare sentences with a partner.

ANSWERS
Students' own answers.

PUZZLE   PAGE 89

- Fast finishers can do Puzzle 7A on page 89.

ANSWERS

2	pop	6	rock
3	jazz	7	country
4	reggae	8	soul
5	rap		

Over to you!

5 Personalization; written practice of simple past regular verbs (affirmative)

- Students work in pairs or as a whole class.
- Students each write a true or false sentence about their past.
- They take turns to read their sentence out aloud. Can their classmates guess if they are true or false?

Extra activity (all classes)

Further practice of past time expressions
- Write this gapped sentence on the board: *The last time I … was … .*
- Read out or write on the board, a number of phrases with regular past tense verbs, e.g. *watched a movie, cooked a meal, chatted online, studied for a test, visited my grandparents, traveled to another country, cried.*
- Students have to complete the sentence with a suitable (true) time expression, e.g. *The last time I chatted online was yesterday. The last time I cooked a meal was a week ago.*

Further practice
Workbook   page W45
MultiROM

Grammar

Aims

Present and practice simple past regular verbs (affirmative)
Talk about actions in the past

1 Grammar chart: Simple past regular verbs (affirmative)

- Look at the chart.

Take note!
- There are some exceptions to the spelling rule for verbs ending in vowel + consonant: if the consonant is -*l*, it is not doubled, e.g. *travel = traveled.*

Grammar reference   page W43

2 Controlled practice of simple past regular verbs (affirmative)

- Complete the sentences.
- Check answers.

3 Further practice of simple past regular verbs (affirmative)

- Look at the pictures.
- Complete the sentences with the verbs in the box.
- Check answers.

Building the topic

Vocabulary

Aims
Present and practice vocabulary for musical instruments
Talk about musical instruments

Warm-up
Ask students if they can play a musical instrument, and which one. Ask them if they would like to learn to play an(other) instrument, and which one?

1 Presentation of vocabulary set: musical instruments ⊚ 2.22
- Label the picture with the words in the box.
- Play the CD.
- Listen, check, and repeat.

2 Vocabulary practice: exposure to words for musical instruments
- Fill in the blanks.
- Check answers.

3 Vocabulary practice: personalization
- Answer the questions.
- Compare with a partner.

ANSWERS
Students' own answers.

> ### Extend your vocabulary
> bass player drummer guitarist
> keyboard player singer
> **Workbook** page W46

> **Further practice**
> **Workbook** page W46
> **MultiROM**

Building the topic

Vocabulary

Musical instruments

1 ◁)) **Label the picture with the correct instruments. Then listen, check, and repeat.**

> bass drums guitar keyboard ~~piano~~
> saxophone trumpet violin

2 **Fill in the blanks with the correct instrument.**

1 Vanessa Mae learned to play the
   __violin__ when she was five.
2 Beethoven's father taught him to play the
   __piano__ .
3 Jason Freese played the __saxophone__ at
   Green Day's concerts last year.
4 George Harrison bought a __guitar__
   when he was a teenager.
5 Stevie Wonder gave his __keyboard__
   to a music teacher in Haiti.
6 Larry Mullen Jr. plays the __drums__ .
   He met Bono in 1976.
7 Justin Bieber taught himself to play the
   __trumpet__ .
8 Paul McCartney played the __bass__
   with the Beatles.

3 **Answer the questions. Compare with a partner.**

1 Which instruments do you like?
2 Which instruments can you play?

Grammar

Simple past irregular verbs (affirmative)

Talking about actions in the past

1 Look at the chart.

Affirmative		
I	**took**	these photos.
You	**won**	the tickets in a competition.
He / She / It	**sang**	for two hours.
We	**saw**	Coldplay.
You	**met**	him last year.
They	**went**	to a concert.

Take note!
- Irregular verbs don't follow a pattern. You need to learn them. There is a list at the back of the book.

2 Fill in the blanks with the simple past verbs below.

had   ran   ~~saw~~   spent   told   went

1 I _saw_ Tom and Sara at the jazz club last night.
2 My grandparents _had_ lunch with us on Sunday.
3 They _told_ their teacher about the problem with the test.
4 Alex _went_ to the Beyoncé concert last night.
5 We were late. We _ran_ all the way to the movie theater.
6 You _spent_ all your money on new sneakers.

3 Write the simple past of these verbs. Two of the verbs are regular. Look at the list of irregular verbs for help.

1 organize _organized_
2 go _went_
3 see _saw_
4 sing _sang_
5 spend _spent_
6 give _gave_
7 take _took_
8 watch _watched_

4 Look at the photo. Fill in the blanks. Use the verbs in exercise 3 in the simple past.

In 2008, Shakira and Miguel Bosé (1) _organized_ two concerts to help 32 million children in Latin America. 380,000 fans (2) _spent_ eight hours listening to their favorite stars. Other people (3) _watched_ the concert live on TV.

The ALAS concerts (4) _took_ place in Buenos Aires and Mexico City at the same time.

In Buenos Aires, music fans (5) _saw_ Alejandro Sanz, Calle 13, Pedro Aznar, and other famous singers and bands.

The stars in Mexico City were David Bisbal, Maná, and Ricky Martin. Ricky (6) _sang_ Livin' La Vida Loca, and the crowd (7) _went_ wild!

Millionaire Carlos Slim Helú and businessman Howard Buffett (8) _gave_ more than $200 million!

Puzzle page 89, puzzle 7B →

5 **Over to you!**

Write a sentence in the simple past, but don't write the verb. Write the verb on a different piece of paper.
Exchange your sentence with another student and keep the paper with the verb. Can you complete your partner's sentence?
I _went_ to Salvador on vacation last year. (go)

Grammar

Aims

Present and practice simple past irregular verbs (affirmative)
Talk about actions in the past

BACKGROUND INFORMATION

The **ALAS** (*Latin America in Solidarity Action / Fundación América Latina en Acción Solidaria*) concerts took place simultaneously in Buenos Aires and Mexico City in May 2008, and raised several million dollars to help Latin American children in need.

1 Grammar chart: Simple past irregular verbs (affirmative)

- Look at the chart.

Take note!
- Regular exposure to irregular past tense verbs will help students learn them more quickly.
- The ten verbs we use most are all irregular: *be, have, do, say, make, go, take, come, see, get*.

Grammar reference (page W43)

2 Review and controlled practice of simple past irregular verbs (affirmative)

- Fill in the blanks.
- Check answers.

3 Controlled practice of simple past regular and irregular verbs (affirmative)

- Write the simple past form of the verbs.
- Check answers.

4 Further practice of simple past regular and irregular verbs (affirmative)

- Look at the photo.
- Fill in the blanks using the verbs in exercise 3.
- Compare answers in pairs.
- Check answers as a class.

PUZZLE PAGE 89
- Fast finishers can do Puzzle 7B on page 89.

ANSWERS
2 My parents gave me a new bicycle!
3 We went to a great movie last night.
4 Fran spent a week in the mountains.
5 Gisela ran ten kilometers in a race.
6 I met Jamie at the Internet café.
7 They built a new school in my town.
8 Pam saw her favorite band in concert last weekend.

Over to you!

5 Personalization; written practice of simple past regular and irregular verbs (affirmative)

- Write a sentence in the simple past about you. Don't write the verb – write it on a separate piece of paper.
- In pairs, exchange your sentences. Can you write the missing verb in your partner's sentence?

Extra activity (all classes)

Further practice of simple past regular and irregular verbs (affirmative)
- Play grammar tennis.
- Divide the class into teams. Team A calls out a verb in the present tense, e.g. *run*.
- Team B responds by giving the correct simple past form (*ran*) and gets a point if it is correct. If it is incorrect, Team A gets a chance to say the correct past tense verb.
- The game continues, with teams taking turns to call out different verbs.

Further practice
Workbook (page W47)
MultiROM

Living English

Reading

🔊 1.23

Aims

Present and practice simple past regular and irregular verbs (affirmative) in a text about *Habbo*, a virtual world

Reading skills: getting the general idea

Warm-up

Ask students what they understand about the term "virtual world". Ask them if they think it means a real world, or an imaginary world (*imaginary*). Ask them which computer or video games they know of that feature virtual worlds (e.g. *The Sims*).

Pre-reading task

Look at the title and the photos. What is the text about?

BACKGROUND INFORMATION

Habbo is a social networking site. It was started in 2000. As it is aimed specifically at teenagers, it attracts many musicians and other celebrities.

Bono and "the Edge" are members of the Irish rock band, U2.

Gorillaz is a "virtual band" consisting of four members.

Big Brother is a reality TV show, with versions in many different countries. Several people live together in a house, watched by TV cameras.

Miley Cyrus (born 1992) is an American actress (she played the lead role in *Hannah Montana*) and pop singer.

Chamillionaire (born 1979) is an American rapper, and **Akon** (born 1973) is a Senegalese-American R&B singer.

1 Reading skills: getting the general idea; global comprehension task (first reading)

- Read the Reading skills box.

> **Reading skills: getting the general idea**
> - When you read a text, read it quickly to understand the general idea.
> - The technique of "skimming" (reading quickly to get the gist, or general idea of a text) is very useful for students to practice as it helps them to know what type of text they are going to read, and what it will be about.

- Read the article quickly.
- What is it about? Choose the correct answer.
- Check answers.

Music in a virtual world

My vacation was awesome. I stayed in a great hotel with my friends. Our rooms were fantastic, and there were a lot of things to see and do in the hotel. There were great pizza restaurants and fast food restaurants, and lots of famous people. One day, we went to a quiz night. Bono from U2 asked the questions. We saw the Edge, and he played the guitar for us. We saw Gorillaz on their world tour. My friends took part in a TV show called *Big Brother*. So, where were we? We were in Habbo.

Habbo is a virtual world. There are 207 million users in over 150 different countries. Record companies use Habbo to tell young people about new bands and new music. For example, 365 is a virtual boy band. It only exists in Habbo. Their record company, Innocent, organized a "street team". The "street team" told people about the band. Then, people started to talk about 365, and they became popular.

Other pop stars visit Habbo, too: Miley Cyrus opened an MTV studio. The rappers, Chamillionaire and Akon, used Habbo to promote their music.

Let's go to Habbo!

Reading ◀))

1 Look at the Reading skills box.

> **Reading skills**
>
> Getting the general idea
> - When you first read a text, read it quickly to understand the general idea.

Now read the article quickly. What is it about?
a Pop bands on vacation
b Virtual bands in a virtual world
c Modern music on the Internet ✓

2 Read the text again. Match the names with the actions.

1 Bono *c*
2 Miley Cyrus *a*
3 Gorillaz *b*
4 365 *d*

a opened an MTV studio there
b had a world tour there
c asked the questons in a quiz there
d became popular there

3 Circle the correct answer.

1 Big Brother is … .
   a a TV show ✓   b a pop star
   c a record company
2 Habbo is … .
   a a real hotel   b a virtual world ✓
   c a virtual band
3 Habbo has … .
   a 207 million users ✓   b 150 different users
   c 365 million places
4 Record companies use Habbo … .
   a to sell music
   b to take people on vacation
   c to tell people about new bands ✓
5 Innocent is … .
   a 365's record company ✓   b a new record by U2
   c U2's record company
6 In Habbo, Chamillionaire and Akon … .
   a sang together   b sold their music
   c promoted their music ✓

70   Workbook p.W48 ◀

---

2 Detailed comprehension task (second reading)

- Read and listen to the article again.
- Match the names with the actions.
- Check answers.

3 Detailed comprehension task (third reading)

- Read the article again.
- Circle the correct answer.
- Check answers.

Further practice
Workbook page W48

Listening

Talking about a concert

1 ◀)) **Listen to the conversation. Which sentence is true?**

(a) Victor went to see Thirty Seconds To Mars last weekend.

b Victor and Joel went to see Thirty Seconds To Mars last weekend.

Thirty Seconds To Mars

Jared Leto

Tomo Miličević   Shannon Leto

2 ◀)) **Listen again. Circle T (True) or F (False).**

1 Victor's parents bought the concert tickets. (T)/ F

2 Tomo played guitar, violin, and the piano. T /(F)

3 Shannon Leto was on bass. T /(F)

4 Jared Leto sang the songs. (T)/ F

5 Jared Leto also played guitar. (T)/ F

3 ◀)) **Listen again. Circle the correct words.**

1 Victor went to the concert last week / (weekend.)

2 The tickets were (expensive) / cheap.

3 His brother / (parents) bought the tickets.

4 The sound was great / (fantastic.)

Speaking

Talking about activities in the past

1 ◀)) **Listen and read.**

"Last night, I went to a concert. We waited for three hours, but when the band arrived, they played all my favorite songs. I loved it!"

"Last weekend, I was at my friend's house. We watched *Sing Stars* on TV. It was awful!"

"Last summer, I went to a concert on the beach. We listened to some great music."

2 ◀)) **Look at the Pronunciation box. Listen to the examples. Then listen again, and repeat.**

Pronunciation
Past tense *-ed* endings
• We only pronounce the *e* in *-ed* after *t* or *d*. For all other verbs the *e* is silent.
-ed   silent *e*
We waited all day.   We watched TV.

3 ◀)) **Put an X (X) next to the words with a silent e. Then listen, check, and repeat.**

1 started __   3 arrived X   5 acted __
2 moved X   4 stopped X

4 **Practice the dialogue in exercise 1.**

5 **Now change the words in blue. Write a new dialogue. Then practice the dialogue in class.**

Listening

Aim

Listen to a phone conversation and find specific information

1 Global comprehension of the listening task (first listening) 🎧 2.24

• Read the sentences.

• Play the CD and choose the true sentence.

• Check answers.

Audioscript

Joel: Hello?

Victor: Hey, Joel, this is Victor.

Joel: Hi, Victor. How are you?

Victor: Great, thanks! I went to see Thirty Seconds To Mars last weekend.

Joel: No way! The tickets were really expensive.

Victor: Yeah, I know but I was lucky … my parents bought them for me.

Joel: So, what was it like? Tomo's my favorite. Was he good?

Victor: Good? He was amazing! He played the guitar, the violin, and the keyboard all night!

Joel: Awesome! And were the other band members good, too?

Victor: Well, the Leto brothers were great. Shannon played the drums, and Jared sang and played the guitar. It was fantastic!

Joel: Wow! Sounds amazing.

Victor: It was! Let's go together next time they play.

Joel: Yeah, sure. That's a great idea.

2 Detailed comprehension of the listening task (second listening) 🎧 2.24

• Play the CD again.

• Listen again. Circle T or F.

• Check answers.

3 Detailed comprehension of the listening task (third listening) 🎧 2.24

• Play the CD again. Listen again.

• Circle the correct words.

• Check answers.

Speaking

Aims

Talking about activities in the past
Pronunciation: past tense *-ed* ending

1 First listening 🎧 2.25

• Play the CD. Listen and read.

2 Presentation of pronunciation point 🎧 2.26

• Look at the Pronunciation box.

• Play the CD.

• Listen to the examples.

Pronunciation: past tense *-ed* endings
• There are three different past tense endings:
• /ɪd/ (waited, started, ended)
• /d/ (arrived, played, listened)
• /t/ (helped, watched, stopped)

• Listen again, and repeat.

3 Pronunciation practice 🎧 2.27

• Play the CD.

• Put an X (X) next to the words with a silent e. Listen, check, and repeat.

4 Dialogue practice

• Practice the dialogue in exercise 1 with a partner.

• Monitor students' pronunciation of past tense *-ed* endings.

5 Dialogue personalization and practice

• Change the words in blue and write a new dialogue in pairs.

• Practice the dialogue with their partner.

• Listen to students' dialogues. Monitor their pronunciation of past tense *-ed* endings.

• Ask stronger students to read their new dialogues out in front of the class.

ANSWERS
Student's own answers.

| Further practice
MultiROM

Round-up

Writing

Aim

Write a profile of your favorite band

1 Global comprehension of model writing text

- Read the band profile.
- Answer the question.
- Check answers.

ANSWER

There are four members in The Killers.

2 Detailed analysis of model writing task

- Read the band profile again.
- Fill in the chart with information about The Killers.
- Check answers.

3 Preparation for personalized writing

- Make notes about your favorite band.
- Use the chart for ideas.
- Check that students are completing the notes correctly.

ANSWERS

Students' own answers.

4 Personalized writing

- Follow the model writing text and the chart. Use your own notes to write about your favorite band.
- Write your band's profile.

ANSWERS

Students' own answers.

I can ...

Aims

Check understanding of simple past regular verbs (affirmative) and simple past irregular verbs (affirmative); self-assessment of own progress

1 Self-assessment of simple past regular verbs (affirmative)

- For items (1–4), students put the sentences in the correct order.
- Students check (✓) *Yes, I can.* if they think they understand the vocabulary or grammar well, or check (✓) *I need more practice.* if they think they need more practice.
- If students have chosen *I need more practice.*, encourage them to review these sections and to do more practice.

2 Self-assessment of simple past irregular verbs (affirmative)

- For items (1–4), students read the sentences and complete them with the correct answers.

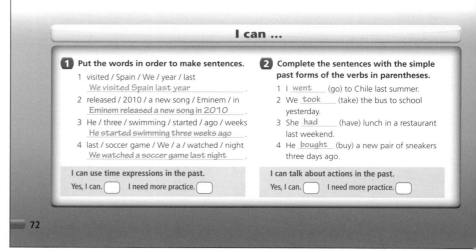

Round-up

Writing

A profile of your favorite band

1 **Read the band profile. How many members are there in The Killers?**

2 **Read again. Fill in the chart with information about The Killers.**

	The Killers	My favorite band
Type of music	rock	
Formed	2002	
Number of members	four	
Instruments	keyboard, guitar, bass, drums	
Number of albums	3	
Favorite song	Mr. Brightside	

3 **Now make notes about your favorite band.**

4 **Write about your favorite band. Use the text and notes in exercise 3 to help you.**

Profile of my favorite band

My favorite band is The Killers. It is a rock band. The band formed in 2002 and they are from Las Vegas. There are four members in the band: Brandon Flowers, Mark Stoermer, Dave Keuning, and Ronnie Vannucci.
In 2001, Brandon Flowers left another band, and he met Dave Keuning. Then they found Stoermer and Vannucci to make a new band. Flowers plays the keyboard and sings, Keuning plays guitar and sings, Stoermer plays the bass and Vannucci plays drums.
Their first album was *Hot Fuss* in 2004. It sold 7,500,000 copies! Their other albums are called *Sam's Town* and *Day and Age*. My favorite song is *Mr. Brightside*.
At the moment, they are working on different things. Vannucci is making a country music album, and Flowers released a solo album in 2010.

I can ...

1 **Put the words in order to make sentences.**

1 visited / Spain / We / year / last
We visited Spain last year.
2 released / 2010 / a new song / Eminem / in
Eminem released a new song in 2010.
3 He / three / swimming / started / ago / weeks
He started swimming three weeks ago.
4 last / soccer game / We / a / watched / night
We watched a soccer game last night.

I can use time expressions in the past.
Yes, I can. ☐ I need more practice. ☐

2 **Complete the sentences with the simple past forms of the verbs in parentheses.**

1 I went (go) to Chile last summer.
2 We took (take) the bus to school yesterday.
3 She had (have) lunch in a restaurant last weekend.
4 He bought (buy) a new pair of sneakers three days ago.

I can talk about actions in the past.
Yes, I can. ☐ I need more practice. ☐

72

- Students check (✓) *Yes, I can.* if they think they understand the vocabulary or grammar well, or check (✓) *I need more practice.* if they think they need more practice.
- If students have chosen *I need more practice.*, encourage them to review these sections and to do more practice.

Further practice
Pairwork pages 120–121
Test pages 100–101; 107

8 Mysteries

Introducing the topic

Unit summary

Vocabulary

Nature: *beaches, deserts, islands, jungles, mountains, oceans, rivers, volcanoes*

Disaster verbs: *break, crash, die, disappear, hit, sink*

Grammar

Simple past (questions and short answers)

Simple past (*Wh-* questions)

Simple past (negative)

Skills

Reading: Reading a text about world mysteries; a real-life mystery

Listening: Listening and identifying specific information in a history talk

Speaking: Talking about yesterday

Writing: Writing an e-mail about a day out

Cross-curricular

Geography

History

Values and topics

Multiculturalism

The environment

Tourism and travel

Vocabulary

Nature

1 🔊 **Look at the photos. Fill in the blanks with the words below. Then listen and repeat.**

beaches deserts islands jungles ~~mountains~~ oceans rivers volcanoes

1 Sahara, Gobi, Atacama, Utah: *deserts*
2 Everest, Fuji, Aconagua: *mountains*
3 Amazon rainforest (Brazil), Ituri rainforest (Congo): *jungles*
4 Fiji, Japan, Borneo *islands*
5 Pacific, Indian, Southern: *oceans*
6 Copacabana (Brazil), Bondi (Australia), Khoa Lak (Thailand) *beaches*
7 Nile, Colorado, Thames, Mekong: *rivers*
8 Popocatapetl, Vesuvius, Krakatoa: *volcanoes*

2 🔊 **Listen to the people (1–4) describe their vacations. What did they visit? Write the correct number in the box.**

beach	☐ 2	volcano	☐ 1
island	☐ 1	jungle	☐ 3
river	☐ 4	ocean	☐ 2
mountain	☐ 4		

3 **Fill in the blanks with places from your country.**

Beaches: _____
Mountains: _____
Rivers: _____

Workbook p.W50 → MultiROM 73

Introducing the topic

Vocabulary

Aim

Present and practice vocabulary for nature

Warm-up

Ask students to look at the pictures. Ask if they can identify any of the places.

1 Presentation of vocabulary set: nature 🔊 2.28

- Look at the photos.
- Fill in the blanks with the words in the box.
- Play the CD.
- Listen, check, and repeat.

2 Vocabulary practice; exposure to vocabulary for nature 🔊 2.29

- Play the CD.
- Write the correct number in the box.
- Check answers.

Audioscript

1 **Boy:** Where did you go on vacation?
  Girl: We went to Hawaii, the Big Island. It was great.
  Boy: Did you see the volcanoes?
  Girl: Yes, we did. They're awesome!
2 **Man:** What did you do on vacation?
  Woman: Well, I went to the beach every day, of course! And I swam in the ocean.
3 **Girl 1:** Did you go into the desert?
  Girl 2: No, we didn't, but we did go to the jungle. It was very hot!
4 **Boy 1:** Did you climb any mountains?
  Boy 2: Yes, we did. Cradle Mountain was huge! The view was beautiful.

Boy 1: Did you see any rivers?
Boy 2: Yes, there are a lot of rivers there. We visited one near Cradle Mountain. It was lovely.

3 Personalization

- Fill in the blanks with places from your own country.
- Compare answers with a partner.

ANSWERS
Students' own answers.

Extend your vocabulary

caves glacier lakes rainforest waterfalls

Workbook page W50

Further practice

Workbook page W50
MultiROM

Exploring the topic

Reading

Aims
Present and practice nature vocabulary through a text about world mysteries

Pre-reading task
Look at the photos. Ask *Do you recognize any of the places?*

Machu Picchu means "Old Mountain" in Quechua. It is a large city built by the Incas (people who lived mainly in Peru, from the 12th century to about 1533). About 500,000 people visit the ruins every year.

The lost city of **Angkor** is a large city built by King Suryavarman II between 1113 and 1150 in Cambodia.

Gávea Rock is 852 meters tall and in one side of the rock there is a carving of a face.

1 Identifying (first reading) 🎧 2.30
- Read and listen to the website text quickly.
- Answer the question.
- Check answers.

ANSWER
The Cambodian people built Angkor in the 12th century.

2 Detailed comprehension task (second reading)
- Read the website text again.
- Match the answers with the questions in the text.
- Check answers as a class.

3 Detailed comprehension task (third reading)
- Read the website text again.
- Answer the questions.
- Check answers.

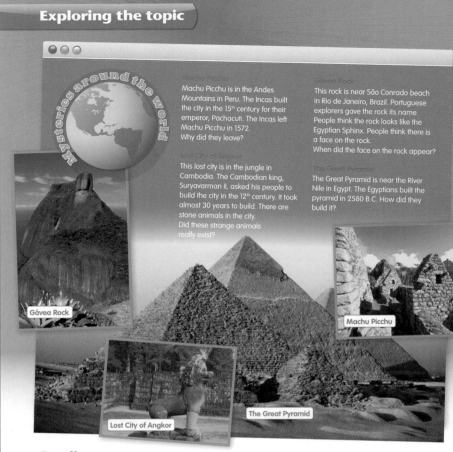

Exploring the topic

Mysteries around the world

Machu Picchu
Machu Picchu is in the Andes Mountains in Peru. The Incas built the city in the 15th century for their emperor, Pachacuti. The Incas left Machu Picchu in 1572. Why did they leave?

Gávea Rock
This rock is near São Conrado beach in Rio de Janeiro, Brazil. Portuguese explorers gave the rock its name. People think the rock looks like the Egyptian Sphinx. People think there is a face on the rock. When did the face on the rock appear?

Lost City of Angkor
This lost city is in the jungle in Cambodia. The Cambodian king, Suryavarman II, asked his people to build the city in the 12th century. It took almost 30 years to build. There are stone animals in the city. Did these strange animals really exist?

The Great Pyramid
The Great Pyramid is near the River Nile in Egypt. The Egyptians built the pyramid in 2580 B.C. How did they build it?

Gávea Rock

Machu Picchu

Lost City of Angkor

The Great Pyramid

Reading

1 🔊 Read and listen to the website quickly. When did the Cambodian people build Angkor?

2 Read the website again. Match the possible answers with the questions in the text.
1. When did the face on the rock appear? *c*
2. Why did they leave? *d*
3. How did they build it? *a*
4. Did these strange animals really exist? *b*

a. They used 10,000 men and big machines.
b. No, they didn't. They were animals from legends.
c. Probably in about 800 B.C.
d. Because there was a war.

3 Read again. Answer the questions.
1. Who built Machu Picchu?
   the Incas
2. When did they build Machu Picchu?
   in the 15th century
3. Where is the lost city of Angkor?
   Cambodia
4. Where is the Gávea Rock?
   Rio de Janeiro, Brazil
5. Who gave the Gávea Rock its name?
   Portuguese explorers
6. When did the Egyptians build the Great Pyramid?
   2580 B.C.

74

Grammar

Simple past (questions and short answers)

Asking and answering questions about things and events in the past

1 Look at the chart.

Questions	Short answers
Did I **visit** the Gávea Rock?	Yes, I **did**. / No, I **didn't**.
Did you **go** to Machu Picchu?	Yes, you **did**. / No, you **didn't**.
Did he / she / it **learn** interesting things?	Yes, he / she / it **did**. / No, he /she / it **didn't**.
Did we **see** the Lost City of Angkor?	Yes, we **did**. / No, we **didn't**.
Did you **read** about the Gávea Rock?	Yes, you **did**. / No, you **didn't**.
Did they **build** the statues?	Yes, they **did**. / No, they **didn't**.
Wh- questions	**Answers**
Why did the Incas **leave** Machu Picchu?	Because there **was** a war.

2 Answer the questions about the past. Then check your answers below.

1 Did people play basketball in the 1700s?
   No, they didn't .
2 Did people take photos in the 1800s?
   Yes, they did .
3 Did people watch TV in the 1950s?
   Yes, they did .
4 Did people listen to rap music in the 1960s?
   No, they didn't .
5 Did cell phones exist in the 1980s?
   Yes, they did .
6 Did people surf the Internet in 1965?
   No, they didn't .
7 Did people travel by airplane in the 1990s?
   Yes, they did .
8 Did people have cars in the 1400s?
   No, they didn't .

Answers
1 ✗ 2 ✓ 3 ✓ 4 ✗
5 ✓ 6 ✗ 7 ✓ 8 ✗

3 Write the questions for the quiz. Do you know the answers?

Ronaldo

1 Brazil / win / the World Cup / in 2002
   Did Brazil win the World Cup in 2002 ?
   Yes, they did
2 When / they / make / the first "talking" movie
   When did they make the first "talking" movie ?
   In 1927
3 When / Martin Cooper / invent / the cell phone
   When did Marin Cooper invent the cell phone ?
   In 1973
4 Where / Marco Polo / travel / in the 13th century
   Where did Marco Polo travel in the
   13th century ?
   He traveled to China
5 people / go on vacation to the moon / in 1969
   Did people go on vacation to the moon
   in 1969 ?
   No, they didn't

Answers
1 Yes, they did.   4 He traveled to China.
2 In 1927.   5 No, they didn't.
3 In 1973.

Puzzle page 89, puzzle 8A →

4 Over to you!
Write some questions about last weekend. Use the ideas below. Ask and answer in class.
you / go out?   you / play sports?
Where / you / go?   What sport / you / play?
you / visit friends?   you / have fun?
Who / you visit?

PUZZLE PAGE 89

- Fast finishers can do Puzzle 8A on page 89.

ANSWERS
1 island
2 river
3 jungle
4 mountain
5 desert
Mystery word: drums

Over to you!

4 Personalization; oral practice of simple past (questions and short answers)

- Students work in pairs or small groups. Write questions about last weekend.
- Take turns to ask and answer questions about last weekend.

Extra activity (stronger classes)

Further practice of simple past questions and short answers

- Students make a sentence about something they did recently, e.g. *I went shopping.*
- Other students ask as many questions as they can to find out more information about the event, e.g. *When did you go? Who did you go with? What did you buy? Did you buy clothes?*, etc.

Further practice
Workbook   page W51
MultiROM

Grammar

Aims

Present and practice simple past (questions, short answers, and *Wh-* questions)

Ask and answer questions about things and events in the past

1 Grammar chart: Simple past (questions, short answers, *Wh-* questions)

- Look at the chart.

Note:
- We form simple past (*yes / no* questions) with *Did* + subject + verb, e.g. *Did you go?* (NOT ~~Did you went?~~)

- We form *Wh-* questions in the simple past by adding the *Wh-* word to the beginning of the *yes / no* question, e.g. *Why did you go?*

Grammar reference   page W49

2 Controlled practice of simple past (questions and short answers)

- Answer the questions.
- Check answers at the bottom of the Student Book page.

3 Further practice of simple past (*yes / no*, *Wh-* questions, and short answers)

- Write the quiz questions.
- Then write the answers.
- Check answers on the Student Book page.

Building the topic

Vocabulary

Aims
Present and practice verbs for disasters
Talk about mysteries

Warm-up
Look at the fact files and the word *legend* in each one. Ask students if they think these fact files are proven true stories, or whether they might be untrue? Teach the meaning of the word *legend*.

BACKGROUND INFORMATION
The **Bermuda Triangle** is an area of about 1.2 million square kilometers between Bermuda, Puerto Rico, and the southern tip of Florida, in the U.S. The phrase was first used in the 1960s by an American journalist writing about various accidents that had happened in the area.

The **Atlantic Ocean** is the second largest ocean in the world and covers about 20% of the earth's surface.

The ***Titanic*** was a British passenger ship. Two days after it set sail on its first trip from England to the U.S., it hit an iceberg in the Atlantic Ocean and sank. Only 706 of the 2,223 passengers on board survived.

The **Great Sphinx** is a statue of a lion with the head of a Pharaoh – a king of Ancient Egypt. It is near the river Nile and the capital of Egypt, Cairo.

Tutankhamun was a Pharaoh of Ancient Egypt. He ruled between 1334 BC and 1325 BC. The British archaeologist, Howard Carter, who was employed by the Egyptologist, **Lord Carnarvon**, discovered Tutankhamun's tomb on November 4th, 1922. For many years, there were rumors of a curse on the tomb, which was responsible for the early death of the people who had first entered the tomb.

1 Presentation of vocabulary set: disaster verbs 🔊 2.31
- Label the pictures (A–F) with the words in the box.
- Play the CD.
- Listen and repeat.

2 Vocabulary practice: exposure to disaster verbs
- Complete the fact files.
- Check answers.

3 Vocabulary practice and extension
- Circle the correct verbs.
- Check answers.

Building the topic

Vocabulary
Disaster verbs

1 🔊 **Label the pictures (A–F) with the words below. Then listen and repeat.**

> break   crash   die   ~~disappear~~   hit   sink

2 **Complete the fact files with the verbs in exercise 1 in the simple past.**

3 Circle the correct verb.
1 Some people **died** / lived when they opened the tomb.
2 Many people appeared / **disappeared** in dangerous expeditions.
3 Bad weather **broke** / died the Sphinx's nose.
4 The ship **hit** / sank a small boat in the sea.
5 The *Titanic* broke / **sank** in the Atlantic Ocean.
6 An airplane hit / **crashed** into an island near Hawaii.

4 **Look at the fact files again. Which mystery do you like? Why? Compare with a partner.**

Historical legends

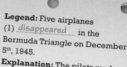

Legend: The *Titanic* (3) _sank_ in the Atlantic Ocean on April 14th, 1912 because there was an Egyptian mummy on the ship.
Explanation: It didn't sink because of a mummy. It (4) _hit_ an iceberg.

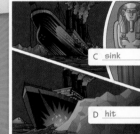

Legend: Five airplanes (1) _disappeared_ in the Bermuda Triangle on December 5th, 1945.
Explanation: The pilots made a mistake, and the airplanes (2) _crashed_ into the ocean. They didn't disappear.

A _disappear_
B _crash_
C _sink_
D _hit_

Legend: Napoleon Bonaparte (5) _broke_ the Sphinx's nose in 1798.
Explanation: The nose (6) _broke_ because of bad weather. Napoleon didn't break it.

E _break_

Legend: Lord Carnarvon (7) _died_ because he opened Tutankhamun's tomb in 1922.
Explanation: He (8) _died_ of pneumonia in 1923. He didn't die because he opened the tomb.

F _die_

76   Workbook p.W52 → MultiROM

4 Vocabulary practice: personalization
- Look at the fact files again.
- Discuss the mystery you like best with a partner.

ANSWERS
Students' own answers.

Extend your vocabulary
drought earthquake fire flood hurricane
Workbook page W52

Further practice
Workbook page W52
MultiROM

Grammar

Simple past (negative)

Talking about things that didn't happen in the past

1 Look at the chart.

Negative		
I	**didn't break** it	yesterday.
You	**didn't disappear**	last night.
He / She / It	**didn't die**	in 1852.
We	**didn't sink** the boat	last week.
You	**didn't crash** the car	last night.
They	**didn't hit** an iceberg	in 1912.

2 Complete the sentences about the first *Sherlock Holmes* movie. Use a negative form and then an affirmative form of the verbs in parentheses.

1 In the movie, Robert Downey, Jr. _didn't play_ the role of Watson. He _played_ the role of Sherlock Holmes. (play)
2 Holmes _didn't believe_ Irene Adler's story. He _believed_ Blackwood was dead. (believe)
3 Holmes and Watson _didn't find_ Lord Blackwood. The police _found_ Lord Blackwood. (find)
4 Lord Blackwood _didn't die_ . Holmes and Watson thought Lord Blackwood _died_ . (die)

3 Make the sentences negative to tell the story from the movie *Sherlock Holmes*.

1 Sherlock Holmes lived on Oxford Street in London.
Sherlock Holmes didn't live on Oxford
Street in London .

2 Sherlock Holmes worked with his brother.
Sherlock Holmes didn't work with
his brother

3 Irene Adler helped Holmes and Watson to solve the mystery.
Irene Adler didn't help Holmes and
Watson to solve the mystery .

4 Lord Blackwood died in London.
Lord Blackwood didn't die in London .

Puzzle page 89, puzzle 8B →

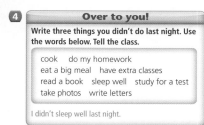

4 **Over to you!**

Write three things you didn't do last night. Use the words below. Tell the class.

cook   do my homework
eat a big meal   have extra classes
read a book   sleep well   study for a test
take photos   write letters

I didn't sleep well last night.

Grammar

Aims

Present and practice simple past (negative)

Talk about things that didn't happen in the past

BACKGROUND INFORMATION

Sherlock Holmes is a fictional detective created by Scottish author, Sir Arthur Conan Doyle. Sherlock Holmes lived at the fictional address of 221b Baker Street, London. In the 2009 movie, *Sherlock Holmes*, Robert Downey Jnr. played the role of Sherlock Holmes, and Jude Law played the role of Dr. Watson, his right-hand man. The story is about a man called Lord Blackwood, who is accused of killing five women, and is believed to have been executed. But a woman called Irene Adler tells Holmes that Blackwood is still alive. It turns out she is right when Holmes is called by the police to help them find Blackwood.

1 Grammar chart: Simple past (negative)

• Look at the chart.

> **Note:**
> • We form the simple past negative with subject pronoun + *didn't* + verb, e.g. *I didn't go*. (NOT ~~I didn't went~~.)
> • We form the simple past negative in the same way for regular and irregular verbs, e.g. *He didn't go. They didn't arrive.*
>
> **Grammar reference** page W49

2 Review and controlled practice of simple past (negative and affirmative)

• Complete the sentences.
• Check answers.

3 Controlled practice of simple past (negative)

• Write the sentences in the negative.
• Compare answers in pairs.
• Check answers as a class.

PUZZLE PAGE 89
• Fast finishers can do Puzzle 8B on page 89.

ANSWERS
hit meet see crash run break
It sank.

> ### Over to you!
>
> ### 4 Personalization; written practice of simple past (negative)
>
> • Write three things you didn't do last night. Use the verbs in the box.
> • Tell the class.

Extra activity (stronger classes)

Further practice of simple past (affirmative, negative, and *yes / no* questions)

• Choose a student to help you demonstrate the activity.
• Ask the student questions in the simple past. They cannot say *Yes* or *No* in their answers, e.g. *Q: Did you watch TV last night? A: I watched TV last night. / I didn't watch TV last night.*
• Invite other students to ask more questions.
• After ten questions or when a student has said *Yes* or *No* by mistake, change roles.

Further practice
Workbook page W53
MultiROM

Living English

Reading

🔊 2.32

Aim

Present and practice the simple past in a text about a real-life mystery

Warm-up

Ask students if they know about any real-life unsolved mysteries, and to tell the class about any they have heard of.

Pre-reading task

Look at the title and the photo. Where would you expect to find this kind of text?

ANSWER

In a newspaper.

BACKGROUND INFORMATION

The story about **Benjaman Kyle** is a true story.

1 Global comprehension task (first reading)

- Read the newspaper article quickly.
- Answer the question.
- Check answers.

ANSWER

He remembered Denver and Indianapolis.

2 Detailed comprehension task (second reading)

- Read and listen to the newspaper article again.
- Match the headings with the paragraphs.
- Check answers.

3 Detailed comprehension task (third reading)

- Read the newspaper article again.
- Answer the questions.
- Check answers.

Further practice
Workbook page W54

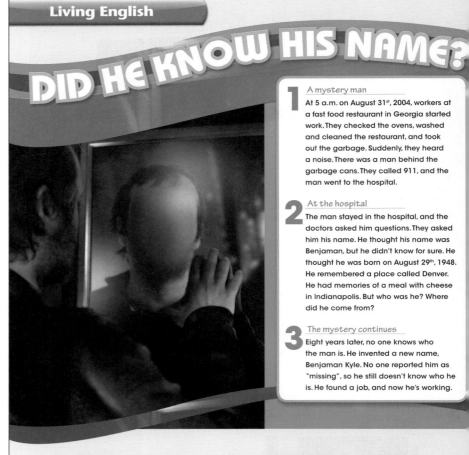

Living English

DID HE KNOW HIS NAME?

1 A mystery man

At 5 a.m. on August 31ˢᵗ, 2004, workers at a fast food restaurant in Georgia started work. They checked the ovens, washed and cleaned the restaurant, and took out the garbage. Suddenly, they heard a noise. There was a man behind the garbage cans. They called 911, and the man went to the hospital.

2 At the hospital

The man stayed in the hospital, and the doctors asked him questions. They asked him his name. He thought his name was Benjaman, but he didn't know for sure. He thought he was born on August 29ᵗʰ, 1948. He remembered a place called Denver. He had memories of a meal with cheese in Indianapolis. But who was he? Where did he come from?

3 The mystery continues

Eight years later, no one knows who the man is. He invented a new name, Benjaman Kyle. No one reported him as "missing", so he still doesn't know who he is. He found a job, and now he's working.

Reading 🔊

1 Read the newspaper article quickly. Which places did the man remember?

2 Read again. Match the headings with the paragraphs.

a At the hospital
b The mystery continues
c A mystery man

3 Read again. Answer the questions.

1 When did the restaurant workers find the man?
   when they took out the garbage
2 Where was he?
   behind the garbage cans
3 What did they do?
   they called 911
4 Where did he go?
   to the hospital
5 What did he remember about Indianapolis?
   a meal with cheese
6 What is he doing now?
   he's working

78 → Workbook p.W54

Listening

Easter Island mystery

Moai statues

1 🔊 **Look at the photo. Listen to the radio show. Where are these statues?**

ⓐ On an island.
b On a beach.
c In a jungle.

2 🔊 **Listen again. Choose the correct answers.**

1 Eva Hunt is a … .
  a doctor ⓑ historian c writer
2 Eva Hunt went to look at the statues … .
  a last year b yesterday ⓒ last week
3 Some of the statues are … meters tall.
  ⓐ 10 b 20 c 12
4 The statues appeared between … .
  ⓐ 1250 and 1500 b 1200 and 1500
  c 1250 and 1300
5 The statues all have … .
  a hands ⓑ faces c feet

3 🔊 **Listen again. Complete the questions with the correct words.**

1 _When_ did you go there?
2 _What_ are the Moai statues?
3 _When_ did they appear?
4 _Do_ the statues have faces of real people?

Speaking

Talking about yesterday

1 🔊 **Listen and read.**

2 🔊 **Look at the Pronunciation box. Listen to the examples. Then listen again, and repeat.**

Pronunciation

Intonation in *yes / no* questions
• **Intonation goes up (↗) at the end of *yes / no* questions.**

Did you use my computer?

Did you break it?

3 🔊 **Practice the questions.**

1 Did you watch TV?
2 Did she go to the movie theater?
3 Did he write a book?
4 Did they do their homework?
5 Did I make a mistake?

4 **Practice the dialogue in exercise 1.**

5 **Now change the words in blue. Write a new dialogue. Then practice the dialogue in class.**

→ MultiROM **79**

Listening

Aim

Listen to a radio show and find specific information

1 Global comprehension of the listening task (first listening) 🔊 2.33

• Look at the photo.
• Play the CD. Where are these statues?
• Check answers.

Audioscript

Radio Presenter: Hi and welcome to the *Mystery Show*. Today, we're talking to Eva Hunt, a historian. Last week she was on Easter Island. Let's ask her some questions about what she learned there. So, Eva, first, welcome to the show.
Eva Hunt: Thanks, it's good to be here.

Radio Presenter: Eva, last week you went to Easter Island. What did you do there?
Eva Hunt: Well, I went there to learn more about the Moai [pron: MO-EYE] statues.
Radio Presenter: What are the Moai statues?
Eva Hunt: They are enormous stone statues. Some of them are ten meters tall and they weigh 75,000 kilograms.
Radio Presenter: When did they appear?
Eva Hunt: Well, people made the statues between the years 1250 and 1500. The real mystery is that the statues all have faces.
Radio Presenter: Do the statues have faces of real people?
Eva Hunt: Well, we still don't know the answer.
Radio Presenter: I see. Well, thanks very much, Eva. We don't have any more time today, but next week …

---

2 Detailed comprehension of the listening task (second listening) 🔊 2.33

• Play the CD again.
• Listen again. Choose the correct answers. Check answers.

3 Detailed comprehension of the listening task (third listening) 🔊 2.33

• Listen again.
• Complete the questions with the correct words. Check answers.

Speaking

Aims

Talk about yesterday
Pronunciation: intonation in *yes / no* questions

1 First listening 🔊 2.34

• Play the CD. Listen and read.

2 Presentation of pronunciation point 🔊 2.35

• Look at the Pronunciation box.
• Play the CD. Listen to the examples.

Pronunciation: intonation in *yes / no* questions

• Intonation goes up at the end of *yes / no* questions.

Note:

• Intonation often goes down on questions where we expect a certain answer, e.g. if we see someone walking towards the library, carrying books, and ask, *Are you going to the library?* intonation may go down, because we <u>expect</u> the answer to be *Yes*.

• Play the CD again.
• Listen again, and repeat.

3 Pronunciation practice 🔊 2.36

• Play the CD.
• Practice the questions. Check answers.

4 Dialogue practice

• Practice the dialogue in exercise 1.
• Listen to students' dialogues. Monitor their intonation on *yes / no* questions.

5 Dialogue personalization and practice

• Change the words in blue and write a new dialogue in pairs.
• Practice the dialogue with their partner.
• Listen to students' dialogues. Monitor their intonation on *yes / no* questions.

ANSWERS
Students' own answers.

Further practice
| MultiROM

Round-up

Writing

Aims
Write an e-mail about a day out
Writing skills: ordering events

1 Writing skills: ordering events
- Read the Writing skills box.

> **Writing skills: ordering events**
> - We use adverbs of order to talk about a series of events.
> - We can use *Then … / Next, … / After, … / After that, …* to talk about something that happened after an earlier event.

- Circle the adverbs of order in the e-mail.
- Check answers.

2 Global comprehension of model writing text
- Read the e-mail.
- Answer the questions.
- Check answers.

ANSWERS
Tom went to New York City. Yes, he did enjoy it.

3 Detailed analysis of model writing task
- Fill in the chart with information about Tom's day.
- Check answers.

4 Preparation for personalized writing
- Ask students to think about a day out they enjoyed recently.
- Fill in the chart about your day out.
- Include places, actions, and opinions.
- Use the chart for ideas.
- Check that students are completing the chart correctly.

ANSWERS
Students' own answers.

5 Personalized writing
- Follow the model writing text and the chart.
- Write an e-mail about your day out.

ANSWERS
Students' own answers.

I can …

Aims
Check understanding of simple past (questions) and simple past (negative); self-assessment of own progress

---

Round-up

Writing

An e-mail about a day out

1 Look at the Writing skills box.

> **Writing skills**
> **Ordering events**
> - We use adverbs of order to talk about a series of events.
>
> | First, we went to … | Later, |
> | Then we … | Finally, |
> | After, we went … | |

Circle the adverbs of order in the e-mail.

2 Read the e-mail about Tom's day out. Where did he go? Did he enjoy it?

3 Complete the chart with information about Tom's day.

NYC!

Hi, Sam!
Did you have a good weekend? We went to New York City for a day out. It was fun!
We left home early, and traveled by train to the Big Apple.
First, we visited the Museum of Modern Art. The Picasso paintings were so cool!
Then we had lunch in a small café near the museum. The food was delicious!
After lunch, we walked in Central Park. It's enormous.
Later we went to a movie theater near Broadway, and watched a movie. It wasn't very good!
Finally, we stopped at a fast food place and had a snack. It was a cool place. Then we went home. We were all so tired.
What did you do?
Love,
Tom

Tom's day out	Action and opinion	Your day out
1 *Museum of Modern Art*	*Picasso paintings; cool*	
2 *small café near the museum*	*food; delicious*	
3 *Central Park*	*enormous; tired*	
4 *movie theater, Broadway*	*movie; not very good*	
5 *fast food restaurant*	*snack; cool place*	
6 *home*	*went home; so tired*	

4 Now fill in the chart about your day out. Remember to include actions and opinions.

5 Write an e-mail about your day out. Use the information you wrote in exercise 4 and Tom's e-mail to help you.

I can …

1 Write questions in the simple past.
1 Shakira / sing / *Waka Waka* / in 2009
 Did Shakira sing Waka Waka in 2009 ?
2 Argentina / win / the World Cup / in 2010
 Did Argentina win the World Cup in 2010 ?
3 people / use / cameras / in the 1950s
 Did people use cameras in the 1950s ?
4 people / download music / in the 19th century
 Did people download music in the 19th century ?

I can ask questions in the past.
Yes, I can. ☐ I need more practice. ☐

2 Write three things that you didn't do last weekend.
1 *I didn't go to math class* .
2 _____ .
3 _____ .
4 _____ .

I can talk about things which aren't true in the past.
Yes, I can. ☐ I need more practice. ☐

---

1 Self-assessment of simple past (questions)
- For items (1–4), students read the sentences and write questions in the simple past.
- Students check (✔) *Yes, I can.* if they think they understand the vocabulary or grammar well, or check (✔) *I need more practice.* if they think they need more practice.
- If students have chosen *I need more practice.*, encourage them to review these sections and to do more practice.

2 Self-assessment of simple past (negative)
- For items (1–4), students read the sentences and complete them with the correct answers.

ANSWERS
Students' own answers.
- Students check (✔) *Yes, I can.* if they think they understand the vocabulary or grammar well, or check (✔) *I need more practice.* if they think they need more practice.
- If students have chosen *I need more practice.*, encourage them to review these sections and to do more practice.

Further practice
Pairwork pages 122–123
Test pages 102–103; 107

Review

Vocabulary

Kinds of music

1 Complete the kinds of music with *a, e, i, o,* or *u.*

1 r a p
2 p o p
3 j a z z
4 s o u l
5 r o c k
6 c l a s s i c a l
7 r e g g a e
8 c o u n t r y

Musical instruments

2 Look at the pictures. Write the musical instruments.

1 keyboard
2 saxophone
3 bass
4 piano
5 violin
6 trumpet
7 guitar
8 drums

Nature

3 Complete the words and the information about the geography of the U.S.

1 Mount Rainier and Mount Whitney are American m ountain s.
2 The Great Basin is a big d esert .
3 The Mississippi, Missouri, Hudson, and Ohio are some of the American r iver s.
4 The b each es in California are beautiful and people surf in the ocean there.
5 Kauai is an i sland in Hawaii.
6 Hawaii is the only place in the U.S. with a j ungle .

Disaster verbs

4 Fill in the blanks with the simple past affirmative of the verbs below.

| break   crash   disappear   hit   sink |

1 Two cars crashed in the fog.
2 The ship *Genesis* disappeared in the Bermuda Triangle on April 23rd, 1999.
3 Richard broke his leg in the soccer game yesterday.
4 The ship *Titanic* hit an iceberg, and it sank in the ocean.

Grammar

Simple past regular (affirmative)

1 Fill in the blanks with the simple past affirmative of the verbs in parentheses.

1 They enjoyed (enjoy) the concert last night.
2 I studied (study) last weekend.
3 He played (play) the guitar for three hours.
4 You visited (visit) your grandparents yesterday.
5 We loved (love) the new Harry Potter movie.
6 She helped (help) her brother with his homework.

Vocabulary

Aim

Present and practice vocabulary for kinds of music, musical instruments, nature, and disasters

1 Review of vocabulary set: kinds of music

• Complete the kinds of music.
• Check answers.

2 Review of vocabulary set: musical instruments

• Look at the pictures.
• Write the musical instruments.
• Check answers.

3 Review of vocabulary set: nature

• Complete the words and information about the geography of the U.S.
• Check answers.

4 Review of vocabulary set: disaster verbs

• Fill in the blanks with the simple past affirmative of the words in the box..
• Check answers.

Grammar

BACKGROUND INFORMATION

The ***Andrea Doria*** was an Italian passenger ship, which collided with a Swedish ship, the *Stockholm*, near New York, in the U.S., in 1956. 1,660 people were rescued, but 46 died.

Taylor Lautner (born February 11th,1992) is an American actor, famous for his role as Jacob Black in the *Twilight* movies.

1 Simple past regular (affirmative)

• Fill in the blanks with the simple past affirmative of the words in parentheses.
• Check answers.

2 Simple past irregular (affirmative)

- Fill in the blanks with the simple past affirmative form of the verbs in parentheses.
- Check answers.

3 Review of simple past (questions)

- Read the statements.
- Make questions in the simple past.
- Check answers.

4 Review of simple past (negative)

- Read the sentences about the actor, Taylor Lautner.
- Rewrite the wrong information (in blue).
- Check answers.

Study skills

Using the right language

It is important that students use the correct language in different situations as it may differ from their own language.

1 Using the correct language

- Make sure you use the correct language for each situation.
- Read through the instructions with the students.
- Students look through their book, using the grammar reference to find the correct language to use in each situation.

ANSWERS
1 Use the present progressive.
2 Use vocabulary for physical description.
3 Use *can* for permission and requests.
4 Use the simple past.

Further practice
MultiROM

Project 4 page 90

Aims

Read about a vacation
Write about and illustrate your vacation

1 Reading

- Read the text.
- Fill in the blanks with the correct headings.
- Check answers.

ANSWERS
2 Who did you go with?
3 How did you travel?
4 What did you take with you?
5 Was it a good journey?
6 What did you do on vacation?

D Review

2 Fill in the blanks with the simple past affirmative form of the verbs in parentheses.

I (1) _went_ (go) to the mountains last weekend with my parents and two of my friends. We stayed in a house there and we (2) _had_ (have) a great time! ☺
On Saturday morning, we (3) _swam_ (swim) in a lake. It was freezing cold, but fun! After that, we (4) _went_ (go) for a walk in the forest. We saw a lot of beautiful birds and butterflies.
In the evening, we (5) _ate_ (eat) outside. We (6) _made_ (make) a campfire and we all (7) _sat_ (sit) round it. My dad played his guitar and we (8) _sang_ (sing) songs until midnight! Awesome!

3 Read the statements about the *Andrea Doria*, then make questions. Use the simple past.

The *Stockholm* in New York Harbor

1 When did the Andrea Doria sink ?
 The *Andrea Doria* sank on July 25th, 1956.
2 Where _did it sink_ ?
 It sank near New York City.
3 Why _did it sink_ ?
 It hit the Swedish ship, the *Stockholm*, because the weather was bad.
4 What _did the captain tell the people_ to do?
 The captain of the *Andrea Doria* told the people to leave the ship immediately.
5 Who _did the captain of the Stockholm take_ on his ship to New York?
 The captain of the *Stockholm* took the people from the *Andrea Doria* to New York on his ship.

Taylor Lautner

Simple past (negative)

4 Read the sentences about the actor, Taylor Lautner. The information in blue is wrong. Correct the sentences.

1 Taylor Lautner went to school in New York until he was eleven. (Michigan)
 He didn't go to school in New York

 He went to school in Michigan
2 He moved to Boston in 2003. (Santa Clarita)
 He didn't move to Boston in 2003

 He moved to Santa Clarita
3 He learned French when he was young. (karate)
 He didn't learn French when he was young

 He learned karate
4 In 2005, he acted in *High School Musical 1*. (*Cheaper By the Dozen 2*)
 In 2005, he didn't act in High School Musical 1
 He acted in Cheaper By the Dozen 2
5 He played Edward Cullen in the *Twilight* movies. (Jacob Black)
 He didn't play Edward Cullen in the Twilight movies
 He played Jacob Black

Study skills

Using the right language
Make sure you use the correct language for each situation. Use the grammar reference at the back of the book to help you.

1 Look at your book. Which language do you use for each of these situations?
1 You want to talk about things that are happening now.
2 You want to talk about someone's physical appearance.
3 You want to ask for permission to do something.
4 You want to talk about things that happened in the past.

---

2 Preparation for writing (first task)

- Think of a vacation you went on. (It could be a recent vacation, or one you went on long ago. It could be a long vacation or a short trip.)

ANSWERS
Students' own answers.

3 Preparation for writing (second task)

- Find a photo, or draw a picture to illustrate your vacation, or some of the things you did. (Look through your own photos, or look on the Internet, or in magazines.)

ANSWERS
Students' own answers.

4 Writing

- Write about your vacation.
- Use the text as a model: answer the questions about your own vacation.

ANSWERS
Students' own answers.

5 Presentation

- Put your description in a class magazine for other students to read.

ANSWERS
Students' own answers.

Project extension

- If you have the facilities, ask students to post their vacation descriptions and photos onto your class or school website. Encourage other students to log on to the website, and to read and compare the descriptions.

Workbook answer key

Welcome

Vocabulary p.W2

1 2 the United States **3** Guatemalan **4** Japanese **5** Australia **6** the United Kingdom

2 2 happy **3** angry **4** bored **5** tired
Mystery word: scared

3 2 bookcase **3** cell phone **4** skateboard **5** closet **6** magazine

4

A	T	H	L	E	T	E	K	L	Z	X	W
S	U	E	T	O	C	T	O	R	S	A
B	W	Y	S	A	R	H	Q	M	N	I	C
R	A	D	B	N	C	Q	F	P	O	N	T
V	X	F	Z	C	D	I	E	J	P	G	O
S	O	C	C	E	R	P	L	A	Y	E	R
C	H	E	G	R	D	M	C	L	B	R	A

p.W3

1 2 father **3** mother **4** brother **5** sister

2 2 f clothes store   **5** e movie theater
3 a cybercafé   **6** c skate park
4 b fast food restaurant

3 2 talk **3** go out **4** go **5** go **6** watch

Grammar p.W4

1 2 You're **3** aren't **4** They're **5** isn't **6** You're

2 2 am **3** Is **4** isn't **5** Are **6** aren't **7** Is **8** is

3 2 Where **3** What **4** How **5** What **6** How

4 2 Their **3** Her **4** Their **5** Your **6** Her

5 2 His **3** Her **4** Their **5** Its **6** Our

p.W5

1 2 Matte's **3** Elise's **4** Angelo's

2 2 this **3** those **4** these **5** that **6** this

3 2 isn't **3** is **4** are **5** aren't **6** is

4 2 can't **3** can **4** Can **5** can't **6** can

p.W6

1 2 Be **3** Read **4** Don't listen **5** sit **6** Don't write

2 2 Wan Ting doesn't lives in Beijing.
3 Does Gilberto go to school every day?
4 Mia and Lisa watch TV in the evening.
5 Shiori plays soccer on Saturdays.
6 Sang-woo doesn't listen to music in the morning.

3 2 Do, go **3** Do, read **4** Does, have **5** Does, stop **5** Do, work

4 2 they do **3** I do **4** she doesn't **5** he does **6** I don't

5 2 c **3** a **4** e **5** d

Unit 1

Vocabulary, p.W8

1 2 snowing **3** cloudy **4** sunny **5** windy **6** stormy **7** cold **8** hot

2 2 hot **3** cold **4** snowing **5** stormy **6** cloudy **7** windy **8** sunny

3 2 It's freezing. **3** It's cool. **4** It's warm.

Grammar, p.W9

1 2 working **3** getting **4** talking **5** sitting **6** sending

2 2 am **3** are **4** aren't **5** are **6** aren't

3 2 's playing **3** is singing **4** are dancing **5** 're making **6** are sitting **7** isn't raining **8** 'm not doing

Vocabulary, p.W10

1 2 chat **3** do **4** get **5** post **6** send **7** sleep **8** wait

2 2 waiting **3** chatting **4** posting **5** doing **6** babysitting **7** sending **8** sleeping

3 2 a **3** d **4** e **5** b

Grammar, p.W11

1 2 Are they getting dressed?
3 Is your friend watching TV?
4 Is Marta doing her homework?
5 What is he doing?
6 Are we waiting for the bus?

2 2 Yes, she is. **3** Yes, they are. **4** No, it isn't. **5** Yes, I am. **6** No, we aren't.

3 2 I'm reading **3** Are you reading **4** I am **5** Is your sister doing **6** she isn't **7** Are your mom and dad sitting **8** No, they aren't. **9** Is your brother playing **10** Yes, he is. **11** Is it raining **12** No, it isn't

Reading, p.W12

1 2 Cindy Becker **3** at the Parkside Mall **4** three

2 2 babysitting **3** shopping **4** studying

3 2 watching TV **3** doing **4** walking

4 2 She's watching TV, writing e-mails, sending text messages, and chatting online.
3 She's doing math and science homework.
4 No, she isn't. Cindy is going to Larissa's house.
5 No, they aren't. They're sending text messages.

Workbook answer key

Unit 2

Vocabulary, p.W14

1 2 glasses 3 pants 4 shirt 5 shoes 6 skirt
7 socks 8 top

2 2 glasses 3 top 4 skirt 5 shirt 6 shoes
7 pants
Mystery word: clothes

3 2 belt 3 gloves 4 scarf 5 swimsuit
6 sandals 7 sunglasses 8 hat

Grammar, p.W15

1 3 Usually 4 Right now 5 Right now 6 Usually
7 Usually 8 Right now

2 2 is chatting 3 clean 4 are having 5 visit
6 is waiting

3 2 visit 3 is snowing 4 wear 5 is sleeping
6 is swimming

Vocabulary, p.W16

1 2 wavy 3 mustache 4 big

2

A	F	B	L	A	C	K	G
E	B	L	U	E	K	H	G
B	R	O	W	N	L	N	R
D	C	N	S	W	O	Y	E
R	I	D	V	P	X	Q	E
E	M	U	B	R	S	Y	N
D	B	T	R	M	M	J	Z

3 2 tall 3 curly 4 good-looking 5 slim
6 overweight 7 strong 8 bald

Grammar, p.W17

1 1 has 2 have 3 is 4 has 5 are 6 is
7 have

2 2 isn't 3 don't have 4 aren't

3 2 doesn't have; has

3 isn't slim; overweight
4 He doesn't have a beard. He has a mustache.
5 They don't have black hair. They have gray hair.

Reading, pW18

1 1 b 2 c

2 1 Betty Malloy 2 Adam Steel 3 Matt Hardy
4 Bill Hyde 5 Joanne Lamb

3 2 T
3 T
4 F. Betty Malloy is wearing a skirt.
5 F. They are all wearing black pants.
6 F. Adam Steel has a mustache.
7 T

4 2 Bill Hyde doesn't have a beard or a mustache.
3 Bill Hyde isn't wearing a white shirt.
4 She usually carries a red bag.
5 He usually has a beard.

Unit 3

Vocabulary, p.W20

1 2 eggs 3 potatoes 4 mangoes 5 pizzas
6 apples

2 2 strawberries 3 bananas 4 apples
5 hamburgers 6 tomatoes

3 1 pear 2 watermelon 3 cookies 4 muffin
5 cakes

Grammar, p.W21

1 2 a 3 are 4 pizzas 5 some 6 any 7 is

2 3 There are some bananas.
4 There are some potatoes.
5 There aren't any hamburgers.
6 There is a cake.

3 3 Are there any sausages? Yes, there are.
4 Are there any French fries? No, there aren't.
5 Is there a pizza? Yes, there is.
6 Is there is a tomato? No, there isn't.

Vocabulary, p.W22

1 2 salt 3 bread 4 oil 5 pasta 6 cheese

2 2 F 3 D 4 D 5 D 6 F

3 2 salad 3 orange 4 soup 5 fruit juice
6 smoothie

Grammar, p.W23

1

Singular	Plural	Uncountable
apple	bananas	bread
egg	books	cheese
hamburger	eggs	milk
mango	lemons	oil
orange	mangoes	soup
sandwich	oranges	water

2 2 an 3 some 4 any 5 any, some 6 a
7 some 8 some

3 2 is a banana   6 There isn't any bread
3 There are some books 8 a teacher
5 any apples   9 Is there any milk

Reading, p.W24

1 1 75 bowls of soup 2 El Akoul – "The Eater"

2 2 drinks some 3 are some 4 are

3 2 Yes, there are. 3 Yes, there are.
4 Yes, he does.

4 1 There's one chair at Salim's table.
2 There's one spoon on the table.
3 There are 1,500 eggs on the table at dinner time.
4 There are two other famous eaters in the world.

Unit 4

Vocabulary, p.W26

1 2 f 3 g 4 a 5 c 6 d 7 h 8 e

2 2 months 3 music 4 furniture 5 desks
6 traffic

3 2 road sign 3 skyscraper 4 stop light
5 billboard 6 sidewalk

Grammar, p.W27

1 2 many 3 much 4 many 5 many 6 much

2 2 aren't 3 a few 4 are 5 a little 6 isn't

3 3 How, cars
4 lot of
5 How many people are there
6 There aren't many
7 How much baggage is there in the hall?
8 There's a lot of baggage in the hall.
9 How much food is there in the refrigerator?
10 There isn't much food in the refrigerator.

Vocabulary , p.W28

1 2 key ring 3 bracelet 4 earrings 5 key
6 ID card 7 sunglasses 8 backpack

2 2 sunglasses 3 key 4 backpack 5 key ring
6 ID card

3 2 watch 3 calculators 4 water bottle
5 wallet 6 coins

Grammar, p.W29

1 2 these; They're 3 this; It's 4 are; They're

2 2 e 3 a 4 f 5 b 6 c

3 3 Whose books are these?
4 They're theirs.
5 Whose jacket is this?
6 It's his.
7 Whose magazines are these?
8 They're mine.

Reading, p.W30

1 1 You can make phone calls.
2 You can make phone calls, send text messages, take pictures, play music, send e-mails, and more.

2 2 doesn't have 3 are a lot of 4 A lot of
5 many

3 2 75% 3 ten hours 4 88% 5 30%

4 2 How much does the 1980s phone cost?
3 How many teenagers send
4 How many teenagers can play games on their cell phone?
5 How much does a cell phone cost today?

Unit 5

Vocabulary, p.W32

1 2 have 3 get 4 borrow 5 stay out 6 buy
7 dye 8 go

2 2 have 3 buy 4 dye 5 get 6 stay out
7 drive 8 borrow

3 2 go skiing 3 go clubbing 4 go snowboarding
5 go fishing 6 go swimming

Grammar, p.W33

1 2 e 3 a 4 c 5 f 6 d

2 2 can't; 2 3 Sorry; 5 4 Yes; 1 5 way; 4
6 can; 6

3 2 Michael come; can 4 Can Sarah go; she can't
3 Can I borrow; can't 5 Can we have; you can't

Vocabulary, p.W34

1 2 coffee shop 3 museum 4 park
5 skating rink 6 amusement park
7 swimming pool 8 clothes store

2 2 shopping mall 3 swimming pool
4 amusement park 5 library 6 park
7 museum 8 skating rink

3 2 hate 3 stand 4 not bad / OK
5 OK / not bad 6 great 7 love 8 crazy

Grammar, p.W35

1 1 so 2 visiting; think 3 doing; No
4 go; a good 5 have; not

2 1 go 2 visit 3 make 4 listening 5 playing
6 go

3 b not; 3 c don't; 1 d No; 6 e That's a; 4
f OK; 2

Reading, p.W36

1 2 She reads 50 e-mails (from teenagers about problems).
3 asking for her permission to do things

2 2 offers advice 3 are 4 permission 5 can't

3 2 Very interesting letters 3 Marcia's answers
4 Teenagers 5 Parents

4 1 Because they are private. You can only read the very interesting letters Marcia chooses for the magazine.
2 She can't give them permission, because she isn't their parent.
3 What about talking to your parents? Why don't you wait and think about it?

Workbook answer key

Unit 6

Vocabulary, p.W38

1 2 architect 3 politician 4 inventor 5 artist
6 musician 7 fashion designer 8 writer

2 2 inventor 3 musician 4 politician
5 fashion designer 6 architect 7 writer
8 scientist

3 2 explorer 3 queen 4 racing driver
5 composer 6 baseball player

Grammar, p.W39

1 1 Were 2 was 3 wasn't 4 Was; wasn't
5 were 6 Were

2 1 was 2 were; was 3 was 4 weren't; were

3 2 was 3 was 4 Were you 5 wasn't 6 was
7 Were 8 were 9 were 10 was

Vocabulary, p.W40

1 2 disgusting 3 awesome 4 fantastic 5 awful
6 boring 7 delicious 8 interesting

2 2 terrible 3 awful 4 fantastic 5 disgusting
6 boring 7 delicious 8 interesting

3 2 scary 3 romantic 4 exhausting
5 disappointing 6 exciting

Grammar, p.W41

1 2 e 3 f 4 h 5 b 6 d 7 g 8 a

2 2 third 3 tenth 4 fifteen 5 ninth 6 two
7 twenty-four 8 hundredth

3 2 first 3 eleven 4 seventh 5 twenty-four
6 twelfth

Reading, p.W42

1 b 1 c 2

2 2 were 3 Amsterdam 4 four

3 2 After the 1936 Olympics, the Dasslers were
world famous.
3 The big argument was in 1948.
4 His new company was called Adidas.

4 2 Dassler shoes weren't popular in 1900. They
were popular in the 1930s.
3 Jesse Owens wasn't a German runner. He was an
American runner.
4 There weren't three Dassler shoe companies
after 1948. There were two.
5 Adidas wasn't Rudi's new company. It was Adi's
new company.

Unit 7

Vocabulary, p.W43

1

M	C	O	U	N	T	R	Y
X	L	L	K	J	I	E	H
I	A	Z	Z	G	J	G	I
D	S	V	K	W	X	G	U
J	S	O	U	L	H	A	R
Z	I	A	M	B	C	E	D
I	C	H	G	T	F	E	S
R	A	P	F	O	R	P	N
G	U	O	D	R	O	C	K
S	R	P	G	H	G	O	Q
C	B	E	F	C	A	Z	Y

2 2 pop 3 reggae 4 classical 5 rock 6 jazz
7 rap 8 soul

3 2 rock and roll 3 folk 4 hip-hop

Grammar, p.W45

1 2 stopped 3 tried 4 formed 5 released

2 2 missed 3 performed 4 danced 5 acted
6 dropped

3 2 arrived 3 studied 4 played 5 started
6 finished 7 visited 8 watched

Vocabulary, p.W46

1 2 drums 3 bass 4 trumpet 5 violin
6 saxophone 7 piano 8 keyboard

2 2 drums 3 guitar 4 keyboard 5 piano
6 saxophone 7 trumpet 8 violin

3 2 drummer 3 singer 4 bass player
5 keyboard player

Grammar, p.W47

1 3 present 4 past 5 present 6 past

2 2 tried 3 took 4 helped 5 won 6 watched

3 2 spent 3 saw 4 bought 5 met 6 ran
7 found 8 gave

Reading, p.W48

1 b

2 2 learned from 3 recorded 4 three 5 was

3 2 Puerto Rico
3 talent
4 Ramon and other Puerto Rican musicians
5 1995

4 2 F. He learned about rap music from rap
musicians.
3 T
4 F. He made his first album in 1995.
5 F. He made his fourth album in 2002.

Unit 8

Vocabulary, p.W50

1 **2** beach **3** volcano **4** desert **5** island **6** river
7 mountain **8** ocean

2 **2** volcano **3** river **4** mountain **5** jungle
6 beach **7** ocean **8** island

3 **2** waterfalls **3** glacier **4** caves **5** rainforest

Grammar, p.W51

1 **2** When did the game start?
3 Who did they visit?
4 Did they eat any apples?
5 What did they eat at their grandfather's house?
6 What did they do in the evening?

2 **2** they didn't. **3** Yes, they did. **4** Yes, he did.
5 No, he didn't.

3 **2** How did you travel? **3** When did you arrive?
4 Did, win the game? **5** What did you do
6 Did you go

Vocabulary, p.W52

1 **2** sink **3** crash **4** hit **5** die **6** break

2 **2** died **3** broke **4** hit **5** sank **6** crashed

3 **2** hurricane **3** earthquake **4** flood **5** fire

Grammar, p.W53

1 **2** didn't break **3** didn't hit **4** didn't sink
5 didn't crash **6** didn't disappear

2 **2** The ship didn't sink in the hurricane.
3 We didn't see the fire.
4 My brother didn't break your computer.
5 You didn't wear your new shoes.
6 We didn't buy any apples.
7 The bus didn't crash into the tree.

3 **2** She didn't buy three jackets. She bought two
T-shirts.
3 She didn't spend $300. She spent $30.
4 Mike and Lucy didn't have lunch at 1 p.m. They
had lunch at 12 p.m.
5 Lucy didn't play the piano in the afternoon. She
played the guitar.
6 She didn't watch a baseball game in the evening.
She watched a soccer game.

Reading, p.W54

1 The *Mary Celeste* was a ship.

2 **2 saw** 3 didn't go 4 watched **5 didn't find**

3 **2** Yes, they did. **3** No, it didn't.
4 No, they didn't. **5** No, it didn't.

4 **2** The *Dei Gratia* found the *Mary Celeste* near the
Azores Islands, in the Atlantic Ocean.
3 They watched the *Mary Celeste*.
4 They waited for two hours.
5 No, they didn't.

Vocabulary

1 Complete the sentences about the weather.

1 It's h _____ in the summer in Australia.
2 It's the winter and it's s _____ .
   Look – it's all white!
3 You can't see the sun because it's gray and
   c _____ .
4 It's w _____ and it's stormy today.
5 I'm wearing my jacket today. It's c _____ .
6 People go to the beach when it's s _____ .

_____ / 12

2 Circle the correct words.

1 sleep / wear / **post** on the sofa
2 babysit / **do** / chat homework
3 do / walk / **get** dressed
4 **chat** / have / wear online
5 post / wait / **start** for the bus
6 sleep / do / **post** a comment
7 read / babysit / **wait** your brother
8 send / go / **do** a text message

_____ / 8

Grammar

1 Fill in the blanks with the present progressive affirmative.

1 I _____ (play) soccer.
2 You _____ (dance) with César.
3 They _____ (swim) right now.
4 It _____ (snow) today.
5 Sara _____ (watch) a movie.
6 She _____ (sit) next to Tomiko.

_____ / 6

2 Write sentences. Use the present progressive negative.

1 I / not listen / to music

_____ .

2 She / not run / fast

_____ .

3 Rafael / not do / his homework

_____ .

4 We / not chat / online

_____ .

5 You / not get / dressed

_____ .

6 They / not talk / on the phone

_____ .

_____ / 6

3 Write questions. Use the present progressive.

1 you / have / breakfast

_____ ?

2 Ana / sleep / on the sofa

_____ ?

3 he / speak / Chinese

_____ ?

4 What / they / do

_____ ?

5 it / rain / today

_____ ?

6 Where / they / play soccer

_____ ?

_____ / 6

4 Write answers for the questions in exercise 3 with the words below.

> In the yard   No, he isn't   No, it isn't
> They're dancing   Yes, I am   Yes, she is

1 _____ .
2 _____ .
3 _____ .
4 _____ .
5 _____ .
6 _____ .

_____ / 6

5 Correct the present progressive questions.

1 Are you watch TV?

_____

_____ ?

2 Is they walking in the park?

_____

_____ ?

3 She is singing a song?

_____

_____ ?

4 Am it raining?

_____

_____ ?

5 Is he talk on the phone?

_____

_____ ?

6 What they eat now?

_____

_____ ?

_____ / 6

Reading

1 Read the e-mail. Are the sentences True or False? Correct the false sentences.

> ● ● ○   **e-mail**
>
> **From:** Maria
> **Date:** July 25,
> **Time:** 12:35
> **To:** Raku
> **Subject:** Today
> _____
>
> Hi Raku!
> How are you? It's hot and sunny today, and I'm in the park with my friends from high school. We're having fun. We're in the cybercafé next to the lake right now, and I'm writing this e-mail to you.
> I'm sitting between Bella and Tom. Bella is chatting online to her friend in San Francisco, and Tom is playing his favorite computer game. He plays it every day. Jane and Pete are sitting on the sofa, but they aren't chatting. Jane is reading a magazine about computers (she loves computer science!), and Pete is sending a text message to Marc. Marc and Katia aren't with us now. They're having lunch in town. They're having a pizza at *Pizzaworld* in the shopping mall.
> Hope you're having fun.
> Love, Maria

1 It's cloudy and it's raining.   **T / F**

_____ .

2 Maria and four of her friends are at school. **T / F**

_____ .

3 Bella, Tom, and Maria are using computers. **T / F**

_____ .

4 Jane isn't talking to Pete.   **T / F**

_____ .

5 Marc and Katia are eating in the cybercafé. **T / F**

_____ .

_____ / 10

Total: _____ / 60

2 Unit test ★★☆

Vocabulary

1 Complete the clothes words.

1 t __ p
2 p __ n __ s
3 sk __ __ t
4 s __ c __ s
5 sh __ r __
6 gl __ ss __ s
7 b __ __ ts
8 sh __ __ s

.... / 8

2 Unscramble the physical description words.

1 g t i h l ....
2 d l o b n ....
3 a g s i t h r t ....
4 d b a r e ....
5 t o h r s ....
6 m l a s l ....

.... / 6

3 Fill in the blanks with the words from exercise 2.

1 She has .... eyes. She doesn't have big eyes.
2 I have .... hair. I don't have long hair.
3 You don't have .... brown eyes. You have dark brown eyes
4 Jed doesn't have .... hair. He has wavy hair.
5 He has .... hair. He doesn't have brown hair.
6 Our dad doesn't have a .... He only has a mustache.

.... / 6

Grammar

1 Fill in the blanks with the simple present or present progressive of the verb in parentheses.

1 (work)
My mom usually .... in an office.
But she .... at home today.

2 (watch)
Jack .... a movie at the moment.
He normally .... TV after school.

3 (not get)
They .... up early today. They're tired.
They .... up early on the weekends.

4 (listen)
.... you .... to rock music now?
.... you .... to rock music every day?

5 (wear)
I always .... black shoes to school.
I .... some new shoes today.

6 (not walk)
Frankie .... to school right now.
He .... to school on Wednesdays.

.... / 12

2 Complete the phone conversation with the simple present or the present progressive. Use the verbs in parentheses.

Elsa: Hi, Carla. What (1) _____ (do) right now?

Carla: We're in the kitchen. David (2) _____ (cook) dinner, and I (3) _____ (read) a magazine.

Elsa: (4) _____ David _____ (cook) every evening?

Carla: No, only on Tuesdays, because I always (5) _____ (get) home late. When (6) _____ you usually _____ (eat) dinner?

Elsa: At seven o'clock. Right now, I (7) _____ (eat) a snack because I'm hungry. But usually I (8) _____ (not eat) snacks.

_____ / 8

3 Fill in the blanks with the affirmative or negative form of _have_.

1 I _____ short hair. (✓)
2 They _____ green eyes. (✓)
3 Anna _____ blond hair. (✗)
4 Robert _____ wavy hair. (✓)
5 You _____ blue eyes. (✗)

_____ / 5

4 Fill in the blanks with the affirmative form of _have_ or _be_.

1 Lionel _____ long dark hair.
2 His hair _____ very straight. It isn't wavy.
3 He _____ a long straight beard, too.
4 Lionel and his brother _____ tall.
5 Lionel and his wife _____ glasses.

_____ / 5

Reading

1 Read the text about Desmond. Then fill in the blanks with words from the text.

Desmond lives in Durban, South Africa. Durban city is near the beach, but Desmond doesn't live near the beach. He lives with his family in a small house in town.

Desmond normally gets up at 6 a.m. every morning. Then he goes to school with his brother and two sisters. They don't take the bus – they walk.

Desmond is carrying his sports bag today because he's playing soccer after school. He normally wears a red top and white shorts in soccer games.

In Durban, school starts early in the morning. Classes start at 8 a.m., and they finish at 2 p.m. Desmond has a good time at school. He studies languages, math, history, geography, and science. He's studying English, science, and math today. His parents don't have a computer at home, but they have a TV, and Desmond has a radio. Desmond listens to British and American music. He watches American movies, too.

1 Desmond has two _____ and a brother.
2 He doesn't go to _____ by bus.
3 He's taking his _____ with him today.
4 Desmond's _____ finish at two o'clock.
5 At home, he has a radio, but he doesn't have a _____ .

_____ / 10

Total: _____ / 60

Vocabulary

1 Unscramble the foods.

1 g e s g ....

2 z s i a p z ....

3 p s p a l e ....

4 r m b h u a r s e g ....

5 t a s o p e t o ....

6 w i s a r s r e t r b e ....

.... / 6

2 Fill in the blanks with the foods from exercise 1.

1 .... are normally red or green.

2 I'm making French fries. Are there any .... ?

3 You use .... to make an omelet.

4 .... are small and red.

5 You eat .... in an Italian restaurant.

6 You eat .... in a fast food restaurant.

.... / 6

3 Find eight items of food and drink. Put the words in the correct column.

pastapplketchupasbreadegsodabercoffeepizcheesemanmilkgowater

Food	Drink

.... / 8

Grammar

1 Circle the correct words.

1 There **is a / are some / is any** potatoes.

2 There **aren't any / isn't any / is some** bananas.

3 There **is a / are a / is an** apple.

4 There **isn't some / isn't a / isn't any** hamburger.

5 There **are any / isn't any / are some** strawberries.

.... / 5

2 Fill in the blanks with *a, an, some,* or *any*.

1 There aren't .... hamburgers.

2 Is there .... egg?

3 There are .... tomatoes.

4 There is .... mango.

5 Are there .... pizzas?

.... / 5

3 Write questions and short answers. Use *Is there a / an* or *Are there any* for the questions.

1 .... fast food restaurant near your school? (✓)

....

2 .... cybercafés in your town? (✓)

....

3 .... egg in the refrigerator? (✗)

....

4 .... sausage under your chair? (✗)

....

5 .... Italian restaurants near here? (✗)

....

.... / 10

4 Write C (for countable) or U (for uncountable).

1 rice ....
2 ketchup ....
3 apple ....
4 bread ....
5 mango ....
6 salt ....

.... **/ 6**

5 Fill in the blanks with the correct form of *be* and *some* or *any*.

1 There .... milk. (✗)
2 There .... sausages. (✓)
3 There .... French fries. (✗)
4 There .... salt. (✓)

.... **/ 4**

Reading

1 Read the blog. Then answer the questions.

My blog

Hi!
My name is Francesca, and my sister's name is Patrizia. Tonight, Patrizia and I want to meet our friends in town for a pizza.
My favorite Italian restaurant is called *Luigi's*. It's a big new restaurant in the town center across from the movie theater. I like it because there's a big menu, and the pizzas are delicious. There are some expensive pizzas, and there are some cheap ones, too. There is other Italian food on the menu like pasta or salad, but I normally have a pizza. My favorite one is a Margarita. There's cheese and tomato on that.
Patrizia's favorite restaurant is called *Buona Sera*. She likes it because it's very small – there are only six tables! They're next to the kitchen and you can watch them cook the pizzas. It's fun! It's a cheap restaurant, and there are only pizzas on the menu, but they're very good.
We can't decide between *Luigi's* and *Buona Sera*!

1 Is *Luigi's* a small restaurant?

....

2 Where exactly is it?

....

3 Are there any cheap pizzas at *Luigi's*?

....

4 Why does Patrizia like *Buona Sera*?

....

5 Is there any pasta on the menu at *Buona Sera*?

....

.... **/ 10**

Total: .... **/ 60**

Vocabulary

1 Match the nouns (1–8) with the noun categories (a–h).

1	$50	a	time
2	backpack	b	music
3	bed	c	furniture
4	buses	d	money
5	apple	e	traffic
6	song	f	travel
7	minute	g	food
8	vacation	h	baggage

...... / 8

2 Unscramble the personal possessions.

1 y k e   n g r i ....
2 k a b p c c a k ....
3 l t a c r e b e ....
4 g r i n r a e s ....
5 n g l s a s u s s e ....
6 l e t b ....

...... / 6

3 Fill in the blanks with the personal possessions from exercise 2.

1 It's sunny today. Where are my

.... ?

2 My pants are too big. I need a

....

3 The key to my house is on my

....

4 She's wearing her gold

.... on her wrist.

5 My .... is very
heavy. It has all my school books in it.

6 My mom has ....
in both ears.

...... / 6

Grammar

1 Put the words in the correct column.

beds   furniture   minutes   music   songs   time

Countable	Uncountable
....	....
....	....
....	....

...... / 6

2 Fill in the blanks with the words in exercise 1.

1 How many ....
are there on your MP3 player?

2 How much ....
is there on your MP3 player?

3 How much ....
is there before classes start?

4 How many ....
are there before classes start?

5 How many ....
are there in the room?

6 How much ....
is there in the room?

...... / 6

3 Look at the answers for the questions in exercise 2. Circle the correct words.

1 There **are a lot / 's a lot.**
2 There **aren't many / isn't much.**
3 There **are none / 's a little.**
4 There **are a few / 's a little.**
5 There **aren't any / isn't any.**
6 There **are a few / 's none.**

...... / 6

4 **Fill in the blanks with the correct possessive pronouns.**

1 It's my book. It's _____ .

2 It's your backpack. It's _____ .

3 They're Anna's earrings. They're _____ .

4 It's David's belt. It's _____ .

5 They're our pens. They're _____ .

6 It's Li and Kenzo's dog. It's _____ .

_____ / 6

5 **Fill in the blanks with *is this* or *are these*. Then write the answer with a possessive pronoun.**

1 Whose key ring **is this** _____ ?
(my key ring) **It's mine** _____ .

2 Whose bags _____ ?
(their bags) _____ .

3 Whose money _____ ?
(her money) _____ .

4 Whose shoes _____ ?
(our shoes) _____ .

_____ / 6

Reading

1 **Read the dialogue. Are the sentences True or False? Correct the false sentences.**

Amanda:	Hello. Welcome to the show *What do you eat?* Here's our reporter, Ben. Whose house are you at today, Ben?
Ben:	I'm at the Turner's house today, Amanda. Mr. and Mrs. Turner have two children, Sarah and Daniel.
Amanda:	And what do the Turners eat? Look in the refrigerator! Is there any fresh food?
Ben:	There's a little. There are some bananas, but they're black. And there's something green.
Amanda:	Is it some salad?
Ben:	No, it isn't. It's some cheese, and it's very old.
Amanda:	Oh, that's not good. Is there anything else?
Ben:	Yes, there are a few sausages.
Amanda:	OK. And is there any milk or water?
Ben:	Well, there is some milk, but it's strawberry milk. And there are six bottles of soda. That's all.
Amanda:	Are there any vegetables in the freezer?
Ben:	Sorry, Amanda. I can see some hamburgers and French fries. But there aren't any vegetables.
Amanda:	So there isn't much food in the Turner's refrigerator, and the food that is in the refrigerator isn't very healthy.
Ben:	That's right, Amanda.

1 There are some apples. T / F

_____ .

2 There aren't any bananas. T / F

_____ .

3 There are some sausages. T / F

_____ .

4 There isn't any water. T / F

_____ .

5 There's a lot of very healthy food. T / F

_____ .

_____ / 10

Total: _____ / 60

Vocabulary

1 Match the verbs (1–6) with the words (a–f).

1	go	a	your hair
2	stay out	b	a sleepover
3	dye	c	your dad's car
4	have	d	late
5	borrow	e	to a party
6	drive	f	money from a friend

.... / 6

2 Unscramble the places to go. Start with the bold letter.

1 r i y b r **l** a

2 e u u m **m** s

3 o e c f e f o h p s

4 n o s p i p h g l m l a

5 n k g i s a t k r n i

6 m w n m g i i s o l o p

7 m t m s e e a u n k p r a

.... / 14

Grammar

1 Fill in the blanks with *can* and the verbs below.

| borrow | buy | drive | eat | come | stay out |

1 .... I .... your dictionary?

2 .... we .... until 1 a.m.?

3 .... I .... some new clothes on the weekend?

4 .... Marc .... the car to the movie theater?

5 .... I .... those potato chips?

6 .... ten friends .... to my house on Saturday?

.... / 6

2 Match the answers (a–f) with the questions in exercise 1. Write the correct number.

a .... Absolutely not! He can't drive.

b .... I'll think about it. How much money do you want?

c .... No way! There are only two beds in your room.

d .... Sure you can. It's Saturday tomorrow.

e .... Sorry you can't. I'm using it.

f .... Sure you can. Are you very hungry?

.... / 6

3 Write suggestions. Then circle the correct answer.

1 A: Let / go / to the beach

   _____ .

   B: **Great! / No way!** It's snowing.

2 A: What about / buy / those jeans ?

   _____ ?

   B: **OK. / I don't think so.** I don't have any money.

3 A: Why / we / play / basketball ?

   _____ ?

   B: **Great! / Let's not.** I love it.

4 A: Let / have / a soda

   _____ .

   B: **That's a good idea. / Let's not.** I'm not thirsty.

5 A: What about / make / a cake ?

   _____ ?

   B: **OK. / No way!** There are some eggs in the refrigerator.

   _____ **/ 10**

4 Fill in the blanks with the words below.

> good idea   go shopping   great   I don't think
> let's   no   not   what about

Amelia: (1) _____ study for the test.

Felipe: (2) _____ way! I don't want to study.

Amelia: Why don't we (3) _____ ?

Felipe: (4) _____ so. Shopping is boring.

Amelia: (5) _____ watching TV?

Felipe: That's a (6) _____ .

Amelia: Let's see what's on TV.

Felipe: (7) _____ ! It's soccer. Why don't we watch this?

Amelia: Let's (8) _____ . I hate soccer!

   _____ **/ 8**

Reading

1 Read the advertisement. Then fill in the blanks.

Come and have fun at THE SUMMER CLUB! We're open from Monday to Thursday every week in August.

Monday: Sports day

Join a team! What about playing soccer or basketball?
Go solo! You can go swimming, running, or ride a mountain bike.

Tuesday: Amusement park

Why don't you come with us to *Fun World Amusement Park?* You can go on the new roller coaster *Fast and Fantastic*. Go up and down 150 meters four times, in just 90 seconds!
It's awesome! Then let's have lunch at a fast food restaurant.

Wednesday: Movie morning

We have over a hundred movies. Why don't you watch a DVD with us? Do you like old movies, new movies, or movies about animals? We have them all!

Thursday: A day in the park

What about spending a relaxing day in the park? You can go on a boat on the lake, play tennis with a friend, take a walk, or read a book under a tree. It's your day!

1 The Summer Club is open _____ days a week in August.

2 You can do different _____ on Mondays.

3 *Fast and Fantastic* is a roller coaster at the _____ .

4 There are a lot of _____ to watch on Wednesday mornings.

5 You can go to the _____ on Thursdays.

   _____ **/ 10**

   Total: _____ **/ 60**

Vocabulary

1 Unscramble the jobs.

1 s t i r a t _____

2 n o i h s a f   e g i s d n r e _____

_____

3 r t i e w r _____

4 i c l p o t a i n i _____

5 c t i a h r e t c _____

_____ / 5

2 Fill in the blanks with the jobs from exercise 1.

1 The Harry Potter books are by J. K. Rowling. She's a British _____ .

2 That picture is by Picasso. He was a Spanish _____ .

3 That's one of Frank Lloyd Wright's buildings. He was an American _____ .

4 That dress is by Christian Dior. He was a French _____ .

5 That book is by Nelson Mandela. He is a South African _____ .

_____ / 5

3 Complete the adjectives of opinion.

1 History is an ____ nt ___ r ___ st ___ g subject.

2 Don't read that book. It's really b ___ r ___ g.

3 Yuck! I can't eat that food. It's d ___ sg ___ t ___ g.

4 The weather is ___ w ___ l today. It's cold and it's raining.

5 Can I have some more pasta? It's d ___ l ___ c ___ s.

_____ / 10

Grammar

1 Read the information. Then fill in the blanks with was, were, wasn't, or weren't.

> **Name:** Michael Jordan
> **Date of birth:** February 17th, 1963
> **Place of birth:** Brooklyn, New York, United States
> **Job:** professional basketball player
> **Club history:** Chicago Bulls (1984–1993, 1995–1998); Washington Wizards (2001–2003)

1 Michael Jordan _____ born in 1966.

2 He _____ born in 1963.

3 He _____ born in the United Kingdom.

4 He _____ a professional tennis player.

5 His clubs _____ Boston Celtics or Los Angeles Lakers.

6 They _____ Chicago Bulls and Washington Wizards.

_____ / 6

2 Write the questions with the past form of be. Then write the short answers.

1 Pelé / a soccer player

Was Pelé a soccer player _____ ?

Yes, **he was** _____ .

2 you / born / in England

_____

_____ ?

No, _____ .

3 Jimi Hendrix / a famous inventor

_____

_____ ?

No, _____ .

4 you and your family / Guatemala / last month

_____

_____ ?

No, _____ .

5   Frida Kahlo / from / Mexico

....

.... ?

Yes, ...

6   Michael Jordan's club / the NBA Champion / in
1998

....

.... ?

Yes, ...

7   your grandparents / famous musicians

....

.... ?

No, ...

.... **/ 12**

3   Write the ordinal numbers in words.

1   1st   ....

2   12th   ....

3   28th   ....

4   46th   ....

5   79th   ....

6   93rd   ....

.... **/ 6**

4   Fill in the blanks with the words below.

> fifth   five hundred   hundredth
> second   two

1   A bird has .... legs.

2   I wasn't first. I was ....

3   E is the .... letter of the English
alphabet.

4   I have .... brothers – Max, Ed, Joe,
Jack, and Kurt.

5   He's 99 years old. It's his ....
birthday next year.

6   There were a .... people at my
birthday party. It was awesome!

.... **/ 6**

Reading

**1   Read the interview. Then correct the sentences
below.**

Interviewer:	Where do you live, Marie?
Marie:	I live in London, England.
Interviewer:	Were you born in London?
Marie:	No, I was born in Sydney, Australia on August 6th, 1994.
Interviewer:	Australia? But you aren't Australian.
Marie:	No, I'm not. My parents are British, but they were in Sydney for ten years. My dad's job was there. He was an architect in the city, and we were there until I was six.
Interviewer:	What was your house like?
Marie:	It was big, and it was near an awesome beach called Manly Beach. There were always a lot of surfers there, and there was a swimming pool with water from the sea.
Interviewer:	And the weather?
Marie:	The weather was fantastic! It was really hot and sunny. It's different in London.
Interviewer:	Do you like London?
Marie:	Yes, of course. I was young when I was in Sydney. London is my home now. But my family and I go back to Australia for a vacation every three years.

1   Marie was born in London.
Marie was born in Sydney .

2   Marie's father was an artist.

....

3   Marie's parents are Australian.

....

4   Marie was in Sydney until she was ten years old.

....

5   The weather was awful in Sydney.

....

6   Marie never goes back to Australia.

....

.... **/ 10**

Total: .... **/ 60**

Vocabulary

1 Complete the kinds of music.

1 r ___ ck
2 j ___ zz
3 s ___ l
4 c ___ ntry
5 cl ___ ss ___ c ___ l
6 p ___
7 re ___ a ___
8 r ___

_____ / 8

2 Unscramble the musical instruments. Then fill in the blanks.

1 Vivaldi was a famous _____ (i o i v n l) player.
2 Larry Mullen Jr. plays the _____ (m r s u d) in U2.
3 Louis Armstrong was a famous _____ (p r m e t u t) player.
4 Chris Martin sometimes plays the _____ (a n i p o) in Coldplay.
5 Jimi Hendrix was an American _____ (t i g u r a) player.
6 John Coltrane was a _____ (n o s e h x a p o) player.

_____ / 12

Grammar

1 Write the simple past form of the verbs.

1 listen – _____
2 study – _____
3 chat – _____
4 arrive – _____
5 stay – _____
6 try – _____
7 watch – _____

_____ / 7

2 Fill in the blanks with the simple past forms in exercise 1.

1 We _____ an awful movie on TV yesterday.
2 The teacher was angry because the students _____ late.
3 I _____ to music on my MP3 player last night.
4 They _____ online for three hours.
5 I _____ to eat snails in the restaurant, but they were disgusting.
6 My mom _____ French and Spanish at college.
7 Josh _____ out late last Saturday.

_____ / 7

3 Circle the correct simple past form of the verbs.

1 go – goed / **went** / goes

2 see – **saw** / sawed / seed

3 win – wind / wan / **won**

4 sing – sung / singed / **sang**

5 spend – spend / **spent** / spended

6 tell – telled / **told** / telld

7 give – **gave** / gove / gived

8 have – **had** / haved / haded

...... / 8

4 Fill in the blanks with the simple past forms of the verbs in exercise 3.

Last July I (1) .... to a music festival. My dad (2) .... four tickets in a competition, and he (3) .... them to me and my friends. There were thousands of people there, and we (4) .... three hours waiting to go in. When it started, we (5) .... a fantastic time. We (6) .... my favorite rap star, Tinie Tempah. He (7) .... *Written in the Stars*, and it was awesome. After the festival, I posted a comment online and (8) .... everyone all about it.

...... / 8

Reading

1 Read the blog. Are the sentences True or False? Correct the false sentences.

○○○ **My blog**

My mom was 40 last Saturday so my dad organized a special birthday party for her. He invited all her friends and family. There were about 80 people there. Our house is very small, so we had the party in a large room at the local sports center. It was great!

A band called Rock On played the music. There are five members in the band. Two girls sang, one man played the guitar, another played the bass, and a boy played the drums. They aren't a famous band, and they don't have an album, but they were awesome! They performed a lot of songs from the 1980s when my mom and dad were at school.

My brother, Ted, plays the saxophone. He played *Happy Birthday* for Mom, and everyone sang for her. Dad took a lot of photos.

Mom spent all night dancing and chatting to people. At the end, she told us it was the best night of her life.

Archie

---

1 80 people went to Archie's mom's birthday party. T / F

....

2 The party was in a hotel. T / F

....

3 Ted isn't a member of the rock band. T / F

....

4 People sang songs from the 1980s for Archie's mom. T / F

....

5 Archie's mom danced for an hour. T / F

....

...... / 10

Total: ...... / 60

Vocabulary

1 Fill in the blanks with the words below.

> beach desert island jungle mountain river
> volcano

1 The Amazon is the longest .... in South America.
2 Mount Fuji in Japan is a ....
3 There are big areas of .... in South America.
4 The Atacama .... is the driest place in the world.
5 Honshu is the biggest Japanese .... , but there are over 6,500 in total!
6 Copacabana is a famous .... in Rio de Janeiro.
7 I skied on a big .... in my winter vacation.

.... / 14

2 Circle the correct word.

1 The boat had a hole so it **crashed / sank / died** in the water.
2 We **sank / crashed / disappeared** into another car.
3 A soccer player **died / sank / broke** his leg yesterday.
4 How many people **hit / broke / died** in accidents last year?
5 The cat **disappeared / broke / crashed** yesterday. I can't find her.
6 He **sank / crashed / hit** a tree with his bike.

.... / 6

Grammar

1 Read Harry's agenda for last Friday and Saturday. Write simple past questions.

Friday	play soccer
	buy some sneakers
	watch a disaster movie with Mick
Saturday	go to the beach
	do geography homework
	go to the shopping mall with Sally
	stay out late with friends

1 Harry / basketball / Friday
   Did Harry play basketball on Friday .... ?
2 Harry / some sneakers / Friday
   .... ?
3 Harry and Mick / movie / Saturday
   .... ?
4 Harry / beach / Saturday
   .... ?
5 Harry / his math homework / Saturday
   .... ?
6 Harry / the shopping mall with Sally / Saturday
   .... ?
7 Harry and his friends / late / Saturday
   .... ?

.... / 6

2 Write short answers for the questions in exercise 1.

1 **No, he didn't** ....
2 ....
3 ....
4 ....
5 ....
6 ....
7 ....

.... / 6

3 Write questions. Use the simple past.

1 Where / you / go / on vacation / last summer

_____ ?

2 you and your family / have / a good time

_____ ?

3 How many islands / you / visit

_____ ?

4 you / learn / about the history of the Bahamas

_____ ?

5 Columbus / discover / the Bahamas

_____ ?

6 What month / he / arrive / there

_____ ?

_____ / 6

4 Match the answers (a–f) with the questions in exercise 3. Write the correct number (1–6).

a _____ Yes, he did. In 1492.

b _____ Two. New Providence and Eleuthera.

c _____ We went to the Bahamas.

d _____ In October.

e _____ Yes, I did. I learned a lot of things.

f _____ Yes, we did. It was awesome!

_____ / 6

5 Write the negative form of the simple past sentences.

1 The *Titanic* sank in 1950.

_____ .

2 The Romans invented cell phones.

_____ .

3 Botticelli painted the *Mona Lisa*.

_____ .

4 Pelé played basketball.

_____ .

5 The Incas built the Great Pyramid.

_____ .

6 Shakespeare wrote the *Sherlock Holmes* books.

_____ .

_____ / 6

Reading

1 Read the blog. Answer the questions.

○ ○ ○   **My blog**

Your questions about … the Pyramids in Egypt

For a long time, the pyramids were one of the world's big mysteries. But today, we know a little more about them. Dr. Daniel Knowles from the Egyptian Museum in Cairo answers your questions.

How old are the pyramids?
About 4,600 years old.

Why did the Egyptians build the pyramids?
The ancient Egyptians built them for their pharaohs, the kings of Egypt. They were their tombs. For example, the Great Pyramid was a tomb for the Pharoah Khufu.

How long did it take to build one?
We think that it took between twenty and thirty years to build one. They didn't have any machines then.

How many people did it take to build a pyramid?
We don't know exactly, but thousands and thousands of people!

How big is the Great Pyramid?
It's very, very big. There are about two million three hundred thousand blocks of stone in this pyramid.

1 Does Dr. Knowles work in a pyramid?

_____ .

2 Did the pyramids exist 20,000 years ago?

_____ .

3 Who were the pharoahs?

_____ .

4 What was the name of Pharoah Khufu's tomb?

_____ .

5 How many people did it take to build a pyramid?

_____ .

_____ / 10

Total: _____ / 60

Unit tests answer key

1 Unit test ★★☆

Vocabulary

1 1 hot 2 snowing 3 cloudy 4 windy 5 cold
6 sunny

2 1 sleep 2 do 3 get 4 chat 5 wait 6 post
7 babysit 8 send

Grammar

1 1 'm playing   4 's snowing
2 're dancing   5 's watching
3 're swimming   6 's sitting

2 1 I'm not listening to music.
2 She isn't running fast.
3 Rafael isn't doing his homework.
4 We aren't chatting online.
5 You aren't getting dressed.
6 They aren't talking on the phone.

3 1 Are you having breakfast?
2 Is Ana sleeping on the sofa?
3 Is he speaking Chinese?
4 What are they doing?
5 Is it raining today?
6 Where are they playing soccer?

4 1 Yes, I am.   4 They're dancing.
2 Yes, she is.   5 No, it isn't.
3 No, he isn't.   6 In the yard.

5 1 Are you watching TV?
2 Are they walking in the park?
3 Is she singing a song?
4 Is it raining?
5 Is he talking on the phone?
6 What are they eating now?

Reading

1 1 F It's hot and sunny.
2 F Maria and four of her friends are in the
cybercafé.
3 T
4 T
5 F Marc and Katia are eating in the shopping mall.

2 Unit test ★★☆

Vocabulary

1 1 top 2 pants 3 skirt 4 socks 5 shirt
6 glasses 7 boots 8 shoes

2 1 light 2 blond 3 straight 4 beard 5 short
6 small

3 1 small 2 short 3 light 4 straight 5 blond
6 beard

Grammar

1 1 works; 's working
2 is watching; watches
3 aren't getting; don't get
4 Are … listening; Do … listen
5 wear; 'm wearing
6 isn't walking; doesn't walk

2 1 are you doing
2 's cooking
3 'm reading
4 Does … cook
5 get
6 do … eat
7 'm eating
8 don't eat

3 1 have 2 have 3 doesn't have 4 has
5 don't have

4 1 has 2 is 3 has 4 are 5 have

Reading

1 1 sisters 2 school 3 sports bag 4 classes
5 computer

3 Unit test ★★☆

Vocabulary

1 **1** eggs **2** pizzas **3** apples **4** hamburgers
5 potatoes **6** strawberries

3 **1** Apples **2** potatoes **3** eggs **4** Strawberries
5 pizzas **6** hamburgers

2
Food	Drink
bread	coffee
ketchup	milk
pasta	soda
cheese	water

Grammar

1 **1** are some **4** isn't a
2 aren't any **5** are some
3 is an

2 **1** any **2** an **3** some **4** a **5** any

3 **1** Is there a; Yes, there is.
2 Are there any; Yes, there are.
3 Is there an; No, there isn't.
4 Is there a; No, there isn't.
5 Are there any; No, there aren't.

4 **1** U **2** U **3** C **4** U **5** C **6** U

5 **1** isn't any **3** aren't any
2 are some **4** is some

Reading

1 **1** No, it isn't (It's big).
2 It's in the town center across from the movie
theater.
3 Yes, there are.
4 Because it's very small.
5 No, there isn't.

4 Unit test ★★☆

Vocabulary

1 **1** d **2** h **3** c **4** e **5** g **6** b **7** a **8** f

2 **1** key ring **4** earrings
2 backpack **5** sunglasses
3 bracelet **6** belt

3 **1** sunglasses **4** bracelet
2 belt **5** backpack
3 key ring **6** earrings

Grammar

1
Countable	Uncountable
beds	furniture
minutes	music
songs	time

2 **1** songs **4** minutes
2 music **5** beds
3 time **6** furniture

3 **1** are a lot **4** are a few
2 isn't much **5** aren't any
3 's a little **6** 's none

4 **1** mine **2** yours **3** hers **4** his **5** ours
6 theirs

5 **2** are these; They're theirs.
3 is this; It's hers.
4 are these; They're ours.

Reading

1 **1** F There aren't any apples.
2 F There are some bananas.
3 T
4 T
5 F There isn't any healthy food.

Unit tests answer key

5 Unit test ★★☆

Vocabulary

1 1 e 2 d 3 a 4 b 5 f (c is also correct) 6 c

2 1 library
2 museum
3 coffee shop
4 shopping mall
5 skating rink
6 swimming pool
7 amusement park

Grammar

1 1 Can … borrow
2 Can … stay out
3 Can … buy
4 Can … drive
5 Can … eat
6 Can … come

2 a 4 b 3 c 6 d 2 e 1 f 5

3 1 Let's go to the beach; No way!
2 What about buying those jeans; I don't think so.
3 Why don't we play basketball; Great!
4 Let's have a soda; Let's not.
5 What about making a cake; OK.

4 1 Let's
2 No
3 go shopping
4 I don't think
5 What about
6 good idea
7 Great
8 not

Reading

1 1 four 2 sports 3 amusement park 4 movies
5 park

6 Unit test ★★☆

Vocabulary

1 1 artist 2 fashion designer 3 writer
4 politician 5 architect

2 1 writer 2 artist 3 architect
4 fashion designer 5 politician

3 1 interesting 2 boring 3 disgusting 4 awful
5 delicious

Grammar

1 1 wasn't 2 was 3 wasn't 4 wasn't
5 weren't 6 were

2 2 Were you born in England; I wasn't
3 Was Jimi Hendrix a famous inventor; he wasn't
4 Were you and your family in Guatemala last
month; we weren't
5 Was Frida Kahlo from Mexico; she was
6 Was Michael Jordan's club the NBA Champion in
1998; it was
7 Were your grandparents famous musicians; they
weren't

3 1 first 2 twelfth 3 twenty-eighth
4 forty-sixth 5 seventy-ninth 6 ninety-third

4 1 two 2 second 3 fifth 4 five 5 hundredth
6 hundred

Reading

1 2 Marie's father was an architect.
3 Marie's parents are British.
4 Marie was in Sydney until she was six years old.
5 The weather was fantastic in Sydney.
6 Maria goes back to Australia every three years.

7 Unit test ★★☆

Vocabulary

1 **1** rock **2** jazz **3** soul **4** country **5** classical
6 pop **7** reggae **8** rap

2 **1** violin **2** drums **3** trumpet **4** piano
5 guitar **6** saxophone

Grammar

1 **1** listened **2** studied **3** chatted **4** arrived
5 stayed **6** tried **7** watched

2 **1** watched **2** arrived **3** listened **4** chatted
5 tried **6** studied **7** stayed

3 **1** went **2** saw **3** won **4** sang **5** spent
6 told **7** gave **8** had

4 **1** went **2** won **3** gave **4** spent **5** had
6 saw **7** sang **8** told

Reading

1 **1** T
2 F The party was at the local sports center.
3 T
4 F People sang *Happy Birthday*.
5 F She danced all night.

8 Unit test ★★☆

Vocabulary

1 **1** river **2** volcano **3** jungle **4** desert **5** island
6 beach **7** mountain

2 **1** sank **2** crashed **3** broke **4** died
5 disappeared **6** hit

Grammar

1 **2** Did Harry buy some sneakers on Friday?
3 Did Harry and Mick watch a movie on Saturday?
4 Did Harry go to the beach on Saturday?
5 Did Harry do his math homework on Saturday?
6 Did Harry go to the shopping mall with Sally on Saturday?
7 Did Harry and his friends stay out late on Saturday?

2 **2** Yes, he did.
3 No, they didn't.
4 Yes, he did.
5 No, he didn't.
6 Yes, he did.
7 Yes, they did.

3 **1** Where did you go on vacation last summer?
2 Did you and your family have a good time?
3 How many islands did you visit?
4 Did you learn about the history of the Bahamas?
5 When did Columbus discover the Bahamas?
6 What month did he arrive there?

4 **a** 5 **b** 3 **c** 1 **d** 6 **e** 4 **f** 2

5 **1** The *Titanic* didn't sink in 1950.
2 The Romans didn't invent cell phones.
3 Botticelli didn't paint the *Mona Lisa.*
4 Pelé didn't play basketball.
5 The Incas didn't build the Great Pyramid.
6 Shakespeare didn't write the *Sherlock Holmes* books.

Reading

1 **1** No, he doesn't.
2 No, they didn't.
3 They were the kings of Egypt.
4 The Great Pyramid.
5 Thousands (and thousands) of people.

What are you doing?

Notes and answers

Aims

to practice the present progressive (affirmative, negative, and questions)
to practice everyday activities and the weather
to review clothes and colors

Instructions

- Copy and cut up the activity sheet.
- Divide the class into A / B pairs.
- Give out the activity sheet, and explain the activity. Go through the example with the class.
- Make sure students have some colored pens / pencils.
- Make sure students understand that they have to ask present progressive questions (*Wh-* and *Yes / No* questions) to find out the details of their partner's picture (what they're doing and what they're wearing). They also need to ask about the weather (*What's the weather like?* / *Is it raining?*).
- Students draw their own picture. Then they ask and answer in pairs and draw their partner's picture.
- Students compare pictures to see if the details are correct.

Answers

Students' own answers.

Extra activity

- Students can repeat the activity with the other profile.

What are you doing?

Student A

1 **Choose a profile (1 or 2). Draw a simple picture to illustrate it. Use the correct colors for the clothes. Don't show your picture to Student B.**

2 **Answer Student B's questions about what you're doing in your picture. Give Student B time to draw the picture.**

Student B:	What are you doing in your picture?
Student A:	I'm waiting for a bus.
Student B:	Are you wearing a jacket?
Student A:	No, I'm not. I'm wearing …
Student B:	What else are you doing?
Student A:	I'm …

3 **Now ask Student B about his / her picture. Remember to ask about the weather, too. Draw Student B's picture.**

4 **Now compare the pictures. Are the details correct?**

1 You're waiting for a bus. You're wearing black shorts, a red T-shirt, and a blue cap. You're sending a text message on your cell phone. It's raining.

2 You're watching TV. You're sitting on a chair. You're wearing blue sweatpants and a yellow sweatshirt. It's cloudy outside.

Your picture

Student B's picture

What are you doing?

Student B

1 **Choose a profile (1 or 2). Draw a simple picture to illustrate it. Use the correct colors for the clothes. Don't show your picture to Student A.**

2 **Ask Student A about his / her picture. Remember to ask about the weather, too. Draw Student A's picture.**

Student B:	What are you doing in your picture?
Student A:	I'm waiting for a bus.
Student B:	Are you wearing a jacket?
Student A:	No, I'm not. I'm wearing …
Student B:	What else are you doing?
Student A:	I'm …

3 **Answer Student A's questions about what you're doing in your picture. Give Student A time to draw the picture.**

4 **Now compare the pictures. Are the details correct?**

1 You're doing your homework. You're sitting at a desk. You're wearing black jeans and an orange T-shirt. It's sunny outside.

2 You're waiting for a taxi. You're talking to a girl. You're wearing a blue jacket. She's wearing a red one. It's snowing.

Student A's picture

Your picture

2 Pairwork activity

Who's who?

Notes and answers

Aims

to practice *has / have* for appearance
to practice physical descriptions

Instructions

- Copy and cut up the activity sheet.
- Divide the class into A / B pairs.
- Give out the activity sheet, and explain the activity. Go through the example with the class.
- Make sure students understand that they have to use *has / doesn't have* to describe the appearance of their six people.
- Students choose names for the people on their activity sheet.
- Then they describe the physical appearance of their people.
- Remind students they have to describe the people in a random order.
- Their partner listens and writes the names under the correct pictures.
- Students compare the pictures to see if the names are correct.

Answers

Students' own answers.

Extra activity

- Students can describe the physical appearance of someone in the class without saying his / her name, e.g. *This person has long hair. This person doesn't have glasses.* Their partner listens and guesses who it is.

Who's who?

Student A

1 Choose a name for each person below. Label the pictures. Don't show Student B.

Barbara   Mick   Helena   Victor   Thomas   Lucy

2 Choose one of your people. Say his / her name. Describe his / her appearance to Student B using *has / doesn't have…* . Then do the same with the other people. Don't follow the order of the pictures.

Student A: Thomas has wavy, blond hair and small eyes. He has a mustache and a beard. He doesn't have glasses.

3 Compare the pictures. Are the names correct?

4 Listen to Student B's descriptions . Label the pictures with the names below.

Ernesto   Joseph   Hannah   Eva   Philip   Julia

5 Compare the pictures. Are the names correct?

Who's who?

Student B

1 Listen to Student A's descriptions. Label the pictures with the names below.

Barbara   Mick   Helena   Victor   Thomas   Lucy

Student A: Thomas has wavy, blond hair and small eyes. He has a mustache and a beard. He doesn't have glasses.

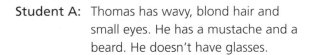

2 Compare the pictures. Are the names correct?

3 Now choose a name for each person below. Label the pictures. Don't show Student A.

Ernesto   Joseph   Hannah   Eva   Philip   Julia

4 Choose one of your people. Say his / her name. Describe his / her appearance to Student A using *has / doesn't have…* . Then do the same with the other people. Don't follow the order of the pictures.

5 Compare the pictures. Are the names correct?

3 Pairwork activity

What's on the menu?

Notes and answers

Aims

to practice asking and answering questions with *there is* / *there are*
to practice food and drink

Instructions

- Copy and cut up the activity sheet.
- Divide the class into A / B pairs.
- Give out the activity sheet, and explain the activity. Go through the example with the class.
- Make sure students understand that they have to ask and answer *Is there …?* / *Are there any …?* questions to find out what's on their partner's menu.
- Students choose and write the things on their menu. Then they ask and answer questions about their menus. They write the things on their partner's menu.
- Students compare menus to see if they are correct.

Answers

Students' own answers.

Extra activity

- Students can talk about the things on the menu in their school cafeteria.

What's on the menu?

Student A

1 Write your menu. Choose from the things below. Don't show Student B.

Main meals:	Extras:	Drinks:
Cheese and tomato pizza Cheese pasta Hamburgers Rice salad Sausages	Bread French fries Fruit salad Tomato salad	Coffee Milk Soda Water

2 Answer Student B's questions about your menu. Tell him / her the price, too. Ask questions about Student B's menu. Write the food and drink on the menu.

Student B: Is there any bread on your menu?

Student A: No, there isn't.

Student B: Are there any sausages?

Student A: Yes, there are. They're $3.

3 Now compare the menus. Are they correct?

Your Menu

Main meals

_____ $4
_____ $3

Extras

_____ $2
_____ $1

Drinks

_____ $1
_____ $1

Student B's Menu

Main meals

_____ $
_____ $

Extras

_____ $
_____ $

Drinks

_____ $
_____ $

What's on the menu?

Student B

1 Write your menu. Choose from the things below. Don't show Student A.

Main meals:	Extras:	Drinks:
Cheese and tomato pizza Cheese pasta Hamburgers Rice salad Sausages	Bread French fries Fruit salad Tomato salad	Coffee Milk Soda Water

2 Ask Student A questions about his / her menu. Write the food and drink on the menu. Answer Student A's questions about your menu. Tell him / her the price, too.

Student B: Is there any bread on your menu?

Student A: No, there isn't.

Student B: Are there any sausages?

Student A: Yes, there are. They're $3.

3 Now compare the menus. Are they correct?

Your Menu

Main meals

_____ $3
_____ $4

Extras

_____ $1
_____ $2

Drinks

_____ $2
_____ $1

Student A's Menu

Main meals

_____ $
_____ $

Extras

_____ $
_____ $

Drinks

_____ $
_____ $

Spot the difference

Notes and answers

Aims

to practice questions with *How much …?* / *How many …?*
to practice quantifiers
to practice countable / uncountable nouns

Instructions

- Copy and cut up the activity sheet.
- Divide the class into A / B pairs.
- Give out the activity sheet, and go through the example with the class.
- Make sure students understand that they have to ask and answer questions with *How much …?* / *How many …?* to find the differences in their pictures.
- Students take turns to ask and answer questions and find the differences in their pictures.
- Students compare pictures and check their answers.

Answers

Student A's picture
There are three people at the bus stop.
There's a lot of baggage.
There aren't any cars.
There are three chairs.
There are five hamburgers.
There are four keys.
There are ten strawberries.

Student B's picture
There are five people at the bus stop.
There's a little baggage.
There are two cars.
There's one chair.
There aren't any hamburgers.
There are five keys.
There are six strawberries.

Extra activity

- Students can add the things below to their pictures. They choose the quantity. They then ask and answer questions about those things.

  eggs   bread   cheese   bananas

Spot the difference

Student A

1 **Take turns to ask and answer questions about Student B's picture. Use *How much ...? / How many ...?* and the words below. Find seven differences. Circle the things on the picture that are different.**

> baggage cars chairs hamburgers ketchup
> keys money people at the bus stop
> skateboarders strawberries water

Student A: How many people are there at the bus stop?

Student B: There are five people at the bus stop.

Student A: That's different. In my picture, there are three people at the bus stop.

Student B: How much money is there in your picture?

Student A: There's none.

Student B: That's the same.

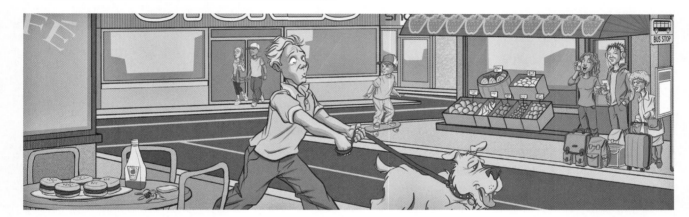

Spot the difference

Student B

1 **Take turns to ask and answer questions about Student A's picture. Use *How much ...? / How many ...?* and the words below. Find seven differences. Circle the things on the picture that are different.**

> baggage cars chairs hamburgers ketchup
> keys money people at the bus stop
> skateboarders strawberries water

Student A: How many people are there at the bus stop?

Student B: There are five people at the bus stop.

Student A: That's different. In my picture, there are three people at the bus stop.

Student B: How much money is there in your picture?

Student A: There's none.

Student B: That's the same.

5 Pairwork activity

Can I ...?

Notes and answers

Aims

to practice asking for permission
to practice giving / refusing permission

Instructions

- Copy and cut up the activity sheet.
- Divide the class into A / B pairs.
- Give out the activity sheet, and explain the activity. Go through the example
- with the class.
- Make sure students understand that this is a fun activity where they have to decide on the answers to the requests *before* their partner asks them.
- Encourage students to be enthusiastic with their answers. Some of them should be sensible, and others should be a bit silly and funny.
- Students take turns to ask for permission and give / refuse permission.
- Ask students how many answers were sensible.

Answers

Students' own answers.

Extra activity

- Students can repeat the activity with their own ideas for requests.

Can I ...?

Student A

1 Look at the key below. Choose and write an answer for Student B's requests (1–6). You don't know what the requests are.

☺	= Sure you can.
☺	= I'll think about it.
☹	= Sorry, you can't.
☹☹	= Absolutely not! / No way!

Request 1 ....

Request 2 ....

Request 3 ....

Request 4 ....

Request 5 ....

Request 6 ....

2 Take it in turns to ask for permission to do something. Use *Can I ...?* and the words below. Answer according to ☺ or ☹ in exercise 1. Are your / Student B's answers sensible, or silly?

> dye / my hair purple?
> borrow / $10?
> eat / your lunch?
> get / a tattoo on my arm?
> go / to the park right now?
> stay out / until 5 a.m.?

Student B: Can I borrow a lot of money?
Student A: I'll think about it. Can I dye my hair purple?
Student B: Sorry, you can't.

Can I ...?

Student B

1 Look at the key below. Choose and write an answer for Student A's requests (1–6). You don't know what the requests are.

☺	= Sure you can.
☺	= I'll think about it.
☹	= Sorry, you can't.
☹☹	= Absolutely not! / No way!

Request 1 ....

Request 2 ....

Request 3 ....

Request 4 ....

Request 5 ....

Request 6 ....

2 Take it in turns to ask for permission to do something. Use *Can I ...?* and the words below. Answer according to ☺ or ☹ in exercise 1. Are your / Student A's answers sensible, or silly?

> borrow / a lot of money?
> get / a tattoo on my leg?
> go / to the coffee shop right now?
> have / a party at your house?
> use / your cell phone?
> use / your computer?

Student B: Can I borrow a lot of money?
Student A: I'll think about it. Can I dye my hair purple?
Student B: Sorry, you can't.

6 Pairwork activity

Who am I?

Notes and answers

Aims

to practice talking about the past
to practice questions and short answers with *was* / *were*
to practice jobs

Instructions

- NB: Students have to know some facts about the famous person they choose. You could ask students to research someone for homework. Tell them not to say who their famous person is.
- Copy and cut up the activity sheet.
- Divide the class into A / B pairs.
- Give out the activity sheet, and explain the activity. Go through the example with the class.
- Make sure students understand that they can only ask *yes* / *no* questions with *Were you …?* to find out information.
- Students take turns to play the guessing game. Give them a time limit.

Answers

Students' own answers.

Extra activity

- Students can repeat the activity, but this time they can only ask five questions.

Who am I?

Student A

1 Choose a famous person from the past. Make sure that you know a few things about this person. Use some of the ideas below, and your own ideas. Imagine that you are this person. Don't tell Student B who you are.

- male / female ?
- nationality ?
- year of birth ?
- job ?
- first person to do something ?
- sports champion ?
- winner of a prize ?

2 Answer Student B's questions. Can he / she guess who you are?

Student B: Were you female?
Student A: Yes, I was.
Student B: Were you born in the 19th century?
Student A: Yes, I was.
Student B: Were you a writer?
Student A: No, I wasn't.

3 Ask Student B questions about his / her person. Can you guess who he / she is?

✂

Who am I?

Student B

1 Choose a famous person from the past. Make sure that you know a few things about this person. Use some of the ideas below, and your own ideas. Imagine that you are this person. Don't tell Student A who you are.

- male / female ?
- nationality ?
- year of birth ?
- job ?
- first person to do something ?
- sports champion ?
- winner of a prize ?

2 Ask Student A questions. Can you guess who he / she is?

Student B: Were you female?
Student A: Yes, I was.
Student B: Were you born in the 19th century?
Student A: Yes, I was.
Student B: Were you a writer?
Student A: No, I wasn't.

3 Answer Student A's questions about your person. Can he / she guess who you are?

Tell me a story

Notes and answers

Aims

to practice simple past (affirmative)
to practice regular and irregular verbs

Instructions

- Copy and cut up the activity sheet.
- Divide the class into A / B pairs.
- Give out the activity sheet, and explain the activity.
- Students read their story to their partner. Their partner numbers the pictures in the cartoon strip 1–6.

Answers

Student A: 1e 2c 3b 4f 5a 6d
Student B: 1d 2f 3a 4e 5b 6c

Extra activity

- Students can write their own mini-stories in the simple past. They read the story to their partner, who has to draw a simple cartoon strip illustrating the story. Students could then vote on which story and comic strip they think is the best.
- Alternatively, students could write their own stories with a cartoon strip for homework.

Tell me a story

Student A

1 The pictures in the cartoon strip are in the wrong order. Listen to Student B's story and number the boxes 1–6.

2 Now read this story slowly to Student B. Give him / her time to number the boxes.

Seth met a girl called Becky at school. He loved her. He went home and created a song about Becky. Then he sent his song to a recording studio. They liked his song! Seth performed his song at a concert, and Becky watched him. Then Becky and Seth went to a party together.

Tell me a story

Student B

1 Read this story slowly to Student A. Give him / her time to number the boxes.

Dolores made a cake for a contest at her school. She was very happy with it. She carried the cake to school. Then she dropped it! But her cake tasted good, and she won the contest. The teachers gave Dolores a prize. "Don't drop it!" everyone said.

2 The pictures in the cartoon strip are in the wrong order. Listen to Student A's story and number the boxes 1–6.

8 Pairwork activity

What did you do last week?

Notes and answers

Aims

to practice simple past (affirmative, negative, questions, short answers)
regular and irregular verbs

Instructions

- Copy and cut up the activity sheet.
- Divide the class into A / B pairs.
- Give out the activity sheet, and explain the activity. Go through the example with the class.
- Students choose what day they did each activity and fill in their agenda.
- Students take turns to ask and answer about their activities last week. When they find out information, they write the activities in the correct place in their partner's agenda.
- Students compare agendas to see if they are correct.

Answers

Students' own answers.

Extra activity

- Students can repeat the activity, but this time with answers that are true for themselves.

What did you do last week?

Student A

1 Look at the activities below. You did all these things last week, but when? Write the activities in your agenda. Use the simple past form of the verbs. Don't show your agenda to Student B.

> buy some shoes   go to a rock concert
> have a sleepover make a cake   play the guitar
> see friends   take some photos

2 Ask and answer simple past questions about what you and your partner did last week. Fill out Student B's agenda with the activities he / she did.

Student A: What did you do on Monday?
Student B: I went to a rock concert. Did you go to a rock concert last week?
Student A: Yes, I did. I went on Thursday. Did you see friends on Wednesday?
Student B: No, I didn't. I saw friends on Saturday.

3 Compare your agendas to see if they are correct. Did you do any activities on the same day?

YOUR AGENDA

Monday
Tuesday
Wednesday
Thursday
Friday
Saturday
Sunday

STUDENT B'S AGENDA

Monday
Tuesday
Wednesday
Thursday
Friday
Saturday
Sunday

- ✂

What did you do last week?

Student B

1 Look at the activities below. You did all these things last week, but when? Write the activities in your agenda. Use the simple past form of the verbs. Don't show your agenda to Student A.

> buy some shoes   go to a rock concert
> have a sleepover make a cake   play the guitar
> see friends   take some photos

2 Ask and answer simple past questions about what you and your partner did last week. Fill out Student A's agenda with the activities he / she did.

Student A: What did you do on Monday?
Student B: I went to a rock concert. Did you go to a rock concert last week?
Student A: Yes, I did. I went on Thursday. Did you see friends on Wednesday?
Student B: No, I didn't. I saw friends on Saturday.

3 Compare your agendas to see if they are correct. Did you do any activities on the same day?

STUDENT A'S AGENDA

Monday
Tuesday
Wednesday
Thursday
Friday
Saturday
Sunday

YOUR AGENDA

Monday
Tuesday
Wednesday
Thursday
Friday
Saturday
Sunday

Word list

Student Book

Welcome

Countries and nationalities

American /əˈmerɪkən/ _____

Australia /ɔˈstreɪlɪə/ _____

Australian /ɔˈstreɪlɪən/ _____

Brazil /brəˈzɪl/ _____

Brazilian /brəˈzɪlyən/ _____

British /ˈbrɪtɪʃ/ _____

Guatemala /ˌgwɑtəˈmɑlə/ _____

_____

Guatemalan /ˌgwɑtəˈmɑlən/ _____

_____

Japan /dʒəˈpæn/ _____

Japanese /ˌdʒæpəˈniz/ _____

The United Kingdom (the U.K.)

/ðə yuˈnaɪtɪd ˈkɪŋdəm/ _____

_____

The United States (the U.S.)

/ðə yuˈnaɪtɪd steɪts/ _____

_____

Feelings

angry /ˈæŋgri/ _____

bored /bɔrd/ _____

happy /ˈhæpi/ _____

sad /sæd/ _____

scared /skɛrd/ _____

tired /ˈtaɪəd/ _____

Things in your bedroom

bedside table /ˈbedsaɪd ˈteɪbl/ _____

bookcase /ˈbʊkkeɪs/ _____

cell phone /ˈsɛl foʊn/ _____

closet /ˈklɑzət/ _____

computer /kəmˈpyuʈər/ _____

desk /dɛsk/ _____

lamp /læmp/ _____

magazine /ˈmægəzin/ _____

MP3 player /ˌɛm pi ˈθri ˈpleɪər/ _____

_____

pencil case /ˈpɛnsl keɪs/ _____

skateboard /ˈskeɪtbɔrd/ _____

Jobs

actor /ˈæktər/ _____

athlete /ˈæθlit/ _____

dancer /ˈdænsər/ _____

doctor /ˈdɑktər/ _____

singer /ˈsɪŋər/ _____

soccer player /ˈsɑkər ˈpleɪər/ _____

_____

Family

brother /ˈbrʌðər / _____

father /ˈfɑðər/ _____

grandfather /ˈgrænfɑðər/ _____

grandmother /ˈgrænmʌðər/ _____

grandparents /ˈgrænperənts/ _____

mother /ˈmʌðər/ _____

sister /ˈsɪstər/ _____

Going out in town

bowling alley /ˈboʊlɪŋ ˈæli/ _____

clothes store /kloʊðz stɔr/ _____

cybercafé /ˈsaɪbərkæfeɪ/ _____

fast food restaurant /fæst fud ˈrɛsʈərənt/

_____

movie theater /ˈmuvi ˈθiəʈər/ _____

_____

skatepark /ˈskeɪtˈpark/ _____

sports store /spɔrts stɔr/ _____

Leisure activities

go online /goʊ ˌɑnˈlaɪn/ _____

go out with friends /goʊ aʊt wɪð frends/

go shopping /goʊ ˈʃɑpɪŋ/ _____

play computer games

/pleɪ kəmˈpyuʈər geɪms/ _____

talk on the phone /tɔk ɑn ðə foʊn/ _____

_____

watch TV /wɑtʃ ˌtiˈvi/ _____

Unit 1
Weather

cloudy /'klaʊdi/ _____
cold /koʊld/ _____
hot /hɑt/ _____
raining /'reɪnɪŋ/ _____
snowing /'snoʊɪŋ/ _____
stormy /'stɔrmi/ _____
sunny /'sʌni/ _____
windy /'wɪndi/ _____

Everyday activities

babysit /'beɪbisɪt/ _____
chat online /tʃæt ˌɑn'laɪn/ _____
do my homework /doʊ maɪ hoʊmwərk/ _____
get dressed /gɛt drɛst/ _____
post a comment /poʊst ə'kɑment/ _____
send a text message /sɛnd ə tɛkst 'mɛsɪdʒ/ _____
sleep /slip/ _____
wait for the bus /weɪt fɔr ðə bʌs/ _____

Nouns

blog /blɑg/ _____
breakfast /brɛkfəst/ _____
coffee /'kɑfi/ _____
dinner /'dɪnər/ _____
fun /fʌn/ _____
kitchen /'kɪtʃɪn/ _____
world /wərld/ _____
youth club /yuθ klʌb/ _____

Verbs

cook /kʊk/ _____
eat /it/ _____
listen /'lɪsn/ _____
love /lʌv/ _____
run /rʌn/ _____
sit /sɪt/ _____
stand /stænd/ _____

Adjectives

favorite /'feɪvərət/ _____
good /gʊd/ _____

Adverbs

outside /'aʊtsaɪd/ _____
right now /raɪt naʊ/ _____
today /tə'deɪ/ _____
tonight /tə'naɪt/ _____

Unit 2
Clothes

boots /buts/ _____
glasses /'glæsɪz/ _____
pants /pænts/ _____
shirt /ʃərt/ _____
shoes /ʃuz/ _____
skirt /skərt/ _____
socks /sɑks/ _____
top /tɑp/ _____

Physical descriptions

beard /bɪrd/ _____
big /bɪg/ _____
blond /blɑnd/ _____
blue /blu/ _____
dark brown /dɑrk braʊn/ _____
green /grin/ _____
light brown /laɪt braʊn/ _____
long /lɔŋ/ _____
mustache /mə'stɑʃ/ _____
red /rɛd/ _____
short /ʃɔrt/ _____
small /smɔl/ _____
straight /streɪt/ _____
wavy /'weɪvi/ _____

Nouns

adventure /əd'vɛntʃər/ _____
agent /'eɪdʒənt/ _____
briefcase /'brifkeɪs/ _____
captain /'kæptɪn/ _____
colonel /'kərnl/ _____
corner /'kɔrnər/ _____
corporal /'kɔrpərəl/ _____
idiot /'ɪdiət/ _____
office /'ɑfɪs/ _____
ogre /'oʊgər/ _____
pajamas /pə'dʒæməz/ _____
party /'pɑrti/ _____
pirate /'paɪrət/ _____
princess /'prɪnsɛs/ _____
snacks /snæks/ _____
sneakers /'snikərs/ _____
suspect /'sʌspɛkt/ _____
sweatpants /'swɛtpænts/ _____
sweatshirt /'swɛtʃərt/ _____
T-shirt /tiʃərt/ _____
uniform /'yunɪfɔrm/ _____
weekend /'wikɛnd/ _____
wizard /'wɪzərd/ _____
woman /'wʊmən/ _____
writer /'raɪtər/ _____

Adjectives

dirty /'dərti/ _____
strange /streɪndʒ/ _____

Verbs

call /kɔl/ _____
carry /'kæri/ _____
follow /'fɑloʊ/ _____
look at /lʊk æt/ _____
see /si/ _____
stay /steɪ/ _____

Adverbs

always /'ɔlweɪz/ _____
normally /'nɔrməli/ _____
sometimes /'sʌmtaɪmz/ _____
usually /'yuʒəli/ _____

Review A
Nouns

art gallery /ɑrt'gæləri/ _____
picture /'pɪktʃər/ _____
trip /trɪp/ _____

Project 1
Nouns

group /grup/ _____
TV host /tivi hoʊst/ _____

Verbs

interview /'ɪntərvyu/ _____

Word list

Unit 3
Food
apples /'æpls/ _____

bananas /bə'nænəz/ _____

eggs /ɛgz/ _____

French fries /frɛntʃ fraɪz/ _____

_____

hamburgers /'hæmbərgərs/ _____

mangoes /'mæŋgoʊs/ _____

pizzas /'pitsəs/ _____

potatoes /pə'teɪtoʊs/ _____

sausages /'sɔsɪdʒɪz/ _____

strawberries /'strɔbɛriz/ _____

tomatoes /tə'meɪtəʊz/ _____

Food and drink
bread /brɛd / _____

cheese /tʃiz/ _____

coffee /'kɑfi/ _____

soda /'soʊdə/ _____

ketchup /'kɛtʃəp/ _____

milk /mɪlk/ _____

oil /ɔɪl/ _____

pasta /'pɑstə/ _____

rice /raɪs/ _____

salad /'sæləd/ _____

salt /sɔlt/ _____

water /'wɑtər/ _____

Nouns
calories /'kæləris/ _____

carrots /'kærəts/ _____

celebration /ˌsɛlɪ'breɪʃn/ _____

chips /tʃɪps/ _____

corn /kɔrn/ _____

ice cream /aɪs krim/ _____

idea /aɪ'diə/ _____

king /kɪŋ/ _____

meals /mils/ _____

omelet /'ɑmlət/ _____

pumpkin pie /pʌmpkɪn paɪ/ _____

radio show host /'reɪdioʊ ʃoʊ hoʊst/

_____

recipe /'rɛsəpi/ _____

refrigerator /rɪ'frɪdʒəreɪtər/ _____

_____

seeds /sidz/ _____

Thanksgiving /ˌθæŋks'gɪvɪŋ/ _____

turkey /'tərki/ _____

vitamins /'vaɪtəmɪnz/ _____

Adjectives
bad /bæd/ _____

important /ɪm'pɔrtnt/ _____

super size /'supər saɪz/ _____

Adverbs
inside /ˌɪn'saɪd/ _____

once /wʌns/ _____

together /tə'gɛðər/ _____

twice /twaɪs/ _____

Verbs
add /æd/ _____

download /'daʊnloʊd/ _____

make /meɪk/ _____

try /traɪ/ _____

Unit 4
Noun categories
baggage /'bægɪdʒ/ _____

food /fud/ _____

furniture /'fərnɪtʃər/ _____

money /'mʌni/ _____

music /'myuzɪk/ _____

time /taɪm/ _____

traffic /'træfɪk/ _____

travel /'trævl/ _____

Personal possessions
backpack /'bækpæk/ _____

belt /bɛlt/ _____

bracelet /'breɪslət/ _____

earrings /'ɪrɪŋs/ _____

ID card /ˌaɪ'di kɑrd/ _____

key /ki/ _____

key ring /ki rɪŋ/ _____

sunglasses /'sʌnglæsɪz/ _____

Nouns
advertisement /ˌædvər'taɪzmənt/ _____

airplane /'erpleɪn/ _____

article /'ɑrtɪkl/ _____

cars /kɑrs/ _____

celebrities /sə'lɛbrəts̬is/ _____

dollars /'dɑlərs/ _____

gadget /'gædʒɪt/ _____

half /hæf / _____

highway /'haɪweɪ/ _____

hours /'aʊərs/ _____

jewelry /'dʒuəlri/ _____

product /'prɑdʌkt/ _____

radio /'reɪdioʊ/ _____

teenager /'tineɪdʒər/ _____

wrist /rɪst/ _____

Verbs
hurry up /'həri ʌp/ _____

prefer /prɪ'fər/ _____

receive /rɪ'siv/ _____

Adjectives
healthy /'hɛlθi/ _____

quiet /'kwaɪət/ _____

Project 2
Nouns
nuts /nʌts/ _____

tea /ti/ _____

Adjectives
diet /'daɪət/ _____

traditional /trə'dɪʃənl/ _____

Adverbs
during /'dʊrɪŋ/ _____

Unit 5

Requests

borrow /'barou/ _____

buy /baɪ/ _____

drive /draɪv/ _____

dye /daɪ/ _____

get /gɛt/ _____

go /gou/ _____

have /hæv/ _____

stay out /steɪ aut/ _____

Places to go

amusement park /ə'myuzmənt park/

_____

coffee shop /'kɑfi ʃɑp/ _____

library /'laɪbreri/ _____

museum /myu'ziəm/ _____

park /park/ _____

shopping mall /ʃɑpɪŋ mɔl/ _____

skating rink /'skeɪtɪŋ rɪŋk/ _____

swimming pool /'swɪmɪŋ pul/ _____

Nouns

advice /əd'vaɪs/ _____

age /eɪdʒ/ _____

ankle /'æŋkl/ _____

body /'bɑdi/ _____

dessert /dɪ'zərt/ _____

exams /ɪg'zæms/ _____

exhibition /ˌɛksɪ'bɪʃn/ _____

glass /glæs/ _____

headphones /'hedfounz/ _____

plans /plænz/ _____

problem /'prɑbləm/ _____

rides /raɪds/ _____

sleepover /'slipouvər/ _____

storyteller /'stɔritɛlər/ _____

tattoo /tæ'tu/ _____

Verbs

date /deɪt/ _____

drop /drɑp/ _____

equal /'ikwəl/ _____

invite /ɪn'vaɪt/ _____

look forward to /lʊk 'fɔrwərd tə/ _____

_____

please /pliz/ _____

Adjectives

amazing /ə'meɪzɪŋ/ _____

cute /kyut/ _____

responsible /rɪ'spɑnsəbl/ _____

unfair /ˌʌn'fɛr/ _____

Adverbs

before long /bɪ'fɔr lɑŋ/ _____

far /far/ _____

right /raɪt/ _____

Unit 6

Jobs

architect /'arkɪtɛkt/ _____

artist /'artɪst/ _____

fashion designer /'fæʃn dɪ'zaɪnər/ _____

inventor /ɪn'vɛntər/ _____

musician /myu'zɪʃn/ _____

politician /ˌpɑlə'tɪʃn/ _____

scientist /'saɪəntɪst/ _____

writer /'raɪtər/ _____

Adjectives of opinion

awesome /'ɔsəm/ _____

awful /'ɔfl/ _____

boring /'bɔrɪŋ/ _____

delicious /dɪ'lɪʃəs/ _____

disgusting /dɪs'gʌstɪŋ/ _____

fantastic /fæn'tæstɪk/ _____

interesting /'ɪntrəstɪŋ/ _____

terrible /'tɛrəbl/ _____

Nouns

character /'kærəktər/ _____

company /'kʌmpəni/ _____

director /daɪ'rɛktər/ _____

discoveries /dɪ'skʌvəriz/ _____

election /ɪ'lɛkʃn/ _____

face /feɪs/ _____

fight /faɪt/ _____

flight /flaɪt/ _____

food can /fud kæn/ _____

guitar /gɪ'tar/ _____

human rights /'hyumən raɪts/ _____

leader /'lidər/ _____

painting /'peɪnʧɪŋ/ _____

perfumes /pər'fyumz/ _____

physics /'fɪzɪks/ _____

pilot /'paɪlət/ _____

politics /'pɑlətɪks/ _____

president /'prɛzɪdənt/ _____

price /praɪs/ _____

prize /praɪz/ _____

race /reɪs/ _____

record holder /'rɛkərd houldər/ _____

snails /'sneɪlz/ _____

space station /speɪs 'steɪʃn/ _____

terror /'tɛrər/ _____

title /'taɪtl/ _____

winner /'wɪnər/ _____

Verbs

be born /bi bɔrn/ _____

design /dɪ'zaɪn/ _____

draw /drɔ/ _____

invent /ɪn'vɛnt/ _____

paint /peɪnt/ _____

set /sɛt/ _____

Adjectives

gross /grous/ _____

national /'næʃnəl/ _____

popular /'pɑpyələr/ _____

rubbish /'rʌbɪʃ/ _____

solo /'soulou/ _____

successful /sək'sɛsfl/ _____

Adverbs

alone /ə'loun/ _____

in line /ɪn laɪn/ _____

Review C

Adjectives

brilliant /'brɪliənt/ _____

Project 3

Nouns

college /'kɑlɪdʒ/ _____

hero /'hɪrou/ _____

taxi /'tæksi/ _____

Word list

Unit 7

Kinds of music

classical /'klæsɪkl/ _____
country /'kʌntri/ _____
jazz /dʒæz/ _____
pop /pɑp/ _____
rap /ræp/ _____
reggae /'rɛɡeɪ/ _____
rock /rɑk/ _____
soul /soʊl/ _____

Musical instruments

bass /beɪs/ _____
drums /drʌmz/ _____
guitar /ɡɪ'tɑr/ _____
keyboard /'kibɔrd/ _____
piano /pi'ænoʊ/ _____
saxophone /'sæksəfoʊn/ _____
trumpet /'trʌmpɪt/ _____
violin /,vaɪə'lɪn/ _____

Nouns

award /ə'wɔrd/ _____
boyfriend /'bɔɪfrɛnd/ _____
businessman /'bɪznəsmæn/ _____
_____
charts /tʃɑrts/ _____
concert /'kɑnsərt/ _____
copies /'kɑpiz/ _____
crowd /kraʊd/ _____
fans /fænz/ _____
hotel /hoʊ'tɛl/ _____
member /'mɛmbər/ _____
midnight /'mɪdnaɪt/ _____
millionaire /,mɪljə'nɛr/ _____
pop star /pɑpstɑr/ _____
quiz /kwɪz/ _____
rapper /'ræpər/ _____
single /'sɪŋɡl/ _____
sound /saʊnd/ _____
studio /'studioʊ/ _____
tour /tʊr/ _____
user /'yuzər/ _____
virtual world /'vərtʃuəl wərld/ _____
_____

Verbs

change /tʃeɪndʒ/ _____
cheat /tʃit/ _____
create /kri'eɪt/ _____
exist /ɪɡ'zɪst/ _____
form /fɔrm/ _____
influence /'ɪnfluəns/ _____
mix /mɪks/ _____
perform /pər'fɔrm/ _____
promote /prə'moʊt/ _____
record /rɪ'kɔrd/ _____
release /rɪ'lis/ _____
top /tɑp/ _____

Adjectives

legendary /'lɛdʒənderi/ _____
modern /'mɑdərn/ _____
wild /waɪld/ _____

Adverbs

early /'ərli/ _____
live /laɪv/ _____

Unit 8

Nature

beaches /bitʃɪz/ _____
deserts /dɪ'zərts/ _____
islands /'aɪləndz/ _____
jungles /'dʒʌŋls/ _____
mountains /'maʊntnz/ _____
oceans /'oʊʃnz/ _____
rivers /'rɪvərs/ _____
volcanoes /vɑl'keɪnoʊs/ _____

Disasters

break /breɪk/ _____
crash /kræʃ/ _____
die /daɪ/ _____
disappear /,dɪsə'pɪr/ _____
hit /hɪt/ _____
sink /sɪŋk/ _____

Nouns

century /'sɛntʃəri/ _____
emperor /'ɛmpərər/ _____
explanation /,ɛksplə'neɪʃn/ _____
_____
garbage cans /'ɡɑrbɪdʒ kænz/ _____
_____
historian /hɪ'stɔriən/ _____
iceberg /'aɪsbərɡ/ _____
legend /'lɛdʒənd/ _____
machines /mə'ʃinz/ _____
moon /mun/ _____
mummy /'mʌmi/ _____
mystery /'mɪstri/ _____
noise /nɔɪz/ _____
nose /noʊz/ _____
ovens /'ʌvnz/ _____
pneumonia /nu'moʊniə/ _____
pyramid /'pɪrəmɪd/ _____
questions /'kwɛstʃənz/ _____
rainforest /'reɪnfɔrɪst/ _____
rock /rɑk/ _____
role /roʊl/ _____
statue /'stætʃu/ _____
tomb /tum/ _____
war /wɔr/ _____
workers /'wərkərs/ _____

Verbs

appear /ə'pɪr/ _____
believe /bɪ'liv/ _____
build /bɪld/ _____
check /tʃɛk/ _____
report /rɪ'pɔrt/ _____
solve /sɑlv/ _____
take out /teɪk aʊt/ _____

Adjectives

lost /lɑst/ _____
stone /stoʊn/ _____

Adverbs

almost /'ɔlmoʊst/ _____
missing /'mɪsɪŋ/ _____

Review D

Nouns

basin /'beɪsɪn/ _____
karate /kə'rɑti/ _____
ship /ʃɪp/ _____
triangle /'traɪæŋɡl/ _____

Adverbs

immediately /ɪ'midiətli/ _____

Project 4

Nouns

journey /'dʒərni/ _____

Workbook

Unit 1
Extend your vocabulary 1
cool /kul/ _____
foggy /ˈfɑgi/ _____
freezing /ˈfrizɪŋ/ _____
warm /wɔrm/ _____

Extend your vocabulary 2
brush your teeth /brʌʃ yər tiθ/ _____
_____
comb your hair /koʊm yər her/ _____
_____
get ready for school /gɛtˈ redi fɔr skul/
_____
say goodbye /seɪ ˌgʊdˈbaɪ/ _____
_____
wash your face /wɑʃ yər feɪs/ _____
_____

Unit 2
Extend your vocabulary 1
belt /bɛlt/ _____
gloves /glʌvz/ _____
hat /hæt/ _____
jacket /ˈdʒækɪt/ _____
sandals /ˈsændls/ _____
scarf /skɑrf/ _____
sunglasses /ˈsʌnglæsɪz/ _____
swimsuit /ˈswɪmsut/ _____

Extend your vocabulary 2
bald /bɔld/ _____
good-looking /gʊdlʊkɪŋ/ _____
overweight /ˌoʊvərˈweɪt/ _____
short /ʃɔrt/ _____
slim /slɪm/ _____
strong /strɔŋ/ _____
tall /tɔl/ _____

Unit 3
Extend your vocabulary 1
cakes /keɪks/ _____
cookies /ˈkʊkis/ _____
muffin /ˈmʌfɪn/ _____
pear /pɛr/ _____
watermelon /ˈwɑtərmɛlən/ _____
_____

Extend your vocabulary 2
fruit juice /frut dʒus/ _____
orange /ˈɑrɪndʒ/ _____
salad /ˈsæləd/ _____
sandwich /ˈsænwɪdʒ/ _____
smoothie /ˈsmuði/ _____
soup /sup/ _____

Unit 4
Extend your vocabulary 1
billboard /ˈbɪlbɔrd/ _____
department store /dɪˈpɑrtmənt stɔr/
_____
road sign /roʊd saɪn/ _____
skyscraper /ˈskaɪskreɪpər/ _____
sidewalk /ˈsaɪdwɔk/ _____
stop light /stɑp laɪt/ _____

Extend your vocabulary 2
calculators /ˈkælkyuleɪʈər/ _____
coins /kɔɪnz/ _____
sunblock /ˈsʌnblɑk/ _____
wallet /ˈwalɪt/ / _____
water bottle /ˈwɑʈərˈbɑtl/ _____
watch /wɑtʃ/ _____

Unit 5
Extend your vocabulary 1
go clubbing /goʊ ˈklʌbɪŋ/ _____
_____
go fishing /goʊ ˈfɪʃɪŋ/ _____
_____
go shopping /goʊ ʃɑpɪŋ/ _____
_____
go skiing /goʊ ˈskiɪŋ/ _____
_____
go snowboarding /goʊ ˈsnoʊbɔrdɪŋ/
_____
go swimming /goʊ ˈswɪmɪŋ/ _____

Extend your vocabulary 2
can't stand /kænt stænd/ _____
crazy /ˈkreɪzi/ _____
great /greɪt/ _____
hate /heɪt/ _____
love /lʌv/ _____
not bad /nɑt bæd/ _____
OK /oʊˈkeɪ/ _____
terrible /ˈtɛrəbl/ _____

Unit 6
Extend your vocabulary 1
baseball player /ˈbeɪsbɔl ˈpleɪər/ _____
_____
composer /kəmˈpoʊzər/ _____
explorer /ɪkˈsplɔrər/ _____
movie director /ˈmuvi daɪˈrɛktər/ _____
_____
queen /kwin/ _____
racing driver /ˈreɪsɪŋ ˈdraɪvər/ _____
_____

Extend your vocabulary 2
disappointing /ˌdɪsəˈpɔɪntɪŋ/ _____
exciting /ɪkˈsaɪtɪŋ/ _____
exhausting /ɪgˈzɔstɪŋ/ _____
romantic /roʊˈmæntɪk/ _____
scary /ˈskeri/ _____
surprising /sərˈpraɪzɪŋ/ _____

Unit 7
Extend your vocabulary 1
folk /foʊk/ _____
grunge /grʌndʒ/ _____
hip-hop /hɪphɑp/ _____
rock and roll /rɑk æn roʊl/ _____
_____

Extend your vocabulary 2
bass player /bæs ˈpleɪər/ _____
_____
drummer /ˈdrʌmər/ _____
guitarist /gɪˈtɑrɪst/ _____
keyboard player /ˈkibɔrd ˈpleɪər/ _____
_____
singer /ˈsɪŋər/ _____

Unit 8
Extend your vocabulary 1
cave /keɪv/ _____
glacier /ˈgleɪʃər/ _____
lake /leɪk/ _____
rainforest /ˈreɪnfɔrɪst/ _____
waterfall /ˈwɑʈərfɔl/ _____

Extend your vocabulary 2
drought /draʊt/ _____
earthquake /ˈərθkweɪk/ _____
fire /ˈfaɪər/ _____
flood /flʌd/ _____
hurricane /ˈhərəkeɪn/ _____